"Out of hundreds of books about improving organizational performance, here is one that is based on extensive empirical evidence and a book that focuses on specific actions managers can take to make their organizations better today! In a world in which managing people provides the differentiating advantage, *First, Break All the Rules* is a must-read."
　—Jeffrey Pfeffer, Professor, Stanford Business School and author of
　　The Human Equation: Building Profits by Putting People First

"This book challenges basic beliefs of great management with powerful evidence and a compelling argument. *First, Break All the Rules* is essential reading."
　　　　—Bradbury H. Anderson, President and COO, Best Buy

"This is it! With compelling insight backed by powerful Gallup data, Buckingham and Coffman have built the unshakable foundation of effective management. For the first time, a clear pathway has been identified for creating engaged employees and high-performance work units. It has changed the way I approach developing managers. *First, Break All the Rules* is a critical resource for every front-line supervisor, middle manager, and institutional leader."
　　　　—Michael W. Morrison, Dean, University of Toyota

"*First, Break All the Rules* is nothing short of revolutionary in its concepts and ideas. It explains why so many traditional notions and practices are counterproductive in business today. Equally important, the book presents a simpler, truer model complete with specific actions that have allowed our organization to achieve significant improvements in productivity, employee engagement, customer satisfaction, and profit."
　　　　—Kevin Cuthbert, Vice President, Human Resources, Swissôtel

"Finally, something definitive about what makes for a great workplace."
　　　　　　—Harriet Johnson Brackey, *Miami Herald*

"Within the last several years, systems and the Internet have assumed a preeminent role in management thinking, to the detriment of the role of *people* in the workplace. Buckingham and Coffman prove just how crucial good people—and specifically great managers—are to the success of any organization."
　　　　—Bernie Marcus, former Chairman and CEO, Home Depot

"The rational, measurement-based approach, for which Gallup has so long been famous, has increased the tangibility of our intangible assets, as well as our ability to manage them. *First, Break All the Rules* shows us how."

> —David P. Norton, President, The Balanced Scorecard
> Collaborative, Inc.; coauthor of *The Balanced Scorecard*

"As the authors put it, 'a great deal of the value of a company lies between the ears of its employees.' The key to success is growing that value by listening to and understanding what lies in their hearts—Mssrs. Buckingham and Coffman have found a direct way to measure and make that critical connection. At Carlson Companies, their skills are helping us become the truly caring company that will succeed in the marketplace of the future."

> —Marilyn Carlson Nelson, President and CEO, Carlson Companies

First, Break All the Rules

What the World's Greatest Managers Do Differently

Marcus Buckingham
and **Curt Coffman**

Simon & Schuster

First published in Great Britain by Simon & Schuster UK Ltd, 1999
A Viacom company

First Published in The United States by
Simon and Schuster Inc.
1230 Avenue of the Americas
New York, NY 10020

1 3 5 7 9 10 8 6 4 2

Simon & Schuster UK Ltd
Africa House
64-78 Kingsway
London WC2B 6AH

Simon & Schuster Australia
Sydney

A CIP catalogue record for this book is available from the British
Library

ISBN 0-684-86139-9

Printed in Great Britain by The Bath Press, Bath

To Janie, who found what was always there

Contents

Breaking All the Rules

The greatest managers in the world do not have much in common. They are of different sexes, races, and ages. They employ vastly different styles and focus on different goals. But despite their differences, these great managers do share one thing: Before they do anything else, they first break all the rules of conventional wisdom. They do not believe that a person can achieve anything he sets his mind to. They do not try to help a person overcome his weaknesses. They consistently disregard the Golden Rule. And, yes, they even play favorites.

Great managers are revolutionaries, although few would use that word to describe themselves. This book will take you inside the minds of these managers to explain why they have toppled conventional wisdom and reveal the new truths they have forged in its place.

We are not encouraging you to replace your natural managerial style with a standardized version of theirs—as you will see, great managers do not share a "standardized style." Rather, our purpose is to help you capitalize on your *own* style, by showing you how to incorporate the revolutionary insights shared by great managers everywhere.

This book is the product of two mammoth research studies undertaken by the Gallup Organization over the last twenty-five years. The first concentrated on employees, asking, "What do the most talented employees need from their workplace?" Gallup surveyed over a million employees from a broad range of companies, industries, and countries. We asked them questions on all aspects of their working life, then dug deep into their answers to discover the most important needs demanded by the most productive employees.

Our research yielded many discoveries, but the most powerful was this: Talented employees need great managers. The talented employee may join a company because of its charismatic leaders, its generous benefits, and its world-class training programs, but how long that employee stays and how productive he is while he is there is determined by his relationship with his immediate supervisor.

This simple discovery led us to the second research effort: "How do the world's greatest managers find, focus, and keep talented employees?" To answer this question we went to the source—large companies and small companies, privately held companies, publicly traded companies, and public sector organizations—and interviewed a cross section of their managers, from the excellent to the average. How did we know who was excellent and who was average? We asked each company to provide us with performance measures. Measures like sales, profit, customer satisfaction scores, employee turnover figures, employee opinion data, and 360-degree surveys were all used to distill the best managers from the rest. During the last twenty-five years the Gallup Organization has conducted, tape-recorded, and transcribed one-and-a-half-hour interviews with over eighty thousand managers.

Some of these managers were in leadership positions. Some were midlevel managers. Some were front-line supervisors. But all of them had one or more employees reporting to them. We focused our analysis on those managers who excelled at turning the talent of their employees into performance. Despite their obvious differences in style, we wanted to discover what, if anything, these great managers had in common.

Their ideas are plain and direct, but they are not necessarily simple to implement. Conventional wisdom is conventional for a reason: It is easier. It is easier to believe that each employee possesses unlimited potential. It is easier to imagine that the best way to help an employee is by fixing his weaknesses. It is easier to "do unto others as you would be done unto." It is easier to treat everyone the same and so avoid charges of favoritism. Conventional wisdom is comfortingly, seductively easy.

The revolutionary wisdom of great managers isn't. Their path is much more exacting. It demands discipline, focus, trust, and, perhaps most important, a willingness to individualize. In this book, great managers present no sweeping new theories, no prefabricated formulae. All they can offer you are insights into the nature of talent and into their secrets for turning talent into lasting performance. The real challenge lies in how you incorporate these insights into *your* style, one employee at a time, every day.

•   •   •

This book gives voice to one million employees and eighty thousand managers. While these interviews ground the book in the real world, their sheer number can be overwhelming. It is hard to imagine what one talented employee or one great manager sounds like. The following excerpt, from a single interview, captures something of both the tone and the content of our in-depth interviews.

As with all the managers we quote, we have changed his name to preserve his anonymity. We will call him Michael. Michael runs a fine-dining restaurant owned by a large hospitality company in the Pacific Northwest. Since Gallup first met Michael fifteen years ago, his restaurant has been in the company's top 10 percent on sales, profit, growth, retention, and customer satisfaction. From the perspective of his company, his customers, and his employees, Michael is a great manager.

Throughout the book you will hear Michael's comments echoed by other managers and employees. But rather than pointing out these echoes, we ask you to make the connections for yourself as you move through the chapters. For the moment we will simply let Michael speak for himself.

GALLUP: Can you tell us about your best team ever?

MICHAEL: You mean my whole team? I have at least thirty people working here.

GALLUP: Just tell us about the core of the team.

MICHAEL: I suppose my best team ever was my wait staff team a few years ago. There were four of them. Brad was about thirty-five, a professional waiter. Took great pride in being the best waiter in town. He was brilliant at anticipating. Customers never had to ask for anything. The moment the thought entered their mind that they needed more water, or a dessert menu, Brad was there at their shoulder, handing it to them.

Then there was Gary. Gary was an innocent. Not naive, just an innocent. He instinctively thought the world was a friendly place, so he was always smiling, cheerful. I don't mean that he wasn't professional, 'cause he was. Always came in looking neat, wearing a freshly pressed shirt. But it was his attitude that so impressed me. Everyone liked to be around Gary.

Susan was our greeter. She was lively, energetic, presented herself very well. When she first joined us, I guessed that she might lack a little common sense, but I was wrong. She handled the customers perfectly. On busy nights she would tell them pleasantly but firmly that last-minute reservations couldn't be accepted. During lunch some customers just want to get their order, pay, and leave. Susan would figure this out and let their server know that, with this particular customer, speed was of the essence. She paid attention, and she made good decisions.

Emma was the unspoken team builder in the crew. Quieter, more responsible, more aware of everyone else, she would get the team together before a busy Saturday night and just talk everyone through the need to put on a good show, to be alert, to help each other get out of the weeds.

These four were the backbone of my best team ever. I didn't really need to interfere. They ran the show themselves. They would train new hires, set the right example, and even eject people who didn't fit. For a good three years they *were* the restaurant.

GALLUP: Where are they now?

MICHAEL: Susan, Emma, and Gary all graduated and moved back east. Brad is still with me.

GALLUP: Do you have a secret to building great teams?

MICHAEL: No, I don't think there is a secret. I think the best a manager can do is to make each person comfortable with who they are. Look, we all have insecurities. Wouldn't it be great if, at work, we didn't have to confront our insecurities all the time? I didn't try to fix Brad, Susan, Gary, and Emma. I didn't try to make them clones of each other. I tried to create an environment where they were encouraged to be more of who they already were. As long as they didn't stomp on each other and as long as they satisfied the customers, I didn't care that they were all so different.

GALLUP: How did you get to know these people so well?

MICHAEL: I spent a lot of time with them. I listened. I took them out for dinner, had a couple of drinks with them. Had them over to my place for holidays. But mostly I was just interested in who they were.

GALLUP: What do you think of the statement "Familiarity breeds contempt?"

MICHAEL: It's wrong. How can you manage people if you don't know them, their style, their motivation, their personal situation? I don't think you can.

GALLUP: Do you think a manager should treat everyone the same?

MICHAEL: Of course not.

GALLUP: Why?

MICHAEL: Because everyone is different. I was telling you about Gary before, how great an employee he was. But I fired him twice. A couple of times his joking around went too far, and he really jerked my chain. I really liked him, but I had to fire him. Our relationship would have been ruined if I hadn't put my foot down and said, "Don't come in on Monday." After each time, he learned a little bit more about himself and his values, so I hired him back both times. I think he's a better person because of what I did.

My firm hand worked with Gary. It wouldn't have worked at all with Brad. If I even raised my voice with Brad, I would get the exact opposite reaction from the one I wanted. He would be crushed. He'd shut down. So when I disagree with him, I have to talk quietly and reason everything through with him quite carefully.

GALLUP: Isn't it unfair to treat people differently?

MICHAEL: I don't think so. I think people want to feel understood. Treating them differently is part of helping them feel unique. If I know that one of my people is the primary breadwinner, then as long as they perform, I will be more likely to give him better hours than someone who is a student. The student might be a little annoyed, but when I explain the situation to him, he usually calms down. Besides, he now knows that I will be paying attention to *his* personal situation when he needs a special favor. That's always a good message to send.

GALLUP: Other than Gary, have you ever fired anyone?

MICHAEL: Unfortunately, I have. Like most managers, sometimes I don't pick the right people and things start to fall apart.

GALLUP: What is your approach to firing an employee?

MICHAEL: Do it fast, the faster the better. If someone is consistently underperforming, you might think you are doing them a favor by waiting. You aren't. You're actually making matters worse.

GALLUP: You've been managing now for fifteen years. If you were going to give any advice to a new manager, what would it be?

MICHAEL: I am not an expert at this, you know. I'm still learning.

GALLUP: That's fine. Just tell us a couple of the ideas that have helped you over the years.

MICHAEL: Well . . . I suppose the first would be, pick the right people. If you do, it makes everything else so much easier.

And once you've picked them, trust them. Everyone here knows that the till is open. If they want to borrow $2 for cigarettes or $200 for rent, they can. Just put an IOU in the till and pay it back. If you expect the best of people, they'll give you the best. I've rarely been let down. And when someone has let me down, I don't think it is right to punish those who haven't by creating some new rule or policy.

Another thing would be, don't overpromote people. Pay them well for what they do, and make it rewarding, in every way, for them to keep doing what they are doing. Brad is a great waiter, but he would make a terrible manager. He loves to perform for an audience he respects. He respects the customers. He is less respectful of some of the new employees. As a manager, these employees would be his audience.

And especially important: Never pass the buck. Never say, "I think this is a crazy idea, but corporate insists." Passing the buck may make your little world easy, but the organism as a whole, sorry, the *organization* as a whole, will be weakened. So in the long run, you are actually making your life worse. Even worse are those who find themselves always promising things that don't come to pass. Since you never know what corporate might spring on you next, I recommend living by this simple rule: Make very few promises to your people, and keep them all.

That's it. That's my list.

GALLUP: Is there anything else that you would like to tell us about your experiences as a manager?

MICHAEL: Maybe just this: A manager has got to remember that he is on stage every day. His people are watching him. Everything he does, everything he says, and the way he says it, sends off clues to his employees. These clues affect performance. So never forget you are on that stage.

So that's Michael. Or, at least, that's an excerpt from Michael. During our research we heard from thousands of managers like Michael and from hundreds of thousands of employees who worked for managers like Michael. Some of Michael's opinions are commonly held—never pass the buck, make few promises and keep them all. But the majority of his testament is revolutionary—his desire to help all employees become more of who they already are; his willingness to treat each person differently; his desire to become close friends with his employees; his acceptance that he cannot change people, that all he can do is facilitate; his trusting nature. Michael, like all great managers, breaks the rules of conventional wisdom.

Like you, we know that change is a fact of modern life. We know that the business climate is in permanent flux and that different approaches to managing people wax and wane. However, in listening to managers like Michael and the employees they manage, we were searching for that which does not change. What will talented employees *always* need? What will great managers *always* do to turn talent into performance? What are the enduring secrets to finding, focusing, and keeping talented employees? What are the constants? These were our questions. On the following pages we present our discoveries.

CHAPTER 1

The Measuring Stick

- **A Disaster Off the Scilly Isles**
- **The Measuring Stick**
- **Putting the Twelve to the Test**
- **A Case in Point**
- **Mountain Climbing**

A Disaster Off the Scilly Isles

"What do we know to be important but are unable to measure?"

In the dense fog of a dark night in October 1707, Great Britain lost nearly an entire fleet of ships. There was no pitched battle at sea. The admiral, Clowdisley Shovell, simply miscalculated his position in the Atlantic and his flagship smashed into the rocks of the Scilly Isles, a tail of islands off the southwest coast of England. The rest of the fleet, following blindly behind, went aground and piled onto the rocks, one after another. Four warships and two thousand lives were lost.

For such a proud nation of seafarers, this tragic loss was distinctly embarrassing. But to be fair to the memory of Clowdisley Shovell, it was not altogether surprising. The concept of latitude and longitude had been around since the first century B.C. But by 1700 we still hadn't managed to devise an accurate way to measure longitude—nobody ever knew for sure how far east or west they had traveled. Professional seamen like Clowdisley Shovell had to estimate their progress either by guessing their average speed or by dropping a log over the side of the boat and timing how long it took to float from bow to stern. Forced to rely on such crude measurements, the admiral can be forgiven his massive misjudgment.

What caused the disaster was not the admiral's ignorance, but his inability to measure something that he already knew to be critically important—in this case longitude.

A similar drama is playing out in today's business world: many companies know that their ability to find and keep talented employees is vital to their sustained success, but they have no way of knowing whether or not they are effective at doing this.

In their book *The Service Profit Chain,* James Heskett, W. Earl Sasser, and Leonard Schlesinger make the case that no matter what your business, the *only* way to generate enduring profits is to begin by building the kind of work environment that attracts, focuses, and keeps talented employees. It is a convincing case. But the manager on the street probably didn't need convincing. Over the last twenty years most managers have come to realize their competitiveness depends upon being able to find and keep top talent in every role. This is why, in tight labor markets, companies seem prepared to go to almost any lengths to prevent employees' eyes from wandering. If you work for GE, you may be one of the twenty-three thousand employees who are now granted stock options in the company. Employees of AlliedSignal and Starbucks can make use of the company concierge service when they forget that their mothers need flowers and their dachshunds need walking. And at Eddie Bauer, in-chair massages are available for all those aching backs hunched over computer terminals.

But do any of these caring carrots really work? Do they really attract and keep only the most productive employees? Or are they simply a catch-all, netting both productive employees and ROAD warriors—the army's pithy phrase for those sleepy folk who are happy to "retire on active duty"?

The truth is, no one really knows. Why? Because even though every great manager and every great company realizes how important it is, they still haven't devised an accurate way to measure a manager's or a company's ability to find, focus, and keep talented people. The few measurements that are available—such as employee retention figures or number of days to fill openings or lengthy employee opinion surveys—lack precision. They are the modern-day equivalent of dropping a log over the side of the boat.

Companies and managers know they need help. What they are asking for is a simple and accurate measuring stick that can tell them how well one company or one manager is doing as compared with others, in terms of finding and keeping talented people. Without this measuring stick, many companies and many managers know they may find themselves high and dry—sure of where they want to go but lacking the right people to get there.

And now there is a powerful new faction on the scene, demanding this simple measuring stick: institutional investors.

Institutional investors—like the Council of Institutional Investors (CII), which manages over $1 trillion worth of stocks, and the California Public Employees Retirement System (CalPERS), which oversees a healthy $260 billion—define the agenda for the business world. Where they lead, everyone else follows.

Institutional investors have always been the ultimate numbers guys, representing the cold voice of massed shareholders, demanding efficiency and profitability. Traditionally they focused on hard results, like return on assets and economic value added. Most of them didn't concern themselves with "soft" issues like "culture." In their minds a company's culture held the same status as public opinion polls did in Soviet Russia: superficially interesting but fundamentally irrelevant.

At least that's the way it used to be. In a recent about-face, they have started to pay much closer attention to how companies treat their people. In fact, the CII and CalPERS both met in Washington to discuss "good workplace practices . . . and how they can encourage the companies they invest in to value employee loyalty as an aid to productivity."

Why this newfound interest? They have started to realize that whether software designer or delivery truck driver, accountant or hotel housekeeper, the most valuable aspects of jobs are now, as Thomas Stewart describes in *Intellectual Capital*, "the most essentially human tasks: sensing, judging, creating, and building relationships." This means that a great deal of a company's value now lies "between the ears of its employees." And this means that when someone leaves a company, he takes his value with him—more often than not, straight to the competition.

Today more than ever before, if a company is bleeding people, it is bleeding value. Investors are frequently stunned by this discovery. They know that their current measuring sticks do a very poor job of capturing all sources of a company's value. For example, according to Baruch Lev, professor of finance and accounting at New York University's Stern School of Business, the assets and liabilities listed on a company's balance sheet now account for only 60 percent of its real market value. And this inaccuracy is increasing. In the 1970s and 1980s, 25 percent of the changes in a company's market value could be accounted for by fluctuations in its profits. Today, according to Professor Lev, that number has shrunk to 10 percent.

The sources of a company's true value have broadened beyond rough measures of profit or fixed assets, and bean counters everywhere are scurrying to catch up. Steve Wallman, former commissioner of the Securities and Exchange Commission, describes what they are looking for:

If we start to get further afield so that the financial statements . . . are measuring less and less of what is truly valuable in a company, then we start to lower the relevance of that scorecard. What we need are ways to measure the intangibles, R&D, customer satisfaction, *employee satisfaction.* (italics ours)

Companies, managers, institutional investors, even the commissioner of the SEC—everywhere you look, people are demanding a simple and accurate measuring stick for comparing the strength of one workplace to another. The Gallup Organization set out to build one.

The Measuring Stick

"How can you measure human capital?"

What does a strong, vibrant workplace look like?

When you walk into the building at Lankford-Sysco a few miles up the road from Ocean City, Maryland, it doesn't initially strike you as a special place. In fact, it seems slightly odd. There's the unfamiliar smell: a combination of raw food and machine oil. There's the decor: row upon row of shelving piled high to the triple ceilings, interspersed with the occasional loading dock or conveyor belt. Glimpses of figures bundled up in arctic wear, lugging mysterious crates in and out of deep freezers, only add to your disquiet.

But you press on, and gradually you begin to feel more at ease. The employees you run into are focused and cheerful. On the way to reception you pass a huge mural that seems to depict the history of the place: "There's Stanley E. Lankford Jr. hiring the first employee. There's the original office building before we added the warehouse. . . ." In the reception area you face a wall festooned with pictures of individual, smiling faces. There are dozens of them, each with an inscription underneath that lists their length of service with the company and then another number.

"They are our delivery associates," explains Fred Lankford, the president. "We put their picture up so that we can all feel close to them, even though they're out with our customers every day. The number you see under each picture represents the amount of miles that each one drove last year. We like to publicize each person's performance."

Stanley Lankford and his three sons (Tom, Fred, and Jim) founded the Lankford operation, a family-owned food preparation and distribution company, in 1964. In 1981 they merged with Sysco, the $15 billion food distribution giant. An important proviso was that Tom, Fred, and Jim would be allowed to stay on as general managers. Sysco agreed, and today all parties couldn't be happier with the decision.

The Lankford-Sysco facility is in the top 25 percent of all Sysco facilities in growth, sales per employee, profit per employee, and market penetration. They have single-digit turnover, absenteeism is at an all-company low, and shrinkage is virtually nonexistent. Most important, the Lankford-Sysco facility consistently tops the customer satisfaction charts.

"How do you do it?" you ask Fred.

He says there is not much to it. He is pleased with his pay-for-performance schemes—everything is measured; every measurement is posted; and every measurement has some kind of compensation attached. But he doesn't offer that up as his secret. He says it is just daily work. Talk about the customer. Highlight the right heroes. Treat people with respect. Listen.

His voice trails off because he sees he is not giving you the secret recipe you seem to be looking for.

Whatever he's doing, it clearly works for his employees. Forklift operators tell you about their personal best in terms of "most packages picked" and "fewest breakages." Drivers regale you with their stories of rushing out an emergency delivery of tomato sauce to a restaurant caught short. Everywhere you turn employees are talking about how their little part of the world is critical to giving the customer the quality that is now expected from Lankford-Sysco.

Here are 840 employees, all of whom seem to thrill to the challenge of their work. Whatever measurements you care to use, the Lankford-Sysco facility in Pocomoke, Maryland, is a great place to work.

You will have your own examples of a work environment that seems to be firing on all cylinders. It will be a place where performance levels are consistently high, where turnover levels are low, and where a growing number of loyal customers join the fold every day.

With your real-life example in mind, the question you have to ask yourself is, "What lies at the heart of this great workplace? Which elements will attract only *talented* employees and keep them, and which elements are appealing to every employee, the best, the rest, and the ROAD warriors?"

Do talented employees really care how empowered they are, as long as they are paid on performance, such as at Lankford-Sysco? Perhaps the opposite is true; once their most basic financial needs have been met, perhaps talented employees care less about pay and benefits than they do about being trusted by their manager. Are companies wasting their money by investing in spiffier work spaces and brighter cafeterias? Or do talented employees value a clean and safe physical environment above all else?

To build our measuring stick, we had to answer these questions.

• • •

Over the last twenty-five years the Gallup Organization has interviewed more than a million employees. We have asked each of them hundreds of different questions, on every conceivable aspect of the workplace. As you can imagine, one hundred million questions is a towering haystack of data. Now, we had to sift through it, straw by straw, and find the needle. We had to pick out those few questions that were truly measuring the core of a strong workplace.

This wasn't easy. If you have a statistical mind, you can probably hazard a pretty good guess as to how we approached it—a combination of focus groups, factor analysis, regression analysis, concurrent validity studies, and follow-up interviews. (Our research approach is described in detail in the appendix.)

However, if you think statistics are the mental equivalent of drawing your fingernails across a chalkboard, the following image may help you envision what we were trying to do.

In 1666 Isaac Newton closed the blinds of his house in Cambridge and sat in a darkened room. Outside, the sun shone brightly. Inside, Isaac cut a small hole in one of the blinds and placed a glass prism at the entrance. As the sun streamed through the hole, it hit the prism and a beautiful rainbow fanned out on the wall in front of him. Watching the perfect spectrum of colors playing on his wall, Isaac realized that the prism had pried apart the white light, refracting the colors to different degrees. He discovered that white light was, in fact, a mixture of all the other colors in the visible spectrum, from dark red to deepest purple; and that the only way to create white light was to draw all of these different colors together into a single beam.

We wanted our statistical analyses to perform the same trick as Isaac's prism. We wanted them to pry apart strong workplaces to reveal the core. We could then say to managers and companies, "If you can bring all of these core elements together in a single place, then you will have created the kind of workplace that can attract, focus, and keep the most talented employees."

So we took our mountain of data and we searched for patterns. Which questions were simply different ways of measuring the same factor? Which were the best questions to measure each factor? We weren't particularly interested in those questions that yielded a unanimous,

"Yes, I strongly agree!" Nor were we swayed by those questions where everyone said, "No, I strongly disagree." Rather, we were searching for those special questions where the most engaged employees—those who were loyal *and* productive—answered positively, and everyone else— the average performers and the ROAD warriors—answered neutrally or negatively.

Questions that we thought were a shoo-in—like those dealing with pay and benefits—fell under the analytical knife. At the same time, innocuous little questions—such as "Do I know what is expected of me at work?"—forced their way to the forefront. We cut and we culled. We rejigged and reworked, digging deeper and deeper to find the core of a great workplace.

When the dust finally settled, we made a discovery: Measuring the strength of a workplace can be simplified to twelve questions. These twelve questions don't capture everything you may want to know about your workplace, but they do capture the *most* information and the most *important* information. They measure the core elements needed to attract, focus, and keep the most talented employees.

Here they are:

1. Do I know what is expected of me at work?
2. Do I have the materials and equipment I need to do my work right?
3. At work, do I have the opportunity to do what I do best every day?
4. In the last seven days, have I received recognition or praise for good work?
5. Does my supervisor, or someone at work, seem to care about me as a person?
6. Is there someone at work who encourages my development?
7. At work, do my opinions seem to count?
8. Does the mission/purpose of my company make me feel like my work is important?
9. Are my co-workers committed to doing quality work?
10. Do I have a best friend at work?
11. In the last six months, have I talked with someone about my progress?
12. At work, have I had opportunities to learn and grow?

These twelve questions are the simplest and most accurate way to measure the strength of a workplace.

When we started this research we didn't know we were going to land on these twelve questions. But after running a hundred million questions through our "prism," these exact questions were revealed as the most powerful. If you can create the kind of environment where employees answer positively to all twelve questions, then you will have built a great place to work.

While at first glance these questions seem rather straightforward, the more you look at them, the more intriguing they become.

First, you probably noticed that many of the questions contain an extreme. "I have a *best* friend at work" or "At work I have the opportunity to do what I do *best every day.*" When the questions are phrased like this, it is much more difficult to say "Strongly Agree," or "5" on a scale of 1 to 5. But this is exactly what we wanted. We wanted to find questions that would discriminate between the most productive departments and the rest. We discovered that if you removed the extreme language, the question lost much of its power to discriminate. Everyone said "Strongly Agree"—the best, the rest, and everyone in between. A question where everyone always answers "Strongly Agree" is a weak question.

Much of the power of this measuring stick, then, lies in the wording of the questions. The issues themselves aren't a big surprise. Most people knew, for example, that strong relationships and frequent praise were vital ingredients of a healthy workplace. However, they didn't know how to measure whether or not these ingredients were present, and if so, to what extent. Gallup has discovered the best questions to do just that.

Second, you may be wondering why there are no questions dealing with pay, benefits, senior management, or organizational structure. There were initially, but they disappeared during the analysis. This doesn't mean they are unimportant. It simply means they are equally important to every employee, good, bad, and mediocre. Yes, if you are paying 20 percent below the market average, you may have difficulty attracting people. But bringing your pay and benefits package up to market levels, while a sensible first step, will not take you very far. These kinds of issues are like tickets to the ballpark—they can get you into the game, but they can't help you win.

Putting the Twelve to the Test

"Does the measuring stick link to business outcomes?"

Gallup had set out to devise a way to measure *strong* workplaces: workplaces that would attract and retain the most productive employees and scare away the ROAD warriors. If these questions were in truth the *best* questions, then employees who answered them positively would presumably work in higher-performing departments. That was our goal when we designed the measuring stick. Would it prove to be true in practice?

Throughout the spring and summer of 1998 Gallup launched a massive investigation to find out.

We asked twenty-four different companies, representing a cross section of twelve distinct industries, to provide us with scores measuring four different kinds of business outcome: productivity, profitability, employee retention, and customer satisfaction. Some companies had difficulty gathering this data, but in the end we managed to include over 2,500 business units in our study. The definition of a "business unit" varied by industry: for banking it was the branch; for hospitality it was the restaurant or the hotel; for manufacturing it was the factory; and so on.

We then interviewed the employees who worked in these branches, restaurants, hotels, factories, and departments, asking them to respond to each of the twelve questions on a scale of 1 to 5, "1" being strongly disagree, "5" being strongly agree. One hundred and five thousand employees took part.

Armed with all this data, we were set to go. We knew the productivity, the profitability, the retention levels, and the customer ratings of these different business units. And we knew how the employees of the business units had answered the twelve questions. We could now see, finally, whether or not engaged employees did indeed drive positive business outcomes, *across 2,500 business units and 24 companies.*

We were optimistic that the links would surface, but, truth be told, it was entirely possible that we wouldn't find them. The links between employee opinion and business unit performance *seem* inevitable—after all, most of us have probably heard ourselves rattle off such clichés as "Happy employees are more productive" or "If you treat your people right, they will treat your customers right." Yet in their attempts to prove these statements, researchers have frequently come up empty-handed. In fact, in most studies, if you test one hundred employee opinion questions, you will be lucky to find five or six that show a strong relationship to any business outcome. Disappointingly, if you repeat the study, you often find that a different set of five or six questions pop up the second time around.

We also knew that no one had ever undertaken this kind of study before, *across many different companies.* Since each of these four business outcomes—productivity, profit, retention, and customer service—is vitally important to every company, and since the easiest lever for a manager to pull is the employee lever, you would have thought the air would be thick with research examining the links between employee opinion and these four business outcomes. It isn't. You can track down research examining these links *within* a particular company—with decidedly mixed results—but never *across* companies and industries. Surprisingly, the Gallup research was the first cross-industry study to investigate the links between employee opinion and business unit performance.

Why does this research vacuum exist? More than likely it's because each company has different ways of measuring the same thing. Blockbuster Video might measure productivity by sales per square foot. Lankford-Sysco might use packages shipped and number of breakages. The Walt Disney Company might include only full-time employees in their retention figures. Marriott might include full-time and part-time. It is frustratingly difficult to pick up on linkages between employee opinion and business performance, when every company insists on measuring performance differently.

Fortunately we had discovered a solution: meta-analysis. A detailed explanation can put even the most ardent number cruncher to sleep, so let's just say that it is a statistical technique that cuts through the different performance measures used by different companies and allows you to zero in on the real links between employee opinion and business unit performance.

So, having entered the performance data from over 2,500 business units and punched in the opinion data from over 105,000 employees, we programmed the meta-analysis formulas, pressed Run, and held our breath.

This is what we found. First, we saw that those employees who responded more positively to the twelve questions also worked in business units with higher levels of productivity, profit, retention, and customer satisfaction. This demonstrated, for the first time, the link between employee opinion and business unit performance, across many different companies.

Second, the meta-analysis revealed that employees rated the questions differently depending on which business unit they worked for rather than which company. This meant that, for the most part, these twelve opinions were being formed by the employees' immediate manager rather than by the policies or procedures of the overall company. We had discovered that the manager—not pay, benefits, perks, or a charismatic corporate leader—was the critical player in building a strong workplace. The manager was the key. We will discuss this finding in more detail later in the chapter. For now let's concentrate on our first discovery, the link between employee opinion and business unit performance.

THE LINKS BETWEEN EMPLOYEE OPINION AND BUSINESS UNIT PERFORMANCE

If you are so inclined, you can find in the appendix a detailed description of all our discoveries and the methodology behind them. This is the top line.

- Every one of the twelve questions was linked to at least one of the four business outcomes: productivity, profitability, retention, and customer satisfaction. Most of the questions revealed links to two or more business outcomes. The twelve questions were indeed capturing those few, vital employee opinions that related to top performance, whether in a bank, a restaurant, a hotel, a factory, or any other kind of business unit. The measuring stick had withstood its most rigorous test.

- As you might have expected, the most consistent links (ten of the twelve questions) were to the "productivity" measure. People have always believed there is a direct link between an employee's opinion and his work group's productivity. Nonetheless, it was good to see the numbers jibe with the theory.

- Eight of the twelve questions showed a link to the "profitability" measure. That means employees who answered these eight questions more positively than other employees also worked in more *profitable* banks, restaurants, hotels, factories, or departments. To some people this might seem a little surprising. After all, many believe that profit is a function of factors that lie far beyond the control of individual employees: factors like pricing, competitive positioning, or variable-cost management. But the more you think about it, the more understandable this link becomes. There are so many things one employee can do to affect profit—everything from turning off more lights, to negotiating harder on price, to avoiding the temptations of the till. Simply put, these will happen more often when each employee feels truly engaged.

- What about employee retention? Strangely enough, only five of the twelve questions revealed a link to retention:
   1. Do I know what is expected of me at work?
   2. Do I have the materials and equipment I need to do my work right?
   3. Do I have the opportunity to do what I do best every day?
   5. Does my supervisor, or someone at work, seem to care about me as a person?
   7. At work, do my opinions seem to count?

   Most people would instinctively agree with the generalization "Engaged employees will stay longer." But our research suggests that the link between employee opinion and employee retention is subtler and more specific than this kind of generalization has allowed. Even more than the rest, these five questions are most directly influenced by the employee's immediate manager. What does this tell us? It tells us that people leave managers, not companies. So much money has been thrown at the challenge of keeping good people—in the form of better pay, better perks, and better training—when, in the end, turnover is mostly a manager issue. If you have a turnover problem, look first to your managers.

- Of the twelve, the most powerful questions are those with a combination of the *strongest* links to the *most* business outcomes. Armed with this perspective, we now know that the following six are the most powerful questions:
   1. Do I know what is expected of me at work?

2. Do I have the materials and equipment I need to do my work right?
3. Do I have the opportunity to do what I do best every day?
4. In the last seven days, have I received recognition or praise for good work?
5. Does my supervisor, or someone at work, seem to care about me as a person?
6. Is there someone at work who encourages my development?

As a manager, if you want to know what you should do to build a strong and productive workplace, securing 5's to these six questions would be an excellent place to start. We will return to these questions in a moment.

MANAGERS TRUMP COMPANIES

Once a year a study is published entitled "The Hundred Best Companies to Work For." The criteria for selection are such factors as Does the company have an on-site day care facility? How much vacation does the company provide? Does the company offer any kind of profit sharing? Is the company committed to employee training? Companies are examined, and the list of the top one hundred is compiled.

Our research suggests that these criteria miss the mark. It's not that these employee-focused initiatives are unimportant. It's just that your immediate manager is *more* important. She defines and pervades your work environment. If she sets clear expectations, knows you, trusts you, and invests in you, then you can forgive the company its lack of a profit-sharing program. But if your relationship with your manager is fractured, then no amount of in-chair massaging or company-sponsored dog walking will persuade you to stay and perform. It is better to work for a great manager in an old-fashioned company than for a terrible manager in a company offering an enlightened, employee-focused culture.

Sharon F., a graduate of Stanford and Harvard, left American Express a little over a year ago. She wanted to get into the world of publishing, so she joined one of the media-entertainment giants in the marketing department of one of their many magazines. She was responsible for devising loyalty programs to ensure that subscription holders would renew. She loved the work, excelled at it, and caught the eye of senior management. Sharon is a very small cog in this giant machine, but according to the chairman of this giant, employees like her—bright, talented, ambitious employees—are "the fuel for our future."

Unfortunately for this giant, the fuel is leaking. After only a year Sharon is leaving the company. She is joining a restaurant start-up as head of marketing and business development. Her boss, it appears, drove her away.

"He's not a bad man," she admits. "He's just not a manager. He's insecure, and I don't think you can be insecure and a good manager. It makes him compete with his own people. It makes him boast about his high-style living, when he should be listening to us. And he plays these silly little power games to show us who's the boss. Like last week he didn't show up for a ten A.M. interview with a candidate who had made a two-hour commute just to see him, because he had stayed out much too late the night before. He called me at nine fifty-five A.M., asked me to break the news to her, and tried to make it seem like he was giving me some kind of compliment, that he could really trust me to cover for him. I can't stand behavior like that."

Listening to Sharon, you might wonder if it is just a personality clash or even whether it is she who is somehow causing the problems. So you ask her, "Does anyone else on the team feel the same way?"

"I'm not sure," she confesses. "I don't like to bad-mouth my boss, so I haven't really talked about it with anyone at work. But I do know this: When I came here there were thirteen of us on his team. Now, a year later, every single one of them has left, except me."

Sharon's company does many things very well, both in terms of its overall business performance and its employee-friendly culture. But deep within this giant, unseen by the senior executives or Wall Street, one individual is draining the company of power and value. As Sharon says, he is not a bad man, but he is a bad manager. Woefully miscast, he now spends his days chasing away one talented employee after another.

Perhaps he is an exception. Or perhaps the giant makes a habit of promoting people into manager roles who are talented individual achievers but poor managers. The giant would certainly hope for the former. But Sharon doesn't care one way or the other. When she told her company that she was considering leaving, they offered her more money and a bigger title, to try to coax her back. But they didn't offer her what she wanted most: a new manager. So she left.

An employee may *join* Disney or GE or Time Warner because she is lured by their generous benefits package and their reputation for valuing employees. But it is her relationship with her immediate manager that will determine *how long she stays* and *how productive* she is while she is there. Michael Eisner, Jack Welch, Gerald Levin, and all the goodwill in the world can do only so much. In the end these questions tell us that, from the employee's perspective, managers trump companies.

Unlike Wall Street and the business press, employees don't put their faith in the myth of "great companies" or "great leaders." For employees, there are only managers: great ones, poor ones, and many in between. Perhaps the best thing any leader can do to drive the whole company toward greatness is, first, to hold each manager accountable for what his employees say to these twelve questions, and, second, to help each manager know what actions to take to deserve "Strongly Agree" responses from his employees.

The following chapters describe the actions taken by the world's great managers.

But first, a case in point: What do all these discoveries mean for a specific company or a specific manager?

A Case in Point

"What do these discoveries mean for one particular company?"

In the winter of 1997 Gallup was asked by an extremely successful retailer to measure the strength of their work environment. They employed thirty-seven thousand people spread across three hundred stores—about one hundred employees per store. Each one of these stores was designed and built to provide the customer with a consistent shopping experience. The building, the layout, the product positioning, the colors, every detail was honed so that the store in Atlanta would have the same distinctive brand identity as the store in Phoenix.

We asked each employee the twelve questions—over 75 percent of all employees chose to participate for a total of twenty-eight thousand. We then looked at the scores for each store. The following table offers an example of what we found: two stores at opposite ends of the measuring stick. (We asked the questions on a 1–5 scale, where "1" equals strongly disagree and "5" equals strongly agree. The numbers in the columns are the percentage of employees who responded "5" to each question.)

	Store A % responding "5"	Store B % responding "5"
Know what is expected of me	69	41
Materials and equipment	45	11
Do what I do best every day	55	19
Recognition last seven days	42	20
Supervisor/someone at work cares	51	17
Encourages development	50	18
Progress in last six months	48	22
My opinions count	36	9
Mission/purpose of company	40	16
Co-workers committed to quality	34	20
Best friend	33	10
Opportunity to learn and grow	44	24

These are startling differences. Whatever the company was trying to do for its employees from the center, at the store level, these initiatives were being communicated and implemented in radically different ways. For the employees, Store A must have offered a much more engaging work experience than Store B.

Look at the different levels of relationship, for example. In Store A, 51 percent of employees said they felt cared about as a person. In Store B, that number sank to 17 percent. Given the pace of change in today's business world, one of the most valuable commodities a company can possess is the employees' "benefit of the doubt." If employees are willing to offer their company the benefit of the doubt, they will give every new initiative a fighting chance, no matter how sensitive or controversial it might be. Store A possesses this precious commodity. Here the employees will tolerate ambiguity, trusting that, as events play out, their manager will be there to support them. Store B doesn't have that luxury. Lacking genuine bonds between manager and employee, any new initiative, no matter how well intended, will be greeted with suspicion.

How about individual performance? In Store A, 55 percent of employees said that they had a chance to do what they do best every day. In Store B, only 19 percent responded "5." What a difference that must make in terms of per person productivity, retention, and workers' compensation claims.

Wherever you look, the differences leap out at you.

"Do your opinions count?" Store A, 36 percent. Store B? A quarter of that, 9 percent.

"Do you have a best friend at work?" Store A, 33 percent. Store B, only 10 percent.

Perhaps the most bizarre discrepancy can be found in the second question. In Store A, 45 percent of employees strongly agreed that they had the materials and equipment they needed to do their work right. In Store B, only 11 percent said "5." The truly odd thing about this is that Store A and Store B had the *same* materials and equipment; yet the employees' perception of them was utterly different. Everything, even the physical environment, was colored by the store manager.

This company didn't have one culture. It had as many cultures as it did managers. No matter what the company's intent, each store's culture was a unique creation of the managers and supervisors in the field.

Some cultures were fragile, bedeviled with mistrust and suspicion. Others were strong, able to attract and keep talented employees.

For this company's leaders, the wide variation in results was actually very good news. Yes, looking only at the negative, it meant there was a limit to what they could control from the center. The challenge of building a strong all-company culture had suddenly turned into a challenge of multiplication.

On the brighter side, however, these results revealed that this company was blessed with some truly exemplary managers. These managers had built productive businesses by engaging the talents and passions of their people. In their quest to attract productive employees, this company could now stop hunting for the magical central fix. Instead they could find out what their newly highlighted cadre of brilliant managers was doing and then build their company culture around this blueprint. They could try to hire more like their best. They could take the ideas of their best and multiply them companywide. They could redesign training programs based upon the practices of their best. To build a stronger culture, this company wouldn't have to borrow ideas from the likes of "best practice" companies like Disney, Southwest Airlines, or Ritz-Carlton. All they would have to do is learn from *their own* best.

"So what if they do learn from their best?" some might ask. "Do more 5's on the twelve questions necessarily translate to higher levels of real performance? Does Store A actually outperform Store B on any of the more traditional performance measures like sales, profit, or retention?"

Of course, our general discoveries would say yes, workplaces where many employees can answer positively to the twelve questions will indeed be more productive workplaces. But this is too general. Like you, we wanted to know the specifics. So we asked the company to supply us with the raw performance data that they would normally use to measure the productivity of a store. We punched in these scores and then compared them with each store's scores on the twelve questions. This is what we found:

- Stores scoring in the top 25 percent on the employee opinion survey were, on average, 4.56 percent over their sales budget for the year, while those scoring in the bottom 25 percent were 0.84 percent below budget. In real numbers this is a difference of $104 million of sales per year between the two groups. If realized, this figure would represent a 2.6 percent increase in the company's total sales.

- Profit/loss comparisons told an even more dramatic story. The top 25 percent of stores on the survey ended the year almost 14 percent over their profit budget. Those stores in the bottom group missed their profit goals by a full 30 percent.

- Employee turnover levels were also vastly different. Each store in the top group retained, on average, twelve more employees per year than each store in the bottom group. Across both groups this means that the top 25 percent scoring stores on the survey retained one thousand more employees per year than the bottom group of stores. If you estimate that the wage of the average store employee is $18,000 and that the cost of finding, hiring, and training each new employee is 1.5 times his salary, then the total cost to the company for the different levels of retention between the two groups is $18,000 x 1.5 x 1,000 = $27,000,000. And that's just the hard cost. The drain of experienced employees who have developed valuable relationships with their customers and their colleagues is harder to measure but is just as significant a loss.

These results are compelling. In this company the business units were measurably more productive where the employees answered positively to the twelve questions. Excellent front-line managers had engaged their employees and these engaged employees had provided the foundation for top performance.

Any measuring stick worth its salt not only tells you where you stand, it also helps you decide what to do next. So what can a manager, any manager, do to secure 5's to these twelve questions and so engage his employees?

First you have to know where to start. Gallup's research revealed that some questions were more powerful than others. This implies that you, the manager, should address these twelve questions in the right order. There is little point attacking the lesser questions if you have ignored the most powerful. In fact, as many managers discover to their detriment, addressing the twelve questions in the wrong order is both very tempting and actively dangerous.

We will show you why, and by way of contrast, we will describe where the world's great managers start laying the foundations for a truly productive workplace.

Mountain Climbing

"Why is there an order to the twelve questions?"

To help us describe the order of these twelve questions, we ask you to picture, in your mind's eye, a mountain. At first it is hard to make out its full shape and color, shifting from blue to gray to green as you approach. But now, standing at the base, you sense its presence. You know there is a climb ahead. You know the climb will vary, sometimes steep, sometimes gradual. You know there will be gullies to negotiate, terrain that will force you to descend before you can resume your climb. You know the dangers, too, the cold, the clouds, and the most pressing danger of all, your own fragile will. But then you think of the summit and how you will feel, so you start to climb.

You know this mountain. We all do. It is the psychological climb you make from the moment you take on a new role to the moment you feel fully engaged in that role. At the base of the mountain, perhaps you are joining a new company. Perhaps you have just been promoted to a new role within the same company. Either way you are at the start of a long climb.

At the summit of this mountain you are still in the same role—the mountain doesn't represent a career climb—but you are loyal and productive in this role. You are the machinist who bothers to write down all the little hints and tips you have picked up so that you can present them as an informal manual to apprentice machinists just learning their craft. You are the grocery store clerk who tells the customer that the grapefruit are in aisle five but who then walks her to aisle five, explaining that the grapefruit are always stocked from the back to the front. "If you like your grapefruit really firm," you say, "pick one from the front." You are the manager who so loves your work that you get tears in your eyes when asked to describe how you helped so many of your people succeed.

Whatever your role, at the summit of this mountain you are good at what you do, you know the fundamental purpose of your work, and you are always looking for better ways to fulfill that mission. You are fully engaged.

How did you get there?

If a manager can answer this, he will know how to guide other employees. He will be able to help more and more individuals reach the summit. The more individuals he can help move up the mountain, one by one, the stronger the workplace. So how *did* you get there? How *did* you make the climb?

Put on your employee hat for a moment. This may be a psychological mountain, but as with an actual mountain, you have to climb it in stages. Read in the right order, the twelve questions can tell you which stage is which and exactly what needs must be met before you can continue your climb up to the next stage.

Before we describe the stages on the climb, think back to the needs you had when you were first starting your current role. What did you want from the role? What needs were foremost in your mind at that time? Then, as time passed and you settled in, how did your needs change? And currently, what are your priorities? What do you need from your role today?

You may want to keep these thoughts in mind as we describe the stages on the climb.

Base Camp: "What do I get?"

When you first start a new role, your needs are pretty basic. You want to know what is going to be expected of you. How much are you going to earn? How long will your commute be? Will you have an office, a desk, even a phone? At this stage you are asking, "What do I get?" from this role.

Of the twelve, these two fundamental questions measure Base Camp:

1. Do I know what is expected of me?
2. Do I have the materials and equipment I need to do my work right?

Camp 1: "What do I give?"

You climb a little higher. Your perspective changes. You start asking different questions. You want to know whether you are any good at the job. Are you in a role where you can excel? Do other people think you are excelling? If not, what *do* they think about you? Will they help you? At this stage your questions center around "What do *I* give?" You are focused on your *individual* contribution and other people's perceptions of it.

These four questions measure Camp 1:

3. Do I have the opportunity to do what I do best every day?
4. In the last seven days, have I received recognition or praise for good work?
5. Does my supervisor, or someone at work, seem to care about me as a person?
6. Is there someone at work who encourages my development?

Each of these questions helps you know not only if you feel you are doing well in the role (Q3), but also if other people value *your individual performance* (Q4), if they value *you as a person* (Q5), and if they are prepared to *invest in your growth* (Q6.) These questions all address the issue of your *individual* self-esteem and worth. As we will see, if these questions remain unanswered, all of your yearnings to belong, to become part of a team, to learn and to innovate, will be undermined.

Camp 2: "Do I belong here?"

You keep climbing. By now you've asked some difficult questions, of yourself and of others, and the answers have, hopefully, given you strength. Your perspective widens. You look around and ask, "Do I belong here?" You may be extremely customer service oriented—is everyone else as customer driven as you? Or perhaps you define yourself by your creativity—are you surrounded by people who push the envelope, as you do? Whatever your basic value system happens to be, at this stage of the climb you really want to know if you fit.

These four questions measure Camp 2:

7. At work, do my opinions seem to count?
8. Does the mission of my company make me feel my job is important?
9. Are my co-workers committed to doing quality work?
10. Do I have a best friend at work?

Camp 3: "How can we all grow?"

This is the most advanced stage of the climb. At this stage you are impatient for everyone to improve, asking, "How can we all grow?" You want to make things better, to learn, to grow, to innovate. This stage tells us that only after you have climbed up and through the earlier three stages can you innovate effectively. Why? Because there is a difference between "invention" and "innovation." Invention is mere novelty—like most of us, you might have devised seventeen new ways of doing things a few weeks after starting in your new role. But these ideas didn't carry any weight. By contrast, innovation is *novelty that can be applied.* And you can innovate, you can apply your new ideas, only if you are focused on the right expectations (Base Camp), if you have confidence in your own expertise (Camp 1), and if you are aware of how your new ideas will be accepted or rejected by the people around you (Camp 2). If you cannot answer positively to all these earlier questions, then you will find it almost impossible to apply all your new ideas.

These two questions measure Camp 3:

11. In the last six months, has someone talked with me about my progress?
12. This last year, have I had opportunities at work to learn and grow?

The Summit

If you can answer positively to all of these twelve questions, then you have reached the summit. Your focus is clear. You feel a recurring sense of achievement, as though the best of you is being called upon and the best of you responds every single day. You look around and see others who also seem to thrill to the challenge of their work. Buoyed by your mutual understanding and your shared purpose, you climbers look out and forward to the challenges marching over the horizon. It is not easy to remain at the summit for long, with the ground shifting beneath your feet and the strong winds buffeting you this way and that. But while you are there, it is quite a feeling.

If this is the psychological climb you made (or failed to make) from the moment you began your current role to the moment you felt fully engaged in this role, then where are you?

Camp 1? Camp 3? The summit?

Ask yourself those twelve questions. Your answers can give you a read on where you are on the mountain. Perhaps your company is going through times of change and you find yourself languishing down at Base

Camp. Change can do that to a person—you genuinely want to commit, but the uncertainty keeps pushing you down and down. ("Quit telling me how great the future is going to be. Just tell me what is expected of me today.")

Perhaps you have just been promoted—you felt as though you were at the summit in your previous role, but now you find yourself right back down at Camp 1, with new expectations and a new manager. ("I wonder what he thinks of me. I wonder how he will define success.") Yes, even when good things happen you can quickly find yourself at the base of a new mountain, with a long climb ahead.

Of course, the climb toward the summit is more complicated than this picture. Not only will people trade one stage off against another, but each individual will also place a slightly different value on each stage of the climb. For example, you might have taken your current role simply because it offered you the chance to learn and grow—in a sense, you flew straight in to Camp 3. And if these higher-level needs are being met, then you will probably be a little more patient in waiting for your manager to make his expectations crystal clear ($\downarrow$ Base Camp). Similarly, if you feel very connected to your team members ($\uparrow$ Camp 2), then you may be prepared to stick this out for a while longer, even though you feel that your role on the team doesn't allow you to use your true talents ($\downarrow$ Camp 1).

However, these kinds of individual trade-offs don't deny the basic truth of the mountain—regardless of how positively you answer the questions at Camp 2 or Camp 3, the longer your lower-level needs remain unmet, the more likely it is that you will burn out, become unproductive, and leave.

In fact, if you do find yourself answering positively to Camps 2 and 3, but negatively to the questions lower down, be very careful. You are in an extremely precarious position. On the surface everything seems fine—you like your team members ($\uparrow$ Camp 2), you are learning and growing ($\uparrow$ Camp 3)—but deep down you are disengaged. Not only are you less productive than you could be, but you would jump ship at the first good offer.

We can give this condition a name: mountain sickness.

In the physical world, mountain sickness is brought on by the lack of oxygen at high altitudes. Starved of oxygen, your heart starts pounding. You feel breathless and disoriented. If you don't climb down to lower altitudes, your lungs will fill with fluid and you will die. There is no way to cheat mountain sickness. There is no vaccine, no antidote. The only way to beat it is to climb down and give your body time to acclimatize.

Inexperienced climbers might suggest that if you have lots of money and not much time, you could helicopter in to Camp 3 and race to the summit. Experienced guides know that you would never make it. Mountain sickness would sap your energy and slow your progress to a crawl. These guides will tell you that to reach the summit you have to pay your dues. During your ascent you have to spend a great deal of time between Base Camp and Camp 1. The more time you spend at these lower reaches, the more stamina you will have in the thin air near the summit.

In the psychological world, their advice still applies. Base Camp and Camp 1 are the foundation. Spend time focusing on these needs, find a manager who can meet these needs, and you will have the strength necessary for the long climb ahead. Ignore these needs and you are much more likely to psychologically disengage.

AN EPIDEMIC OF MOUNTAIN SICKNESS

Now put your manager's hat back on.

This metaphorical mountain reveals that the key to building a strong, vibrant workplace lies in meeting employees' needs at Base Camp and Camp 1. This is where you should focus your time and energy. If your employees' lower-level needs remain unaddressed, then everything you do for them further along the journey is almost irrelevant. But if you can meet these needs successfully, then the rest—the team building and the innovating—is so much easier.

It almost sounds obvious. But over the last fifteen years most managers have been encouraged to focus much higher up the mountain. Mission statements, diversity training, self-directed work teams—all try to help employees feel they belong (Camp 2). Total quality management, reengineering, continuous improvement, learning organizations—all address the need for employees to innovate, to challenge cozy assumptions and rebuild them afresh, every day (Camp 3).

All of these initiatives were very well conceived. Many of them were well executed. But almost all of them have withered. Five years ago the

Baldrige Award for Quality was the most coveted business award in America—today only a few companies bother to enter. Diversity experts now bicker over the proper definition of "diversity." Process reengineering gurus try to squeeze people back into process. And many of us snort at mission statements.

When you think about it, it is rather sad. An important kernel of truth lay at the heart of all of these initiatives, but none of them lasted.

Why? An epidemic of mountain sickness. They aimed too high, too fast.

Managers were encouraged to focus on complex initiatives like reengineering or learning organizations, without spending time on the basics. The stages on the mountain reveal that if the employee doesn't know what is expected of him as an individual (Base Camp), then you shouldn't ask him to get excited about playing on a team (Camp 2). If he feels as though he is in the wrong role (Camp 1), don't pander to him by telling him how important his innovative ideas are to the company's reengineering efforts (Camp 3). If he doesn't know what his manager thinks of him as an individual (Camp 1), don't confuse him by challenging him to become part of the new "learning organization" (Camp 3).

Don't helicopter in at seventeen thousand feet, because sooner or later you and your people will die on the mountain.

THE FOCUS OF GREAT MANAGERS

Great managers take aim at Base Camp and Camp 1. They know that the core of a strong and vibrant workplace can be found in the first six questions:

1. Do I know what is expected of me at work?
2. Do I have the materials and equipment I need to do my work right?
3. At work, do I have the opportunity to do what I do best every day?
4. In the last seven days, have I received recognition or praise for good work?
5. Does my supervisor, or someone at work, seem to care about me as a person?
6. Is there someone at work who encourages my development?

Securing 5's to these questions is one of your most important responsibilities. And as many managers discover, getting all 5's from your employees is far from easy. For example, the manager who tries to curry favor with his people by telling them that they should all be promoted may receive 5's on the question "Is there someone at work who encourages my development?" However, because all his employees now feel they are in the wrong role, he will get 1's on the question "At work, do I have the opportunity to do what I do best every day?"

Similarly, the manager who tries to control his employees' behavior by writing a thick policies and procedures manual will receive 5's to the question "Do I know what is expected of me at work?" But because of his rigid, policing management style, he will probably receive 1's to the question "Does my supervisor, or someone at work, seem to care about me?"

To secure 5's to all of these questions you have to reconcile responsibilities that, at first sight, appear contradictory. You have to be able to set consistent expectations for all your people yet at the same time treat each person differently. You have to be able to make each person feel as though he is in a role that uses his talents, while simultaneously challenging him to grow. You have to care about each person, praise each person, and, if necessary, terminate a person you have cared about and praised.

F. Scott Fitzgerald believed that "the test of a first-rate intelligence is the ability to hold two opposed ideas in mind at the same time, and still maintain the ability to function." In this sense, great managers possess a unique intelligence. In the following chapters we will describe this intelligence. We will help you look through the eyes of the world's great managers and see how they balance their conflicting responsibilities. We will show you how they find, focus, and develop so many talented employees, so effectively.

CHAPTER 2

The Wisdom of Great Managers

- Words from the Wise
- What Great Managers Know
- What Great Managers Do
- The Four Keys

Words from the Wise

"Whom did Gallup interview?"

How do the best managers in the world lay the foundations of a strong workplace? The flood of answers is rising and threatens to swamp even the most level-headed managers. In 1975 two hundred books were published on the subject of managing and leading. By 1997 that number had more than tripled. In fact, over the last twenty years authors have offered up over nine thousand different systems, languages, principles, and paradigms to help explain the mysteries of management and leadership.

This barrage of conflicting, impressionistic, and largely anecdotal advice is overwhelming, but it rarely enlightens. It lacks precision and simplicity. Something is missing, even from the most persuasive advice. There are volumes of case studies and "here's how I did it" personal success stories, but very little quantitative research and virtually no standard of measurement. No one has ever interviewed the best managers in the world and then compared systematically their answers with the answers of average managers. No one has ever allowed great managers to define themselves. No one has tapped the source. So Gallup did.

This second research effort was the inevitable companion to the first. In the previous chapter we described the link between engaged employees and business unit outcomes and revealed the critical role played by managers everywhere. In this chapter we seek to delve into the minds of the world's great managers and find out how they engaged, so successfully, the hearts, minds, and talents of their people.

Year after year we asked our clients to give us their great managers to interview. It was not always easy to identify who the best ones were, so we began by asking, "Which of your managers would you dearly love to clone?" In some organizations this was the only criterion available. However, in the great majority of organizations there were performance scores: scores measuring productivity and profit; scores for shrinkage, for absenteeism, for employee accidents; and, most important perhaps, scores reflecting the feedback of customers and of the employees themselves. We used these performance scores to sort out the great managers from the rest.

We interviewed hotel supervisors, sales managers, general agents, senior account executives, manufacturing team leaders, professional sports coaches, pub managers, public school superintendents, captains, majors, and colonels in the military, even a selection of deacons, priests, and pastors. We interviewed over eighty thousand managers.

Each great manager was interviewed for about an hour and a half, using open-ended questions. For example:

- "As a manager, which would you rather have: an independent, aggressive person who produced $1.2 million in sales or a congenial team player who produced about half as much? Please explain your choice."
- "You have an extremely productive employee who consistently fouls up the paperwork. How would you work with this person to help him/her be more productive?"
- "You have two managers. One has the best talent for management you have ever seen. The other is mediocre. There are two openings available: the first is a high-performing territory, the second is a territory that is struggling. Neither territory has yet reached its potential. Where would you recommend the excellent manager be placed? Why?"

(You can find out what great managers said to these questions in Appendix B.)

The answers to these, and hundreds of similar questions, were tape-recorded, transcribed, read, and reread. Using the same questions, we then interviewed their rather less successful colleagues. These managers were neither failing nor excelling. They were "average managers." Their answers were tape-recorded, transcribed, read, and reread.

Then we compared. We listened to 120,000 hours of tape. We combed through 5 million pages of transcript. We searched for patterns. What, if anything, did the best have in common? And what, if anything, distinguished them from their less successful colleagues?

It turns out that great managers share less than you might think. If you were to line them all up against a wall, you would see different sexes, races, ages, and physiques. If you were to work for them, you would feel different styles of motivation, of direction, and of relationship building. The truth is they don't have much in common at all.

However, deep within all these variations, there was one insight, one shared wisdom, to which all of these great managers kept returning.

What Great Managers Know

"What is the revolutionary insight shared by all great managers?"

An old parable will serve to introduce the insight they shared.

There once lived a scorpion and a frog.

The scorpion wanted to cross the pond, but, being a scorpion, he couldn't swim. So he scuttled up to the frog and asked: "Please, Mr. Frog, can you carry me across the pond on your back?"

"I would," replied the frog, "but, under the circumstances, I must refuse. You might sting me as I swim across."

"But why would I do that?" asked the scorpion. "It is not in my interests to sting you, because you will die and then I will drown."

Although the frog knew how lethal scorpions were, the logic proved quite persuasive. Perhaps, felt the frog, in this one instance the scorpion would keep his tail in check. So the frog agreed. The scorpion climbed onto his back, and together they set off across the pond. Just as they reached the middle of the pond, the scorpion twitched his tail and stung the frog. Mortally wounded, the frog cried out: "Why did you sting me? It is not in your interests to sting me, because now I will die and you will drown."

"I know," replied the scorpion as he sank into the pond. "But I am a scorpion. I have to sting you. It's in my nature."

Conventional wisdom encourages you to think like the frog. People's natures do change, it whispers. Anyone can be anything they want to be if they just try hard enough. Indeed, as a manager it is your duty to direct those changes. Devise rules and policies to control your employees' unruly inclinations. Teach them skills and competencies to fill in the traits they lack. All of your best efforts as a manager should focus on either muzzling or correcting what nature saw fit to provide.

Great managers reject this out of hand. They remember what the frog forgot: that each individual, like the scorpion, is true to his unique nature. They recognize that each person is motivated differently, that each person has his own way of thinking and his own style of relating to others. They know that there is a limit to how much remolding they can do to someone. But they don't bemoan these differences and try to grind them down. Instead they *capitalize* on them. They try to help each person become *more* and *more* of who he already is.

Simply put, this is the one insight we heard echoed by tens of thousands of great managers:

> *People don't change that much.*
> *Don't waste time trying to put in what was left out.*
> *Try to draw out what was left in.*
> *That is hard enough.*

This insight is the source of their wisdom. It explains everything they do with and for their people. It is the foundation of their success as managers.

This insight is revolutionary. It explains why great managers do not believe that everyone has unlimited potential; why they do not help people fix their weaknesses; why they insist on breaking the "Golden Rule" with every single employee; and why they play favorites. It explains why great managers break all the rules of conventional wisdom.

Simple though it may sound, this is a complex and subtle insight. If you applied it without sophistication, you could quickly find yourself suggesting that managers should ignore people's weaknesses and that all training is a complete waste of time. Neither is true. Like all revolutionary messages, this particular insight requires explanation: How do great managers apply it? What does it ask of employees? What does it mean for companies?

Over the next chapters we will answer these questions, but before we do, we have to agree on what a manager, any manager, actually does. What is their unique function in a company? What role do they play?

What Great Managers Do

"What are the four basic roles of a great manager?"

Tony F., a senior executive in a large entertainment conglomerate, has a familiar complaint: "Smart individual performers keep getting moved into manager positions without the slightest idea of what the manager role is, let alone the ability to play it. We send them off to one of these leadership development courses, but they come back more impressed with their miniexecutive status than with the day-to-day challenges of being a good manager. No one knows what being a good manager is anymore."

Maybe Tony is right. No one knows what being a good manager is anymore. And on top of that, nobody cares. Conventional wisdom tells us that the manager role is no longer very important. Apparently managers are now an impediment to speed, flexibility, and agility. Today's agile companies can no longer afford to employ armies of managers to shuffle papers, sign approvals, and monitor performance. They need self-reliant, self-motivated, self-directed work teams. No wonder managers were first against the wall when the reengineering revolution came.

Besides, continues conventional wisdom, every "manager" should be a "leader." He must seize opportunity, using his smarts and impatience to exert his will over a fickle world. In this world, the staid little manager is a misfit. It is too quick for him, too exciting, too dangerous. He had better stay out of the way. He might get hurt.

Conventional wisdom has led us all astray. Yes, today's business pressures are more intense, the changes neck-snappingly fast. Yes, companies need self-reliant employees and aggressive leaders. But all this does not diminish the importance of managers. On the contrary, in turbulent times the manager is more important than ever.

Why? Because managers play a vital and distinct role, a role that charismatic leaders and self-directed teams are incapable of playing. The manager role is to reach inside each employee and release his unique talents into performance. This role is best played one employee at a time: one manager asking questions of, listening to, and working with one employee. Multiplied a thousandfold, this one-by-one-by-one role is the company's power supply. In times of great change it is this role that makes the company robust—robust enough to stay focused when needed, yet robust enough to flex without breaking.

In this sense, the manager role is the "catalyst" role. As with all catalysts, the manager's function is to speed up the reaction between two substances, thus creating the desired end product. Specifically the manager creates performance in each employee by speeding up the reaction between the employee's talents and the company's goals, and between the employee's talents and the customers' needs. When hundreds of managers play this role well, the company becomes strong, one employee at a time.

No doubt, in today's slimmed-down business world, most of these managers also shoulder other responsibilities: they are expected to be subject matter experts, individual superstars, and sometimes leaders in their own right. These are important roles, which great managers execute with varying styles and degrees of success. But when it comes to the *manager* aspect of their responsibilities, great managers all excel at this "catalyst" role.

Think back to the six questions measuring Base Camp and Camp 1.

1. Do I know what is expected of me at work?
2. Do I have the materials and equipment I need to do my work right?
3. At work, do I have the opportunity to do what I do best every day?
4. In the last seven days, have I received recognition or praise for good work?
5. Does my supervisor, or someone at work, seem to care about me as a person?
6. Is there someone at work who encourages my development?

These questions provide the detail for the catalyst role. To warrant positive answers to these questions from his employees, a manager must be able to do four activities extremely well: *select a person, set expectations, motivate the person, develop the person.* These four activities are the manager's most important responsibilities. You might have all the vision, charisma, and intelligence in the world, but if you cannot perform these four activities well, you will never excel as a manager.

I.   To secure "Strongly Agree" responses to the question "At work, do I have the opportunity to do what I do best every day?" you must know how to select a person. This sounds straightforward, but to do it well demands clearheadedness. Most important, you must know how much of a person you can change. You must know the difference between talent, skills, and knowledge. You must know which of these can be taught and which can only be hired in. You must know how to ask the kinds of questions that can cut through a candidate's desire to impress and so reveal his true talents. If you don't know how to do these things, you will always struggle as a manager. Cursed with poorly cast employees, all your efforts to motivate and develop will be diminished.

II.   If you want "Strongly Agree" responses to the questions "Do I know what is expected of me at work?" and "Do I have the materials and equipment I need to do my work right?" you must be able to set accurate performance expectations. This activity encompasses more than simple goal setting. You must be able to keep the person focused on performance today, no matter how tempting it is to stare at the changes massing over the horizon. You must know on which parts of a job you will enforce conformity and on which parts you will encourage your employee to exercise her own style. You must be able to balance today's need for standardization and efficiency with a similarly pressing need for flair and originality. If you don't know how to set these kinds of performance expectations, you will always be off balance, lurching haphazardly between enforcing too many rules and enduring too much chaos.

III.   "Strongly Agree" responses to the questions "In the last seven days, have I received recognition and praise for good work?" and "Does my supervisor, or someone at work, seem to care about me?" are driven by your ability to motivate each employee. As a manager, you have only one thing to invest: your time. Whom you spend it with, and how you spend it with him, determines your success as a manager. So should you spend more time with your best people or your strugglers? Should you help a person fix his weaknesses, or should you focus on his strengths? Can you ever give someone too much praise? If so, when? If not, why not? You must be able to answer these questions if you are to excel at helping each employee excel.

IV. "Does my supervisor, or someone at work, seem to care about me?" is also driven by your ability to develop the employee, as is the question "Is there someone at work who encourages my development?" When an employee comes up to you and asks the inevitable "Where do I go from here? Can you help me grow?" you need to know what to say. Should you help each person get promoted? If you tell her to attend some training classes and pay her dues, is that the right thing to say? Perhaps you feel as though you are too close to your people. Can you ever get too close to them? What happens if you have to terminate someone you have come to care about? What do you owe your people, anyway? Your answers to all of these questions will guide you as you try to set up each person for success, both in the current role and beyond.

Select a person, set expectations, motivate the person, and *develop the person:* these are the four core activities of the "catalyst" role. If a company's managers are unable to play this role well, then no matter how sophisticated its systems or how inspirational its leaders, the company will slowly start to disintegrate.

In the early nineties one of the leading hospitality companies began experimenting with self-managed work teams as a replacement for the traditional manager role. It was the brainchild of a top industry executive whose flood of new ideas was matched only by his passion in presenting them. He envisioned a hotel of teams. Each team would comprise a balanced roster of housekeepers, front-desk clerks, bellhops, maintenance staff, and table servers. The employees on each team would manage themselves, setting schedules, assigning duties, and disciplining colleagues. To encourage mutual support, all praise and recognition would be meted out at the team level. To encourage individual growth, each employee would be able to increase his pay only by learning how to play each of the other roles on the team—the more roles he learned, the more he would earn. All of this would be monitored by a couple of managers whose chief responsibility was not to manage the people, but to ensure the smooth running of the new team structure. It was an inspired plan, with only one flaw:

It didn't work.

The employees liked the idea of supporting one another, as all great hotel employees do, but the team structure threw them into confusion.

The best housekeepers didn't want to become front-desk clerks. They liked housekeeping. Front-desk clerks didn't like table serving, and the table servers, looking up from their own troubles behind the reception desk, didn't appreciate the mess the front-desk clerks were making of their precious restaurant. Each employee came to feel as though he were in the wrong role. He no longer knew clearly what was expected of him. He no longer felt competent, and with the focus on team rather than individual excellence, he no longer felt important. Arguments broke out, guests complained, and the few remaining managers, forced to support novices in every role, dashed around and about, fighting fires, spinning plates.

It was a mess. The chief designer kept trying to rally the troops, but the slide continued. In the end the hotel was forced to revert back to the traditional system, and its parent company was sold to an even larger hotel conglomerate.

This company paid a hefty price for substituting an elaborate team structure for the elegant power of great managers.

Unfortunately, many other companies seem to be heading for a similar fate, albeit down a slightly different path. These companies have decided to hand off the "catalyst" role to other departments, like human resources or training. These departments then devise sophisticated selection systems or skills development classes and leave the manager to concentrate on "getting the job done." The thinking seems to be that managers have enough to do without having to worry about things like selecting the right people or developing them.

This thinking is laced with good intentions; but, in fact, taking these activities away from managers actually starts to bleed the life out of the company. Healthy companies need strong bonds to develop between each manager and each employee. If the manager has not had a say in selecting his people and if he is not invested in their current success and future growth, then those bonds wither.

This doesn't mean that human resources or training departments should not give managers access to tools, systems, and classes. They should. But the chief focus should be on educating managers on how to use these tools, not on substituting the tools, or the department, for the manager. The core of the manager role consists of those four activities: selecting a person, setting expectations, motivating him, and developing him. You cannot centralize activities that can be done well only one to one, individual manager to individual employee.

MANAGERS ARE NOT JUST LEADERS-IN-WAITING

"Managers do things right. Leaders do the right things." Conventional wisdom is proud of maxims like this. As we mentioned earlier, it uses them to encourage managers to label themselves "leaders." It casts the manager as the dependable plodder, while the leader is the sophisticated executive, scanning the horizon, strategizing. Since most people would rather be a sophisticated executive than a dependable plodder, this advice *seems* positive and developmental. It isn't: it demeans the manager role but doesn't succeed in doing much else. The difference between a manager and a leader is much more profound than most people think. The company that overlooks this difference will suffer for it.

The most important difference between a great manager and a great leader is one of focus. Great managers look *inward.* They look inside the company, into each individual, into the differences in style, goals, needs, and motivation of each person. These differences are small, subtle, but great managers need to pay attention to them. These subtle differences guide them toward the right way to release each person's unique talents into performance.

Great leaders, by contrast, look *outward.* They look out at the competition, out at the future, out at alternative routes forward. They focus on broad patterns, finding connections, cracks, and then press home their advantage where the resistance is weakest. They must be visionaries, strategic thinkers, activators. When played well, this is, without doubt, a critical role. But it doesn't have much to do with the challenge of turning one individual's talents into performance.

Great managers are not miniexecutives waiting for leadership to be thrust upon them. Great leaders are not simply managers who have developed sophistication. The core activities of a manager and a leader are simply different. It is entirely possible for a person to be a brilliant manager and a terrible leader. But it is just as possible for a person to excel as a leader and fail as a manager. And, of course, a few exceptionally talented individuals excel at both.

If companies confuse the two roles by expecting every manager to be a leader, or if they define "leader" as simply a more advanced form of "manager," then the all-important "catalyst" role will soon be undervalued, poorly understood, and poorly played. Gradually the company will fall apart.

KEEP IT SIMPLE

Mike K., a senior trader for a large merchant bank, was stunned. The thirty traders under him were having their best year ever. The atmosphere on the desks was positive and supportive. His boss had given him a very generous bonus. Yet he had just been told by Human Resources that he was the worst manager in the firm. They had come right out and said it, just like that. "You're the worst manager in the firm."

"What on earth gave you that idea?" Mike had shot back.

"This 360-degree survey," they had replied. "Your direct reports rated you on these twenty-five different competencies, and although you scored very well on some of them, by our calculations your overall average was the lowest in the firm. Over the next few months you need to work on all of these low areas because this time next year we're going to send this survey out again." It wasn't a threat—not quite—but Mike knew he was going to be in for a long year.

Mike is the unfortunate victim of good intentions. Some companies, not wanting to fall into the trap of overlooking the importance of the manager, have rushed to the other extreme. They have tried to define the manager role in so much detail that they have ended up overburdening the poor manager with a frighteningly long list of "behavioral competencies." Here, for example, is a sampling of manager competencies used by a number of Fortune 50 companies:

- Manage change
- Self-knowledge
- Establish plans
- Compelling vision
- Inspiration
- Strategic agility
- Troop rallying
- Risk taking
- Take charge
- Business practices and controls
- Results orientation
- Manages diversity
- Broad perspective

- Calm under fire
- Interpersonally sensitive

Managers like Mike are rated on these competencies by their supervisor, direct reports, and sometimes their peers. Areas where they are doing well are given a cursory once-over. Areas where they score poorly are labeled "areas of opportunity" and become the focus for next year's "individual development plan."

You can just imagine how all this is received by managers on the front line: "How can I have a 'compelling vision' yet also maintain a 'broad perspective'!? How can I 'take charge' and be 'interpersonally sensitive' at the same time!?" These are bizarre, backbreaking contortions. Creating supermanager may seem like a good idea at the time, but as with Dr. Frankenstein's plan, the results always end up looking faintly ridiculous and a little scary.

In the end, however well intentioned, this kind of overdefinition is unnecessary. A company should not force every manager to manage his people in exactly the same way. Each manager will, and should, employ his own style. What a company can, and should, do is keep every manager focused on the four core activities of the catalyst role: *select a person, set expectations, motivate the person,* and *develop the person.* No matter how many different styles are used, when managers play this role well, the foundations are laid. As far as is humanly possible, every single employee's talent is being released into performance. The company becomes strong.

The Four Keys

"How do great managers play these roles?"

The catalyst role describes *what* great managers do. It tells us nothing about *how* they do it.

So how do they do it? How do great managers release the potential energy of their people? How do they select a person, set expectations, and then motivate and develop each and every one of their employees?

There is a scene in *Raiders of the Lost Ark* where a frustrated Indiana Jones is trying to discover where to start digging for the Ark of the Covenant. His adversaries, the Nazis, have already begun their excavations, and he is desperate to beat them to the prize. The location of the Ark is inscribed on an archaic ornamental headpiece, and a gnarled Egyptian fakir is turning it over in his hands, translating the Sanskrit symbols, slowly, exactly. Suddenly Indy stops his pacing. Hearing the translation, he realizes that the Nazis have misunderstood the ancient text. Their calculations are flawed. Their measuring stick is too short. He turns to his partner and grins. "They're digging in the wrong place."

When it comes to a manager's four core activities, conventional wisdom is "digging in the wrong place." Its advice is close, very close. But when you look through the eyes of great managers you realize that each element ever so slightly, but so significantly, misses the mark. Conventional wisdom encourages you to

1. select a person . . . *based on his experience, intelligence, and determination.*
2. set expectations . . . *by defining the right steps.*
3. motivate the person . . . *by helping him identify and overcome his weaknesses.*
4. develop the person . . . *by helping him learn and get promoted.*

On the surface there seems to be nothing wrong with this advice. In fact, many managers and many companies follow it devoutly. But all of it misses. You cannot build a great team simply by selecting people based on their experience, intelligence, and determination. Defining the right steps and fixing people's weaknesses are not the most effective ways to generate sustained performance. And preparing someone for the next rung on the ladder completely misses the essence of "development."

Remember the revolutionary insight common to great managers:

> *People don't change that much.*
> *Don't waste time trying to put in what was left out.*
> *Try to draw out what was left in.*
> *That is hard enough.*

If you apply their insight to the core activities of the catalyst role, this is what you see:

- When selecting someone, they **select for talent** . . . not simply experience, intelligence, or determination.
- When setting expectations, they **define the right outcomes** . . . not the right steps.
- When motivating someone, they **focus on strengths** . . . not on weaknesses.
- When developing someone, they help him **find the right fit** . . . not simply the next rung on the ladder.

We've labeled this revolutionary approach, "the Four Keys" of great managers. Taken together, the Four Keys reveal how these managers unlock the potential of each and every employee.

Let's examine how each of these Four Keys works and how you can apply them to your own people.

C H A P T E R   3

The First Key:
Select for Talent

- **Talent: How Great Managers Define It**

- **The Right Stuff**

- **The Decade of the Brain**

- **Skills, Knowledge, and Talents**

- **The World According to Talent**

- **Talent: How Great Managers Find It**

- **A Word from the Coach**

Talent: How Great Managers Define It

"Why does every role, performed at excellence, require talent?"

Normally we associate talent only with celebrated excellence—with a strong emphasis on the word "celebrated." We look at Michael Jordan, swaying and knifing his way to the basket, and we know that neither his training nor his dogged determination is the prime source of his brilliance. He may have both of these, but then so do most other NBA players. Alone, these cannot explain why Michael shines. Deep down we know that his secret weapon is his talent. We look at Robert De Niro and we think the same: He has talent. Tiger Woods, Jay Leno, Maya Angelou, they are all part of the talent club. They are blessed with a secret gift. For most of us talent seems a rare and precious thing, bestowed on special, faraway people. They are different, these people with talent. They are "not us."

Great managers disagree with this definition of talent. It is too narrow, too specialized. Instead they define a talent as "a recurring pattern of thought, feeling, or behavior that can be productively applied." The emphasis here is on the word "recurring." Your talents, they say, are the behaviors you find yourself doing *often*. You have a mental filter that sifts through your world, forcing you to pay attention to some stimuli, while others slip past you, unnoticed. Your instinctive ability to remember names, rather than just faces, is a talent. Your need to alphabetize your spice rack and color-code your wardrobe is a talent. So is your love of crossword puzzles, or your fascination with risk, or your impatience. Any *recurring* patterns of behavior that can be productively applied are talents. The key to excellent performance, of course, is finding the match between your talents and your role.

This definition of talent is deceptively neutral, almost bland. Nevertheless it guides great managers toward a momentous discovery: *Every* role, performed at excellence, requires talent, because *every* role, performed at excellence, requires certain *recurring* patterns of thought, feeling, or behavior. This means that great nurses have talent. So do great truck drivers and great teachers, great housekeepers and great flight attendants. (We will describe some of these talents later in this chapter.)

Whether the excellence is "celebrated" or anonymous, great managers know that excellence is impossible without talent.

The Right Stuff

"Why is talent more important than experience, brainpower, and willpower?"

For most roles, conventional wisdom advises managers to select for experience, for intelligence, or for determination. Talent, if mentioned at all, is an afterthought.

Conventional wisdom says:

"Experience makes the difference." Managers who place a special emphasis on experience pay closest attention to a candidate's work history. They pore over each person's résumé, rating the companies who employed him and the kind of work he performed. They see his past as a window to his future.

"Brainpower makes the difference." These managers put their faith in raw intelligence. They say that as long as you are smart, most roles can be "figured out." Smart people simply "figure it out" better than the rest. When selecting people, they tend to favor articulate applicants blessed with high-powered academic records.

"Willpower makes the difference." This is the "Success is 10 percent inspiration, 90 percent perspiration" school of thought. Managers from this school believe that the technical part of most roles can be taught, whereas the desire to achieve, to persist in the face of obstacles, cannot. When selecting people, they look for past evidence of grit.

As far as it goes, great managers would agree with all of this advice—experience *can* teach valuable lessons; intelligence *is* a boon; and willpower—which great managers actually label a talent—*is* almost impossible to teach. But conventional wisdom stops there. It fails to take into account that there are so many other kinds of talents and that the *right talents,* more than experience, more than brainpower, and more than willpower alone, are *the* prerequisites for excellence in all roles—talents such as a waiter's ability to form opinions, empathy in nurses, assertiveness in salespeople, or, in managers, the ability to individualize.

Conventional wisdom assumes either that these behaviors can be trained after the person has been hired or that these characteristics are relatively unimportant to performance on the job.

Both assumptions are false. First, you cannot teach talent. You cannot teach someone to form strong opinions, to feel the emotions of others, to revel in confrontation, or to pick up on the subtle differences in how best to manage each person. You have to select for talents like these. (We shall explain why this is true later in the chapter.)

Second, talents like these prove to be the driving force behind an individual's job performance. It's not that experience, brainpower, and willpower are unimportant. It's just that an employee's full complement of talents—what drives her, how she thinks, how she builds relationships—is *more* important.

No matter how carefully you select for experience, brainpower, or willpower, you still end up with a *range* in performance. In the retail company described in chapter 1, all store managers faced the same conditions and were provided the same training, yet some were 15 percent over their P/L budget and some were 30 percent below.

In a large telecommunications company, the lower-performing customer service representatives take three times as many calls as the best reps to resolve the same customer complaint—and since millions of customers call in each year, and each call costs the company $10, this range in performance rightly gets management's attention.

Similarly, a nationwide trucking company reports that their average drivers cover 125,000 miles per year and suffer four accidents per year—yet one of their best drivers has just celebrated his four millionth mile of accident-free driving.

There is range in every role, no matter how simple it seems. While experience, brainpower, and willpower all affect performance significantly, only the presence of the right talents—recurring patterns of behavior that fit the role—can account for this *range* in performance. Only the presence of talents can explain why, all other factors being equal, some people excel in the role and some struggle.

Let's take an extreme example where candidates were carefully selected for experience, brainpower, and willpower. They were expertly trained, and yet they still performed very differently from one another.

Brigadier General Don Flickinger faced one of the more daunting management challenges in history. He had to find and train seven men to perform an extremely difficult role. No one had ever performed this role before, and each man would have the opportunity to do it only once. The stakes were very high. Succeed in their role, and these men would restore America's faith in America. Fail, and they would add fuel to the Eastern bloc's swelling self-confidence.

As any manager would, the general spent a great deal of time and energy trying to find the right men for the job. First he laid out his minimum criteria: They had to be no older than thirty-nine, no taller than five feet eleven, in excellent physical condition, and graduates of a military test-pilot school, with at least 1,500 hours of flying experience in jets.

After passing muster, all successful applicants were subjected to the most exacting physical and psychological tests. Tests of physical endurance—how long can you support a column of mercury with one lungful of breath? Tests of mental stability—how long can you endure being locked up in a pitch-black, soundproof "sensory deprivation chamber" with no idea when you will be released? Tests of pain suppression—if we drive a long needle into the big muscle at the base of your thumb and pass an electric current through it, what will you do?

Eventually the general found his seven men.

He found Alan Shepard, Gus Grissom, John Glenn, Scott Carpenter, Wally Schirra, Gordon Cooper, and Deke Slayton. He found the seven astronauts of the Mercury Space Program.

And like any good manager, after having found them, he trained them. They were taught everything from the esoterics of gravitation and rocket propulsion to the very practical matter of how to control yaw, roll, and pitch in the vacuum of space. They were given the best teachers, the most up-to-date equipment, and the time to focus. Over two years they acquired a wealth of new skills and knowledge.

By May 5, 1961, they were ready. Alan Shepard's fifteen-minute suborbital flight was the first of six successful missions (Deke Slayton fell foul of a preexisting heart condition), which culminated in Gordon Cooper's thirty-four-hour, twenty-two-orbit marathon.

By the time Cooper splashed down on May 17, 1963, the Russians had been caught up with, America's pride had been restored, and the platform had been laid for the leap to the moon.

From almost every angle, the MISS program (Man in Space Soonest) was a model of project execution excellence: superior technology combined with carefully selected and well-trained employees, all focused on a specific mission and buoyed by the hopes of a nation. No wonder it succeeded.

But look closer. When you examine the Mercury Program through a strictly managerial lens, you do not see a picture-perfect project. You see six very different missions. And putting aside for a moment the spectacular dimension of the endeavor and the inspirational bravery of each astronaut, the quality of the performance in each of the six missions can be comparatively ranked—two textbook, two heroic, and two mediocre. Look closer still and you realize that, in most instances, the individual astronauts themselves caused this variation.

Alan Shepard and Wally Schirra, both career military men, executed their duties perfectly: no drama, no surprises, textbook missions.

John Glenn and Gordon Cooper were a little special. Glenn was the heroes' hero. Cooper was so laid-back, he actually fell asleep on the launchpad. But both of them faced severe mechanical difficulties and then responded with cool heroism and technical brilliance—Cooper even managed to achieve the most accurate splashdown of all, despite the complete failure of his automatic reentry guidance systems.

The performances of Gus Grissom and Scott Carpenter were rather less impressive. Grissom piloted a clean flight, but he appeared to panic after his capsule splashed down. It seems he blew the escape hatch too early, the capsule filled with water, and it sank to the sea floor sixteen thousand feet below. NASA never recovered the three-thousand-pound capsule.

Carpenter, meanwhile, was so excited to be up in space that while in orbit he maneuvered his capsule this way and that until he had used up almost all his fuel. When it came time to reenter the earth's atmosphere, he was unable to make the appropriate corrections to his angle of reentry and ended up splashing down 250 miles from his designated landing sight. He was lucky. If he had been a couple of degrees shallower in his approach, the capsule would have bounced off the atmosphere and spun off into space for eternity.

NASA must have looked at the performance of their astronauts and wondered, "Why this *range* in performance? We selected for experience, for intelligence, and for determination. They all had the same training and the same tools. So why didn't they perform the same? Why did Cooper excel while Carpenter struggled? Why did Glenn behave so calmly and Grissom less so?"

The answer is that despite being similar in many ways—and all exceptionally accomplished, in comparison with the rest of us—these six men possessed different talents.

What does that mean? It means that although each of these men faced the same stimuli, the way they reacted to these stimuli and then behaved was very different. During orbit, Carpenter was so excited that he couldn't stop playing with the altitude jets; yet Cooper felt so calm, he actually slept through some of his orbits. At takeoff, Grissom's pulse rate spurted to 150. Glenn's never climbed above 80.

Same stimuli, vastly different reactions. Why? Because each man filtered the world differently. Each man's mental filter sorted and sifted, making one man acutely aware of stimuli to which another was blind. Bobbing in the water after splashdown, the dependable Wally Schirra was so focused on "doing it right" that he stayed in the capsule for four hours in order to complete every step of his postflight routine. His mental filter blocked out any twinges of claustrophobia. Gus Grissom's didn't. All indications are that barely five minutes after splashing down, he felt the tiny little capsule closing in around him. His mental filter, no longer able to dampen his growing panic, told him to get out, to escape, now, *now*. The hatch blew.

You have a filter, a characteristic way of responding to the world around you. We all do. Your filter tells you which stimuli to notice and which to ignore; which to love and which to hate. It creates your innate motivations—are you competitive, altruistic, or ego driven? It defines how you think—are you disciplined or laissez-faire, practical or strategic? It forges your prevailing attitudes—are you optimistic or cynical, calm or anxious, empathetic or cold? It creates in you all of your distinct patterns of thought, feeling, and behavior. In effect, your filter is the source of your talents.

Your filter is unique. It sorts through every stimulus and creates a world that only you can see. This filter can account for the fact that the same stimulus produces vastly different reactions in you from those in the person next to you.

For example, imagine you are asleep on a long flight when the plane encounters some high-level turbulence. Do you wake up, convinced that the main reason you haven't heard any explanation from the cockpit is that the pilots are too busy strapping on their parachutes? Or do you stay sleeping, a slightly more vigorous head nodding the only sign that your body notices the bumps?

Imagine you are at a party with some people you know and some you don't. Do you find yourself compelled to dive into the crowd of strangers and swim easily through the throng, remembering names, telling stories, turning strangers into friends? Or do you hug the corner with your significant other, scanning the room for anyone else you might know and nervously rehearsing the one joke you might have to tell tonight?

Imagine you are arguing with your boss. As the argument intensifies, do you find yourself becoming colder, clearer, more articulate, as your brain hands you one perfect word after another? Or, despite all your preparations, does your emotion rise and your brain shut down, separating you from all of those carefully rehearsed words?

Because every human being is guided by his unique filter, the same situation produces very different reactions. What is ridiculously easy for him is excruciatingly difficult for you. What is stimulating to you is tedious for someone else.

All truck drivers face the same situation—miles of road, an unwieldy load, and swarms of little cars buzzing around them. They all have the same training, the same experience. But some of these drivers drive twice as many miles as their colleagues yet suffer half as many accidents. Why? Their filter. When you ask the best drivers, "What do you think about when you are driving?" they all say the same thing. They all say, "I think about what would I do *if* . . . *if* that car pulled out right now. *If* that pedestrian decided to try to cross before the light changed. *If* my brakes failed." While the other drivers are thinking about the next rest stop, how much longer they have to go today, or other, more diverting subjects, the best drivers are playing "what if?" games, anticipating scenarios, planning evasive maneuvers. Same stimuli, different reactions, very different performance.

Likewise all customer service representatives face the same situation—thousands of telephone calls coming in from disgruntled customers. They all have the same technology, the same experience and training. Yet the best take a third fewer calls than the average to solve the same complaint. Why? Because for the best, many of whom are shy in person, the phone is an instrument of intimacy. It offers them shelter from the customer while at the same time giving them the chance to reach through the phone and connect more quickly and more closely than if they were standing face-to-face with her. They picture what room the customer is in. They imagine what the customer looks like. They smile and wave their hands even though they know that the customer cannot see what they are doing. Instinctively their filter takes every disembodied voice and fashions a full human being. On the other end of the line, the customer feels the difference.

This filtering of their world is not a conscious, rational process. It does not happen once a week, allowing them the luxury of sitting back and weighing up all alternatives before deciding on the most "sensible" course of action. Rather, their filter is constantly at work, sorting, sifting, creating their world in real time.

Yours does the same. It's happening now, as you read this book. Maybe, just at this moment, you have looked up from the page to pause and think through something. Maybe you haven't. Maybe you are speed-reading this so that you can get to the end of the chapter before your plane flight ends. Maybe the flight has nothing to do with it; you are simply a compulsive speed reader. Maybe you have just picked up your pen to underline this paragraph or to make a scrawled note in the margin. Maybe you hate it when people mark up books.

Your filter is always working. Of all the possibilities of things you could do or feel or think, your filter is constantly telling you the few things *you must* do or feel or think.

Your filter, more than your race, sex, age, or nationality, is You.

The Decade of the Brain

"How much of a person can the manager change?"

How much of You can be changed?

If you hate meeting new people, can you learn to love the icebreaking with strangers? If you shy away from confrontation, can you be made to revel in the cut and thrust of debate? If the bright lights make you sweat, can you be taught to thrill to the challenge of public speaking? Can you carve new talents?

Many managers and many companies assume that the answer to all these questions is "Yes." With the best of intentions they tell their employees that everyone has the same potential. They encourage their employees to be open and dedicated to learning new ways to behave. To help them climb up the company hierarchy, they send their employees to training classes designed to teach all manner of new behaviors—empathy, assertiveness, relationship building, innovation, strategic thinking. From their perspective, one of the most admirable qualities an employee can possess is the willingness to transform herself through learning and self-discipline.

The world's great managers don't share this perspective. Remember their mantra:

> *People don't change that much.*
> *Don't waste time trying to put in what was left out.*
> *Try to draw out what was left in.*
> *That is hard enough.*

They believe that a person's talents, his mental filter, are "what was left in." Therefore no amount of "smile school" training is going to transform the person who is intimidated by strangers into a smooth wooer. Despite his best efforts, the person who becomes less articulate the angrier he gets will never acquire what it takes to excel at debate. And no matter how much he understands the value of "win-win" scenarios, the intense competitor will never learn to love them.

A person's mental filter is as enduring and as unique as her fingerprint. This is a radical belief, one that flies in the face of decades of self-help mythology. But over the last ten years, neuroscience has started to confirm what these great managers have long believed.

In 1990 Congress and the president declared the nineties the decade of the brain. They authorized funding, sponsored conventions, and generally did everything within their power to help the scientific community unravel the mysteries of the human mind.

Their encouragement accelerated ongoing efforts by industry, academia, and research organizations. According to Lewis L. Judd, former director of the National Institute of Mental Health: "The pace of progress in neuroscience is so great that 90 percent of all we know about the brain we learned in the last ten years."

In the past we had to infer the workings of the brain from the behavior of the patient. Today new technologies like positron emission tomography (PET) and magnetic resonance imaging (MRI) actually allow scientists to see the brain at work. Armed with these and other tools, we have taken giant leaps in learning.

We have learned that the causes of mental illness are as biological as any physical disease. We have learned why the neurotransmitter dopamine calms us down and why serotonin fires us up. We have learned that, contrary to what we used to think, our memories are not stored in one particular place but are scattered like clues on every highway and back alley of our brain.

And we have learned how the brain grows. Given the pace of scientific discovery in this arena, we shall surely advance our knowledge dramatically over the next few years. But this is what we know today.

At birth the child's brain contains one hundred billion neurons, more brain cells than there are stars in the Milky Way. These cells will grow and die regularly throughout the child's life, but their number will remain roughly the same. These cells are the raw material of the mind. But they are not the mind. The mind of the child lives between these cells. In the connections between the cells. In the synapses.

During the first fifteen years of life, the carving of these synaptic connections is where the drama unfolds.

From the day she was born, the child's mind begins to reach out, aggressively, exuberantly. Beginning at the center of the brain, every neuron sends out thousands and thousands of signals. They are trying to talk to one another, to communicate, to make a connection. Imagine everyone alive today simultaneously trying to get in touch with 150,000 other people and you will get some idea of the wonderful scale, complexity, and vitality of the young mind.

By the time the child reaches her third birthday the number of successful connections made is colossal—up to fifteen thousand synaptic connections for each of its one hundred billion neurons.

But this is too many. She is overloaded with the volume of information whirling around inside her head. She needs to make sense of it all. Her sense. So during the next ten years or so, her brain refines and focuses its network of connections. The stronger synaptic connections become stronger still. The weaker ones wither away. Dr. Harry Chugani, professor of neurology at Wayne State University Medical School, likens this pruning process to a highway system:

"Roads with the most traffic get widened. The ones that are rarely used fall into disrepair."

Scientists are still arguing about what causes some mental highways to be used more regularly than others. Some contend that the child's genetic inheritance predisposes her toward certain mental pathways. Others claim that the way she is raised has a significant effect on which pathways will survive the Darwinian pruning and which will die.

These views are not mutually exclusive. But whatever their nature-nurture bias, few disagree on the outcome of this mental pruning. By the time the child reaches her early teens, she has half as many synaptic connections as she did when she was three. Her brain has carved out a unique network of connections. She has some beautiful, frictionless, traffic-free, four-lane highways, where the connections are smooth and strong. And she has some barren wastelands, where no signal at all makes it across.

If she ends up with a four-lane highway for empathy, she will feel every emotion of those around her as though it were her own. By contrast, if she has a wasteland for empathy, she will be emotionally blind, forever saying the wrong thing at the wrong time to the wrong person— not out of malice, but simply out of an inability to pick up the frequency of the emotional signals being sent. Likewise if she has a four-lane highway for confrontation, she will be that lucky person whose brain just hands her one perfect word after another during the heat of a debate. If she has a wasteland for confrontation, she will find that her brain always shuts her mouth down at the most critical moments.

These mental pathways are her filter. They produce the recurring pattern of behaviors that makes her unique. They tell her which stimuli to respond to and which to ignore. They define where she will excel and where she will struggle. They create all of her enthusiasms and all of her indifferences.

The carving of these pathways is the carving of her character. Neuroscience is telling us that beyond her mid-teens there is a limit to how much of her character she can recarve.

This does not mean that she cannot change. As we will describe later, she can learn new skills and new knowledge. She can alter her values. She can develop a greater sense of self-awareness and a greater capacity for self-regulation. And if she does indeed have a wasteland for confrontation, then with enough training, coaching, and encouragement, she can probably be helped to build a thin path so that she is at least able to cope with confrontation. But it does mean that in terms of these mental pathways, no amount of training, coaching, or encouragement will enable her to turn her barren wastelands into frictionless four-lane highways.

Neuroscience confirms what great managers know. Her filter, and the recurring patterns of behavior that it creates, is enduring. In the most important ways she is permanently, wonderfully, unique.

So are you. And, of course, so are the people you hire.

Skills, Knowledge, and Talents

"What is the difference among the three?"

Great managers are not troubled by the fact that there is a limit to how much they can rewire someone's brain. Instead they view it as a happy confirmation that people are different. There is no point wishing away this individuality. It's better to nurture it. It's better to help someone understand his filter and then channel it toward productive behavior.

So if you can't carve out new talents for your people, what, if anything, can you change about them?

First, you can help them discover their hidden talents. As we shall discuss in more detail in chapter 5, the best managers are adept at spotting a glimpse of a talent in someone and then repositioning him so that he can play to that talent more effectively.

Second, a manager can teach her employees new skills and new knowledge. Here we come to one of the most profound insights shared by great managers: Skills, knowledge, and talents are distinct elements of a person's performance. The distinction among the three is that skills and knowledge can easily be taught, whereas talents cannot. Combined in the same person, they create an enormously potent compound. But you must never confuse talents with skills and knowledge. If you do, you may waste a great deal of time and money trying to teach something that is fundamentally unteachable.

Skills are the how-to's of a role. They are capabilities that can be transferred from one person to another. For accountants, arithmetic is a skill. If, for some strange reason, the neophyte accountant doesn't know how to do arithmetic, he can still be taught. For pilots, the mechanics of yaw, roll, and pitch are a skill. For administrative assistants, Microsoft Word or Excel are skills. For nurses, the details of how to give a safe injection are a skill. The best way to teach a skill is to break down the total performance into steps, which the student then reassembles. And, naturally, the best way to learn a skill is to practice.

Your knowledge is simply "what you are aware of." There are two kinds of knowledge: *factual knowledge*—things you know; and *experiential knowledge*—understandings you have picked up along the way.

Factual knowledge for an accountant would be knowing the rules of double-entry bookkeeping. For flight attendants, the Federal Aviation Administration's safety regulations are factual knowledge. For salespeople, their products' features and benefits are factual knowledge. For engineers, the National Bureau of Standards' electrical frequencies are factual knowledge. Factual knowledge can and should be taught.

Experiential knowledge is a little different. It is less tangible and therefore much harder to teach. Acquiring it is your responsibility. You must discipline yourself to stop, look back on past experiences, and try to make sense of them. Through this kind of musing or reflection, you can start to see patterns and connections. You can start to understand.

Some of these understandings are practical. For example, over a number of years an accountant comes to know a variety of ways to shield a client's assets from excessive taxation. A retail store manager, reflecting back on customer buying patterns, now knows which products to highlight during the holiday seasons. A teacher, remembering the glazed eyes of past students, is now prepared with videos and field trips to spice up the particularly stodgy sections of the course.

Some understandings are more conceptual. Your awareness of who you are and how you come across to others is experiential knowledge. It comes with time, if you are listening. In the same way, your values—those aspects of life that you hold dear—are experiential knowledge. As you make your choices, sometimes compromising, sometimes holding firm, you come to realize that certain aspects of your life are more important than others. These critical aspects become your values, guiding the choices you make in the future. Some of these values will remain constant throughout your life. Others will change with time and reflection.

Talents are different phenomena altogether. Talents are the four-lane highways in your mind, those that carve your recurring patterns of thought, feeling, or behavior. Through Gallup's studies of great accountants, we have discovered that one of their most important talents is an innate love of precision. Ask a great accountant—not any accountant, but a great accountant—when he smiles and he will tell you, "When the books balance." When the books balance, his world is perfect. He may not show it, but inside he is aglow. All he can think about is, Oh, when can I do that again! This might seem rather odd to you. But if you think about it, for the person blessed with an innate love of precision, accountancy must be a wonderful job. Every time his books balance he experiences absolute perfection in his work. How many of us can claim that?

A love of precision is not a skill. Nor is it knowledge. It is a talent. If you don't possess it, you will never excel as an accountant. If someone does not have this talent as part of his filter, there is very little a manager can do to inject it.

THREE KINDS OF TALENT

At Gallup we have studied the talents of over 150 distinct roles and, in the process, have identified a multitude of different talents (some of which are described in the appendix). As you would imagine, the talents needed to excel at these roles vary greatly—an all-star goalie in the NHL possesses rather different talents than an excellent Catholic deacon; the best nurses are not cut from the same cloth as the best stockbrokers.

Fortunately we have found a way to simplify these diverse talents into three basic categories: **striving** talents, **thinking** talents, and **relating** talents.

Striving talents explain the *why* of a person. They explain *why* he gets out of bed every day, *why* he is motivated to push and push just that little bit harder. Is he driven by his desire to stand out, or is good enough good enough for him? Is he intensely competitive or intensely altruistic or both? Does he define himself by his technical competence, or does he just want to be liked?

Thinking talents explain the *how* of a person. They explain *how* he thinks, *how* he weighs up alternatives, *how* he comes to his decisions. Is he focused, or does he like to leave all of his options open? Is he disciplined and structured, or does he love surprises? Is he a linear, practical thinker, or is he strategic, always playing mental "what if?" games with himself?

Relating talents explain the *who* of a person. They explain *whom* he trusts, *whom* he builds relationships with, *whom* he confronts, and *whom* he ignores. Is he drawn to win over strangers, or is he at ease only with his close friends? Does he think that trust must be earned, or does he extend trust to everyone in the belief that most will prove worthy of it? Does he confront people dispassionately, or does he avoid confrontation until finally exploding in an emotional tirade?

Striving, thinking, and relating: these are the three basic categories of talent. Within each you will have your own combination of four-lane highways and barren wastelands. No matter how much you might yearn to be different, your combination of talents, and the recurring behaviors that it creates, will remain stable, familiar to you and to others throughout your life.

A COUPLE OF MIND GAMES

If you want to experience firsthand the distinct properties of skills, knowledge, and talents, try this little game.

Can you see the well-known phrase or saying in this word:

MILL1ON

The solution: "One in a million."

If the answer leapt out at you, then you probably have an innate talent for finding word patterns. We have seen this kind of thinking talent in great computer programmers. Like them, you might also love crossword puzzles and brainteasers.

But perhaps you didn't see the answer immediately. If so, don't worry. We will try to teach you a skill that will help you to improve your pattern-finding performance. The skill has three steps:

1. Identify what seems out of place within the word.
2. Evaluate where it is in relation to the whole word.
3. Combine steps 1 and 2 and discover the phrase.

Thus, with this first puzzle, the number **1** is out of place. Where is it in relation to the whole word? It is in the middle. So by combining these two facts, you discover the phrase: "One in a million." Simple, really.

Now try gaining some experience at applying this new skill. Can you see the well-known phrase in this word:

P ^A Y

What is out of place? The letter **A.** Where is it in relation to the rest of the word? It is raised and in the middle.

The solution: "A raise in pay."

How about this one:

$$TEMPER_ATURE$$

What is out of place? The letter **A** again. Where is it in relation to the rest of the word? It is dropped and in the middle.

The solution: "A drop in temperature."

One more:

$$GR_ACE$$

Hopefully the solution is starting to come a little quicker: "A fall from grace."

Okay, you have been given the opportunity to learn a new skill and to gain some experiential knowledge at applying this skill, just as you provide your people in the real world. But now we are going to change the rules on you, just as in the real world.

Can you see the well-known phrase in these words:

	BUT
1) THOUGHT	2) THOUGHT

This one is a little harder, but if you have the innate thinking talent for perceiving patterns, then once again the solution should gradually emerge:

"But on second thought."

But if you don't have this talent, then the skills and knowledge you just acquired didn't help you at all, did they? Lacking the talent, your performance suffered when you were confronted with a novel situation not covered in your training.

The same thing happens in the real world. Let's say you have just trained some new associates in the skills and knowledge they need to provide good customer service. You send them out into the field. As long as the customers' requests stay within the guidelines covered in training, most of them perform acceptably well.

But what happens when, all of a sudden, they are confronted by a customer request that they have never heard before? If they have the relating talent of empathy and/or persuasion, they will perform well. Instinctively they will find just the right words and just the right tone to calm the customer down and resolve the situation.

But if they lack these talents, all the skills and knowledge they have just acquired will be of little help. Their performance will suffer.

The power of skills and knowledge is that they are transferable from one person to another. Their limitation is that they are often situation-specific—faced with an unanticipated scenario, they lose much of their power.

In contrast, the power of talent is that it is transferable from situation to situation. Given the right stimulus, it fires spontaneously. If you have the striving talent of competitiveness, then almost any kind of contest can spark you. If you have the relating talent of empathy, then every emotion speaks to you. If you have the relating talent of assertiveness, then no matter what the subject, you will be able to state your case plainly and persuasively.

The limitation of talent, of course, is that it is very hard to transfer from one person to another. You cannot teach talent. You can only select for talent.

SIMPLE LANGUAGE, SMART THINKING

Now that you know the difference between skills, knowledge, and talents, you can use these terms to throw light on all the other words used to describe human behavior—words like "competencies," "habits," "attitude," and "drive." At present many of us assume that they all mean virtually the same thing. We use phrases like "interpersonal skills," "skill set," "work habits," or "core competencies" so naturally that we rarely question their true meaning.

This isn't just careless language. It's careless thinking. It leads managers astray. It leads them to waste precious time, effort, and money try-ing, with the best of intentions, to train characteristics that are funda-mentally untrainable.

So let's look more closely at competencies, habits, attitude, and drive. Which of these are skills, or knowledge, and therefore can be changed in a person? And which are talents and therefore cannot?

Competencies

Developed by the British military during World War II to define the perfect officer, competencies are now used in many companies to de-scribe behaviors that are expected from all managers and leaders. Although no one really believes that this perfect manager/leader exists, competencies can occasionally be useful if they help a company think through the ideal set of behaviors for a particular role.

But if you do use them, be careful. Competencies are part skills, part knowledge, and part talent. They lump together, haphazardly, some characteristics that can be taught with others that cannot. Consequently, even though designed with clarity in mind, competencies can wind up confusing everybody. Managers soon find themselves sending people off to training classes to learn such "competencies" as strategic thinking or attention to detail or innovation. But these aren't competencies. These are talents. They cannot be taught.

If you are going to use competencies, make it clear which are skills or knowledge and therefore can be taught, and which are talents and therefore cannot. For example, a competency such as "Implements business practices and controls" is a skill—all managers can learn it to some minimum degree of proficiency. A competency such as "Calm under fire" is a talent—you cannot teach someone to be cool.

Habits

"Habit" is another potentially confusing term. We have been told that our habits are second nature. We have been told that we can all change this nature and acquire new habits. Again, this advice is well intended but inaccurate. Most habits are our *first* nature. Most habits are talents.

If you are habitually assertive or habitually empathic or habitually competitive, then you are going to have a tough time changing these habits. They are enduring. They make you You. It's potentially disastrous to suggest that the only way to become more effective is to try to change your first nature.

Of course, this doesn't mean that you cannot change some of your behaviors. You can. Over time, through reflection, you might change your values and so learn a more positive and productive way to apply your talents. You might choose to play to one talent more than another. You might combine your talents with relevant skills. You might learn to accept your unique combination of talents and so become less defensive or insecure. There is a great deal you can change.

But whatever you do, the beauty of this approach is that it relies on *self-awareness*, rather than self-denial, to help you become more effective. Some of your behaviors may have changed, but you haven't been forced to contort yourself into someone else. You have simply cultivated your unique set of talents.

Attitudes

Many managers say they select for attitude—a positive attitude, a team-focused attitude, a service-oriented attitude. They are right to do so, because a person's prevailing attitudes are part of her mental filter. They are created by the interplay of her unique pattern of highways and wastelands. Her attitudes are talents.

She may be cynical or trusting. She may be an optimist or a malcontent. She may be experimental or conservative. None of these attitudes are necessarily better than any of the others. None of them will prevent a person from playing certain roles extremely well—for example, the malcontent might be a powerful entrepreneur, driven by her dissatisfaction with the status quo. The cynic might fit right into a role in law, policing, or investigative reporting, anywhere a healthy mistrust is a prerequisite.

But *all* of these attitudes form part of the person's recurring patterns of thought, feeling, or behavior. Managers may be able to change someone's mood from one day to the next. However, managers will always struggle to change that person's prevailing attitudes. As Mick K., a manager in a large consulting company, describes it: "If I find myself telling the same person to 'look on the bright side' time and time and time again, I should take a hint. He's not a bright-sider. He's a dark-sider. I should stop wasting my breath and try to find a role where skepticism is key to success."

Drive

Many managers make a distinction between talent and drive. They often find themselves counseling someone by saying: "Look, you are very talented. But you need to apply yourself or that talent will go to waste."

This advice sounds helpful. More than likely it is well intended. But fundamentally it is flawed. A person's drive is not changeable. What drives him is decided by his mental filter, by the relative strength or weakness of the highways in his mind. His drives are, in fact, his striving talents.

Take the striving talent of competitiveness as an example. Some people have a four-lane highway for competition. Show them scores and they will instinctively try to use these scores to compare their performance with that of their peers. They love scores, because what you can measure you can compare; and if you can compare, you can compete.

However, people with a wasteland for competition will see the same scores and not feel any jolt of energy at all. Putting themselves on a level playing field, pitting their best efforts against their peers, and winning . . . means nothing to them. They rationalize their behavior by opining, "I don't like competition; I prefer win-win scenarios," or the classic, "I prefer to compete with myself." But these comments are just signs that their filter is, understandably, trying to describe itself in the most positive light.

The truth is that they are not competitive. There is nothing good or bad about this. It is simply who they are. And there is not much that either they or you, their manager, can do about it.

Similarly, some people have a four-lane highway for constant achievement, a striving talent we call achiever. They may not have to win, but they do feel a burning need to achieve something tangible every single day. And these kind of people mean "every single day." For them, every day—workday, weekend, vacation—every day starts at zero. They have to rack up some numbers by the end of the day in order to feel good about themselves. This burning flame may dwindle as evening comes, but the next morning it rekindles itself, spurring its host to look for new items to cross off his list. These people are the fabled "self-starters."

Not all roles require employees to possess this striving talent of achiever. Nurses, for example, do not have to generate all of their drive from within. Instead they have to *respond* caringly and efficiently to the urgent needs that face them every day—for nurses the altruistic striving talent mission is much more important than achiever. But if you manage roles that do require achiever—like an insurance agent, a pharmaceutical salesperson, or any role where the person must initiate rather than respond—then remember: You had better select for it. Because if a person does not feel this burning fire, you cannot light it for him.

The same applies to all striving talents: the need to be of service, the need to be on stage, the need to be seen as competent, the need to help others grow. All of these drives are talents, and therefore they have the same characteristics as other talents. Namely, they are part of each person's mental filter. They are unique and enduring.

A manager can never breathe motivational life into someone else. All she can do is try to identify each employee's striving four-lane highways and then, as far as is possible, cultivate these. (More on this in chapter 5.)

When describing human behavior, we would advise you to stick with the clarity of skills, knowledge, and talents. Tread carefully when using habits or competencies—they lump too much together rather haphazardly. Likewise, if you feel a need to use attitude or drive, be cautious. Remember that a person's drive and her prevailing attitudes are talents, and as such, they are very hard to change. When you hear yourself berating the person to "get a better attitude," watch out. You might be asking her to tackle the impossible.

None of this implies that a person cannot change. Everyone can change. Everyone can learn. Everyone can get a little better. The language of skills, knowledge, and talents simply helps a manager identify where radical change is possible and where it is not.

The World According to Talent

"Which myths can we now dispel?"

Guided by their own beliefs, and supported by recent scientific advances, great managers can now dispel two of the most pervasive management myths.

MYTH #1: "TALENTS ARE RARE AND SPECIAL"

There is nothing very special about talent. If talents are simply recurring patterns of thought, feeling, or behavior, then talents are actually rather commonplace. Everyone has certain recurring patterns of behavior. No one can take credit for these talents. They are an accident of birth, "the clash of the chromosomes," as the ethologist Robert Ardrey described them. However, each person can and should take credit for cultivating his unique set of talents.

The best way to help an employee cultivate his talents is to find him a role that plays to those talents. Employees who find such roles *are* special. These people are naturally able to do what someone is prepared to pay them to do. We rightly label these people "talented."

Take nursing as an example. Working with a large health care provider, Gallup had a chance to study some of the best nurses in the world. As part of our research we asked a study group of excellent nurses to inject one hundred patients and a control group of less productive nurses to perform the same injection on the same population of one hundred patients. Although the procedure was exactly the same, the patients reported feeling much less pain from the best nurses than from the rest. Why? What were the best nurses doing to lessen the pain? Did they have some special technique with the needle? Did they apply the disinfectant using a firmer hand or a softer swab?

Apparently not. Apparently it all came down to what the nurse said to the patient right before the needle punctured the skin. The average nurses introduced themselves with a brisk, "Oh, don't worry, this won't hurt a bit," and then plunged in the needle with businesslike efficiency.

The best nurses opted for a very different approach. They were just as efficient with the needle, but they set the stage rather more carefully. "This is going to hurt a little," they admitted. "But don't worry, I'll be as gentle as I can."

The best nurses were blessed with the relating talent empathy. They knew the injection would hurt, and each of them, in their own style, felt compelled to share that knowledge with the patient. Surprisingly, this confession eased the patients' pain. To the patients it seemed as though the nurse were, in some small way, going through the experience with them. The nurse was on their side. The nurse understood. So when the needle broke the skin, somehow it didn't feel as bad as they thought it would.

The relating talent of empathy is not particularly special. Many people have it and call upon it in all aspects of their life. But those people with empathy who become nurses *are* special. They can share a patient's pain. They are "talented."

Similarly, some people are fascinated with risk. This striving talent is neither a good thing nor a bad thing, although it can prompt some otherwise normal people to hurl themselves out of planes or swim with great white sharks just for the fun of it. However, if these people become anesthesiologists or surgeons, then their four-lane highway for risk becomes a positive strength. For them, the literal life-or-death quality of their work is a thrill, not a pressure. They are special, these people. They are "talented."

The same goes for the person with the talent for remembering names as well as merely faces. This talent is nice to have, but it becomes particularly valuable if she is hired as the concierge in a hotel.

In all of these situations the talent alone isn't special. It is the matching of the talent with the role that is special. As with the performing arts, the secret to great performances is all in the casting.

Of course, in today's highly specialized business world, finding the right fit between the person and the role is a good deal more challenging than it used to be. It is not enough to say, "This person has a talent for assertiveness; I think I'll hire him to sell." You have to know very specifically what kind of selling you are going to be asking him to do. For example, to be a great salesperson for IBM, as in many sales roles, you have to love pushing for the close—a striving talent—and you have to know exactly when and how to do it—a relating talent. These talents, among others, are critical to an individual's success in the role.

But if you are a salesperson for Merck, the pharmaceutical giant, you'd better not have these talents, because you'll never have a chance to use them. The job will quickly frustrate you. The goal of pharmaceutical sales is for the sales representative to build up influence with the doctor or the HMO gradually, so that, over time, more of *your* drugs are prescribed. Here, success has a great deal to do with the sales rep's relating talent for patience and influence and almost nothing to do with a talent for closing.

As a manager your job is not to teach people talent. Your job is to help them earn the accolade "talented" by matching their talent to the role. To do this well, like all great managers, you have to pay close attention to the subtle but significant differences between roles.

MYTH #2: "SOME ROLES ARE SO EASY, THEY DON'T REQUIRE TALENT"

The famous management theorist Oscar Wilde once said:

"A truth ceases to be a truth as soon as two people perceive it."

All right, so Mr. Wilde was better known for his wit than for his management advice; nonetheless, every manager should be required to remember this one remark. Although he phrased it in the extreme, Mr. Wilde simply meant that the only truth is your own. The world you see is seen by you alone. What entices you and what repels you, what strengthens you and what weakens you, is part of a pattern that no one else shares. Therefore, as Mr. Wilde said, no two people can perceive the same "truth," because each person's perspective is different.

This can be both a blessing and curse. You are blessed with a wonderfully unique filter but cursed with a systematic inability to understand anybody else's. True individuality can be lonely.

One way to cope with this loneliness is to succumb to the illusion that other people operate under many of the same assumptions as you. Your ambitions, passions, likes, and dislikes are not special or distinct. They are "normal." So you are "normal." In moments of calm objectivity, you may concede that your point of view is not the only one, but day to day it is simply easier if you assume that everyone shares yours.

Of course, this is a generalization—some people, particularly empathic people, seem able to walk a genuine mile in someone else's moccasins. Nonetheless it is a generalization that pervades our working world. Managers look at "lower-level" roles like housekeeping or outbound telemarketing and wonder, "How could anyone want to do that job? That job must be so demoralizing." Misled by the illusion that everyone shares their filter, they make two false assumptions: first, that virtually anyone with the right training could do the job adequately; and second, that everyone, regardless of who they are, will want to be promoted out of the job as soon as possible. With the best of intentions, they then define these roles as "entry-level" and build career paths and compensation plans that reward top performers with speedy promotion out of the "drudgery."

Great managers do not believe that their filter is common to everyone. Instead, when they select for a role, they are guided by the belief that some people are probably wired to excel at this role and to derive enduring satisfaction from doing it well. The Gallup research confirms this belief. Let's take hotel housekeepers as an example.

Most of us haven't spent much time mulling over the details of housekeeping. But consider, for a moment, what hotel housekeepers do and how often they have to do it. Put yourself in their shoes.

Okay.

Two things might have occurred to you: first, that this is an easy job anyone with a modicum of responsibility can do; and second, that this is a terrible job that everyone, including housekeepers, must hate to do.

If these thoughts crossed your mind, then you would be wrong on both counts.

We shouldn't devalue housekeepers. Anyone can probably clean a hotel room once in a while, but great housekeepers are special. Every day they vacuum themselves out of each room knowing that the next day they will return to find the room hit by the usual tornado of towels, toiletries, and bed linen. It is enough to make Sisyphus weary, endlessly pushing his rock up the hill. But great housekeepers don't get weary. They get stronger. They are not beaten down by the relentless grind of their work. On the contrary, they seem to be energized by it. In their mind, their work asks them to be accountable, to be creative, and to achieve something tangible each and every day. They *want* to come in and attack their section of rooms. The challenge gives them strength.

All this is so because great housekeepers possess a certain special set of talents. Does this sound incongruous? What follows may give you a clearer sense of some of the talents needed to be a great housekeeper.

Gallup was asked by a large entertainment company to help them find more housekeepers like their best. This company already knew how special housekeepers were. Leaders in service quality the world over, they had over fifteen thousand hotel rooms, cleaned by over three thousand housekeepers. But to maintain their edge over competitors, they wanted to learn more about what made their best the best.

Sitting around the table we had assembled eight of this company's best housekeepers. Some were shy, perplexed by being asked to talk about their work. Others were completely relaxed, chatting away in English or Haitian Creole or Portuguese. One of them had been a housekeeper for only eighteen months, while another had cleaned the same section of rooms in the same hotel for twenty-three years. They were of different races, sexes, and ages. But they were all great housekeepers.

Our goal was to encourage them to talk about their work to see what, if anything, these eight great housekeepers had in common.

"How do you know if a room is clean?" we asked them. They said that the last thing they did before leaving a room was to lie on the guest's bed and turn on the ceiling fan.

"Why?"

"Because," they explained, "that is the first thing that a guest will do after a long day out. They will walk into the room, flop down on the bed, and turn on the fan. If dust comes off the top of the fan, then no matter how sparkling clean the rest of the room was, the guest might think it was as dirty as the top of the fan."

We asked them if they were front-of-house or back-of-house. (In many hotel companies housekeepers are considered back-of-house staff.)

"Front-of-house. I am always on stage, always, always." A grumpy chorus of English, Creole, and Portuguese.

"Why do you say you are on stage?"

"Because we make a show for our guests. Unless the guests object, we will take the toys that the children leave on the bed and every day we will make a little scene with them. We will put Pooh and Piglet on the pillows together. Pooh will have his arm in a chocolate candy box. Piglet will have his on the remote control. When the children come back, they imagine that all day long Pooh and Piglet just hung out on the bed, snacking and watching TV. The next day they find Donald and Goofy dancing on the windowsill. We make a show."

These eight great housekeepers were not just trying harder, nor did they simply "take more pride in their work." These great housekeepers had talent. They shared a unique filter. Seen through this filter, a hotel room wasn't just another chore to be completed. It was a world, a guest's world. When they cleaned the room, they looked through the guests' eyes and imagined how the world should look. Making each guest's world just right brought them strength and satisfaction.

No one told these housekeepers to behave like this. But for some reason their mental filter drove them to these behaviors and to gain enduring satisfaction from the outcome. These individuals were probably some of the best housekeepers in the world.

The managers of these housekeepers knew that the best way to recognize these Michael Jordans of housekeeping was not necessarily to promote them out of it. They looked for other ways—more specific praise, better compensation, tighter selection criteria for aspiring housekeepers—to highlight these superstars. Guided by the knowledge that great housekeepers possessed talent, they did everything in their power to make excellence in housekeeping publicly revered and a genuine career choice.

In the minds of great managers, every role performed at excellence deserves respect. Every role has its own nobility.

Talent: How Great Managers Find It

"Why are great managers so good at selecting for talent?"

Even if you know to select for talent, it is not always easy to identify those who have it. First off, many people don't know what their true talents are. They may be experts in their chosen field, but when it comes to listing their unique set of talents, they are stumped. As Peter Drucker, the elder statesman of management wisdom, says:

"Even today, remarkably few Americans are prepared to select jobs for themselves. When you ask, 'Do you know what you are good at? Do you know your limitations?' they look at you with a blank stare. Or they often respond in terms of subject knowledge, which is the wrong answer."

This confusion is understandable. Your own skills and knowledge are relatively easy to identify. You had to acquire them, and therefore they are apart, distinct. They are "not You." But your talents? Your talents are simply your recurring patterns of behavior. They are your very essence. It takes a rare objectivity to be able to stand back from yourself and pick out the unique patterns that make you You.

Second, when someone applies for a job, he naturally wants to impress. Therefore those few recurring behaviors of which he is aware will be painted in as rosy a hue as possible. In the job interview he labels himself "assertive," not "aggressive." He describes himself as "ambitious" rather than "pushy." More often than not these are not deliberate misrepresentations. They are genuine attempts to describe himself to you positively. But whatever his true motivations, his instinct to try to impress you makes your job—the talent scout—that much more difficult.

These barriers to talent scouting are a fact of life. Human nature being what it is, people will always struggle to know themselves, and they will always sell themselves in job interviews. Despite these barriers, great managers still do much better than their colleagues at selecting people with the right talents for the role. They have discovered some simple techniques to cut through the barriers and so find the match between the person and the role.

KNOW WHAT TALENTS YOU ARE LOOKING FOR

In the early nineties Gallup began work with two of the largest retail brokerage firms in the United States. Both companies wanted help in selecting brokers. And both of them defined the role in exactly the same way—the broker was not paid to be a money manager, doing financial analysis, picking stocks. Instead he was paid to be a money *gatherer*, identifying high-potential prospects and then persuading them to invest their money with his firm. He was a salesperson.

Although the definition of both roles was the same, each company organized itself differently. One was extremely structured. Each broker spent months learning how to represent the same suite of meticulously packaged products, and regular refresher courses helped keep him from straying too far from the company's mandate.

By comparison, the other company was wildly entrepreneurial. Licensed brokers were told, "Here's a phone, here's a phone book. I want to see $500,000 in assets under management by this time next year. Best of luck."

Both strategies had their strengths. And as it turns out, both strategies have proven very successful. However, both could not be executed by the same kind of person. Although the job title was the same—"broker"—and the job description was the same—"gather money"—the talent profiles were significantly different.

For the structured company, the critical striving talent was achiever, the burning inside-out push; in this environment of frequent supervision, other striving talents, like the need for independence, were actually weaknesses. The critical thinking talent was discipline—an ability to work in a highly regimented environment. Thinking talents like focus or strategic thinking were much less important because the company, not the broker, set the direction and determined the best routes forward. Any broker who wanted to do this for himself would quickly start to butt heads with the company. He would lose.

In the entrepreneurial company, the opposite was true. The critical striving talent was desire—a burning need for independence—and the critical thinking talent was focus—the ability to pick out a genuine prospect from the phone book, to sort out whom to call from everyone who could be called. Lacking these talents, the unfortunate broker would feel lost and lonely, a company man in an entrepreneur's world.

A broker with lots of desire and focus is not necessarily a better broker than one with lots of achiever and discipline. But she would certainly fit better in the entrepreneurial company, just as the broker blessed with achiever and discipline would be better cast in the more structured company. Lacking this knowledge, both companies might have ended up hiring each other's brokers, with disastrous repercussions.

As a manager you need to know exactly which talents you want. To identify these talents, look beyond the job title and description. Think about the culture of the company. Is your company the kind that uses scores to drive performance and makes heroes out of those with the highest scores? If so, make sure that the striving talent competition is in your profile. Or maybe yours is an organization that emphasizes the underlying purpose of its work and confers prestige only on those who manifestly live the values of the company. If so, search for people who possess the striving talent mission, people who *must* see the greater purpose of which their efforts are a part.

Think about how expectations will be set and how closely the person will be supervised. Think about who you are as a manager and who will mesh with your style. Do you prefer to set short-term goals and expect to check in regularly with each person to monitor incremental progress? If so, you need to surround yourself with direct reports who yearn for structure and detail and regular updates, the thinking talent discipline. Or are you the kind of manager who likes to hand off as much responsibility as possible, who sets long-term goals and then expects employees to orient themselves toward those goals without much help from you? If so, your direct reports will need the thinking talent focus, which we described previously.

Think about the other people on the team. Think about the total work environment into which this person must fit. Perhaps the team is filled with solid but serious performers who are in need of drama and excitement—find a person with the relating talent stimulator, a person who can find the drama in almost any milestone or achievement. Perhaps the team is friendly but lacks the ability to confront one another with the truth—look for a person who leads with her relating talent assertiveness, so that you have at least one team member who feels compelled to bring every issue, no matter how sensitive, to the surface. Perhaps your organization has a strong human resources department that can give your managers detailed feedback on the strengths and weaknesses of each of their direct reports. In this case you may not need to select managers who possess the relating talent individualized perception, defined as the ability to identify and capitalize upon the uniqueness in people. Or perhaps your organization offers no HR support at all. In this case relating talents like individualized perception, or relator—the need to build bonds that last—or developer—the need to invest in other people's growth and to derive satisfaction from doing so—will need to serve as the cornerstones of your desired talent profile.

Pondering all of these variables can become overwhelming. So simplify, bring things down to size. Try to identify *one critical talent* in each of the three talent categories, striving, thinking, and relating. Use these three talents as your foundation. Focus on them during the interviewing process. Mention them when asking people for referrals. Do not compromise on them, no matter how alluring a candidate's résumé might appear.

STUDY YOUR BEST

If you want to be sure that you have started with the right three talents, study your best in the role. This may sound obvious, but beware: conventional wisdom would advise the opposite.

Conventional wisdom asserts that good is the opposite of bad, that if you want to understand excellence, you should investigate failure and then invert it. In society at large, we define good health as the absence of disease. In the classroom, we talk to kids on drugs to learn how to keep kids off drugs and delve into the details of truancy to learn how to keep more kids in school.

And in the working world, this fascination with pathology is just as pervasive. Managers are far more articulate about service failure than they are about service success, and many still define excellence as "zero defects."

When it comes to understanding talent, this focus on pathology has caused many managers to completely misdiagnose what it takes to excel in a particular role. For example, many managers think that because bad salespeople suffer from call reluctance, great salespeople must not; or that because bad waiters are too opinionated, great waiters must keep their opinions in check.

Reject this focus on pathology. You cannot infer excellence from studying failure and then inverting it. Why? Because excellence and failure are often surprisingly similar. Average is the anomaly.

For example, by studying the best salespeople, great managers have learned that the best, just like the worst, suffer call reluctance. Apparently the best salesperson, as with the worst, feels as if he is selling himself. It is this striving talent of feeling personally invested in the sale that causes him to be so persuasive. But it also causes him to take rejection personally—every time he makes a sales call he feels the shiver of fear that someone will say no to him, to *him*.

The difference between greatness and failure in sales is that the great salesperson is not paralyzed by this fear. He is blessed with another talent, the relating talent of confrontation, that enables him to derive immense satisfaction from sparring with the prospect and overcoming resistance. Every day he feels call reluctance, but this talent for confrontation pulls him through it. His love of sparring outweighs his fear of personal rejection.

Lacking this talent for confrontation, the bad salesperson simply feels the fear.

The average salesperson feels nothing. He woodenly follows the six-step approach he has been taught and hopes for the best.

By studying their best, great managers are able to overturn many similarly long-standing misconceptions. For example, they know that the best waiters, just like the worst, form strong opinions. The difference between the best and the worst is that the best waiters use their quickly formed opinions to tailor their style to each particular table of customers, whereas the worst are just rude—average waiters form no opinions and so give every table the same droning spiel.

And the best nurses, contrary to popular opinion, do form strong emotional relationships with their patients. The difference between the best and the worst is that the best nurses use their emotions to take control and smooth the patient's world as far as is possible, whereas the worst are overwhelmed by their emotions. Average nurses? Average nurses protect themselves by keeping their distance. They are emotionally disengaged.

Take time to study your best, say great managers. Learn the whys, the hows, and the whos of your best and then select for similar talents.

In the end, much of the secret to selecting for talent lies in the art of interviewing. When interviewing for talent, most managers are aware of the more obvious pitfalls: don't put the candidate under undue stress; don't evaluate people on their appearance alone; don't rush to judgment. Avoiding these will certainly lay the foundations for a productive interview.

However, if you want to excel in the art of interviewing you will need to do more. In chapter 7 we will describe in detail the interviewing techniques that have enabled great managers to select for talent so unerringly.

A Word from the Coach

"John Wooden, on the importance of talent."

Selecting for talent is the manager's first and most important responsibility. If he fails to find people with the talents he needs, then everything else he does to help them grow will be as wasted as sunshine on barren ground. John Wooden, the legendary coach of the UCLA Bruins, puts it more pragmatically:

"No matter how you total success in the coaching profession, it all comes down to a single factor—talent. There may be a hundred great coaches of whom you have never heard in basketball, football, or any sport who will probably never receive the acclaim they deserve simply because they have not been blessed with the talent. Although not every coach can win consistently with talent, no coach can win without it."

According to everything we have heard from great managers, the coach is right. But he is also a little humble. What made John Wooden so successful was not just the talents on his teams, but also his own ability to create the right kind of environment to allow those talents to flourish. After all, talent is only potential. This potential cannot be turned into performance in a vacuum. Great talents need great managers if they are to be turned into performance.

Selecting for talent is only the first of the Four Keys. In the chapters that follow we will present the others and describe how great managers focus, recognize, and develop the talents they have so carefully selected.

The Second Key: Define the Right Outcomes

- **Managing by Remote Control**
- **Temptations**
- **Rules of Thumb**
- **What Do You Get Paid to Do?**

Managing by Remote Control

"Why is it so hard to manage people well?"

"I am ultimately responsible for the quality of all teaching in my district. Yet every day, in every classroom, there is a teacher and there are students . . . and the door is shut."

Gerry C., a superintendent for a large public school district, captures the manager's challenge perfectly: How can you get people to do what you want them to do when you are not there to tell them to do it? Gerry knows what all great managers know: As a manager, you might think that you have more control, but you don't. You actually have *less* control than the people who report to you. Each individual employee can decide what to do and what not to do. He can decide the hows, the whens, and the with whoms. For good or for ill, he can make things happen.

You can't. You can't make anything happen. All you can do is influence, motivate, berate, or cajole in the hope that most of your people will do what you ask of them. This isn't control. This is remote control. And it is coupled, nonetheless, with all of the accountability for the team's performance.

Your predicament is compounded by the fact that human beings are messy. No matter how carefully you selected for certain talents, each of your people arrived with his own style, his own needs, and his own motivations. There is nothing wrong with all this diversity—it is often a real benefit to have a team of people who all look at the world in slightly different ways. But this diversity does make your job significantly more complicated. Not only do you have to manage by remote control, but you have to take into account that each employee will respond to your signals in slightly but importantly different ways.

If it's any consolation, great managers are in the tightest spot of all. They are further hemmed in by two fervent beliefs. First, as we described in chapter 2, they believe that people don't change that much. They know that they cannot force everyone in a particular role to do the job in exactly the same way. They know that there is a limit to how much each employee's different style, needs, and motivation can be ground down.

Second, they believe that an organization exists for a purpose and that that purpose is performance—with "performance" defined as any outcome that is deemed valuable by either an external or internal customer. In their view, the manager's most basic responsibility is not to help each person grow. It is not to provide an environment in which each person feels significant and special. These are worthy methods, but they are not the point. The point is to focus people toward performance. The manager is, and should be, totally responsible for this. This explains why great managers are skeptical about handing all authority down to their people. Allowing each person to make all of his own decisions may well result in a team of fully self-actualized employees, but it may not be a very productive team.

So this is their dilemma: The manager must retain control and focus people on performance. But she is bound by her belief that she cannot force everyone to perform in the same way.

The solution is as elegant as it is efficient: Define the right outcomes and then let each person find his own route toward those outcomes.

This solution may sound simple. But study it more closely and you can begin to see its power.

First, it resolves the great manager's dilemma. All of a sudden her two guiding beliefs—that people are enduringly different and that managers must focus people on the same performance—are no longer in conflict. They are now in harmony. In fact, they are intertwined. The latter frees her up to capitalize on the former. To focus people on performance, she must define the right outcomes and stick to those outcomes religiously. But as soon as she does that, as soon as she standardizes the required outcomes, she has just avoided what she always knew was impossible anyway: forcing everyone to follow the same path toward those outcomes. Standardizing the ends prevents her from having to standardize the means.

If a school superintendent can keep focused on his teachers' student grades and ratings, then he need not waste time evaluating them on the quality of their lesson plans or the orderliness of their classrooms. If a hospitality manager can measure her front-desk clerks' guest ratings and the repeat visits they created, then she won't have to monitor how closely they followed the preset welcome script. If the sales manager can define very specifically the few outcomes he wants from his salespeople, then he can ignore how well they filled out their call-reporting sheets.

Second, this solution is supremely efficient. The most efficient route that nature has found from point A to point B is rarely a straight line. It is *always* the path of least resistance. The most efficient way to turn someone's talent into performance is to help him find his own path of least resistance toward the desired outcomes.

With his mind firmly focused on the right outcomes, the great sales manager can avoid the temptation of correcting each person's selling style so that it fits the required mold. Instead he can go with each person's flow, smoothing a unique path toward the desired result. If one salesperson closes through relationship building, one through technical competence and detail orientation, and another through sheer persuasiveness, then the great sales manager doesn't have to interfere . . . so long as quality sales are made.

Third, this solution encourages employees to take responsibility. Great managers want each employee to feel a certain tension, a tension to achieve. Defining the right outcomes creates that tension. By defining, and more often than not measuring, the required outcomes, great managers create an environment where each employee feels that little thrill of pressure, that sense of being out there by oneself with a very definite target. This kind of environment will excite talented employees and scare away the ROAD warriors. It is the kind of environment where a person must *learn*. She must learn the unique combination of plays that work for her time and time again. She must learn how she responds to pressure, how she builds trust with people, how she stays focused, how and when she needs to rest. She must discover her own paths of least resistance.

Defining the right outcomes *does* expect a lot of employees, but there is probably no better way to nurture self-awareness and self-reliance in your people.

Temptations

"Why do so many managers try to control their people?"

If defining outcomes rather than methods is so elegant and so efficient, why don't more managers do just that? When faced with the challenge of turning talent into performance, why do so many managers choose, instead, to dictate how work should be done? Every manager has his own reasons, but in the end it is probably that the allure of control is just too tempting. On the surface these temptations seem justifiable, but play them out, and each one soon saps the life out of the company and shrivels its value.

TEMPTATION: "PERFECT PEOPLE"

This first temptation is very familiar.

Imagine an expert, a well-intentioned expert. He wants to help all employees rise above their imperfections. He looks at all the fumbling inefficiency around him, and he knows, he just knows, that if only people would learn his simple steps, the world would be a better place. And everyone would thank him.

This expert believes that there is "one best way" to perform every role. With time and study, he will find this "one best way" and teach it to all employees. He will make them more efficient and more successful. You, the manager, will simply have to monitor each person to ensure that they are all sticking to the regimen.

Many managers can frequently be seduced by the idea that there is "one best way" and that it can be taught. Thus they dispatch the salesperson to learn the ten secrets of effective negotiation and then evaluate him based upon how closely he followed the required steps. They send the budding executive off to acquire the twenty competencies of successful leadership and then grade him on his ability to demonstrate each and every one. And, with the best of intentions, they encourage every employee to develop the nine habits for effective living.

Although their areas of interest differ, these scientific experts all base their ideas on the same premise: namely, that each person's uniqueness is a blemish. If you want to make your people perform, they say, you must teach the perfect method, remove the blemishes, and so perfect the person.

Frederic Taylor, of the infamous time-and-motion studies, is considered the father of "one best way" thinking, but despite some formidable competition of late, the most *influential* "one best way" expert is probably a woman by the name of Madelaine Hunter.

Virtually every educator in the United States knows her name. Having studied effective teaching practices at UCLA's University Elementary School, Madelaine Hunter identified what she considered to be the seven most basic components of an effective lesson:

- Step 1: A brief review
- Step 2: Introduction
- Step 3: Explanation
- Step 4: Demonstration
- Step 5: Check for understanding
- Step 6: Q&A session
- Step 7: Independent study

She gave each of the steps a unique moniker (for example, step 5 she called "Dipsticking;" step 6 became "Monitored Practice"). But by her own admission all she was basically doing was repackaging what talented teachers had always done. Not that there was anything wrong with this. In fact, for any educator interested in learning from the best, it was an extremely valuable analysis.

If she had left it at that, she would probably have attracted a little less attention and much less criticism. But she didn't leave it at that. She couldn't. She had become convinced that her seven steps were not just a perceptive summary of what most good teachers did in the classroom; they were a formula, a strict formula. Anyone who took the time to learn and apply her formula would be transformed into an excellent teacher. She was sure of it.

"I used to think that teachers were born, not made. But I know better now," she claimed in an interview with the *Los Angeles Times*. "I've seen bumblers turned into geniuses."

It is doubtful that she had, but since she believed that her formula could indeed transform "bumblers into geniuses," then couldn't she fix the entire education system? Couldn't she make a better world for teachers and students and parents? Well, in her mind, yes, she could. She was on a mission.

Beginning in the late sixties and continuing until her death in 1994, she expanded her formula into books and videotapes. She raced around and around the lecture circuit. She courted school superintendents and administrators. She spread her good word. "At University Educational School," she announced, "we identified the nutrients required for a successful school situation. We showed teachers what those learning nutrients are, how to put everything together to make a nourishing meal. We have made some darned good cooks."

As you can imagine, these optimistic claims were a sweet song for many embattled educators. Thousands of school administrators became disciples. They decided not only to train teachers in the seven steps, but also to evaluate each teacher based upon how closely and how well he or she followed the required sequence. What began as a thoughtful message about great teachers quickly became a creed that every teacher was forced to recite. Today hundreds of thousands of teachers have been indoctrinated in the "Madelaine Hunter method," and sixteen states still, to some degree, officially embrace her methods.

However, the tide is beginning to turn against the scientific doctrine of Madelaine Hunter. Some critics point out that her research was faulty—she didn't study thousands of great teachers; she studied a few teachers working at her school at UCLA. Some comment on the unimpressive results of Hunterized school districts—over the years, student achievement scores were either no higher than regular school districts or, in some cases, significantly lower.

Some are quite forgiving of the woman herself: "I don't think that Madelaine meant for all this to happen," said Gerry C., the school superintendent. "Her seven steps were meant to be ideas that each teacher could then incorporate into his own style. They were never meant to be rules which everyone had to follow."

Others judge her more harshly. Here's Amy F., another school superintendent: "I think Madelaine suckered us into it. We liked the teach-by-the-numbers feel of it all. Teachers can be insecure, and she made teaching seem like a science, a real profession. We forgot that the essence of great teaching is to treat every child as an individual. You can't train that. There aren't seven steps to discovering that Billy learns by doing, while Sally learns by reading. It's a talent. Madelaine distracted us from this. She led the whole of teaching astray."

Whatever the criticism, most educators agree: In ten years' time her theories will still be known, and probably revered, as a perceptive study of great teaching. But they will no longer carry the force of dogma that they do today.

This is a teaching example, but it could apply to any role. Any attempt to impose the "one best way" is doomed to fail. First, it is inefficient—the "one best way" has to fight against the unique, grooved four-lane highways possessed by each individual. Second, it is demeaning—by providing all the answers, it prevents each individual from perfecting and taking responsibility for her own style. Third, it kills learning—every time you make a rule you take away a choice and choice, with all of its illuminating repercussions, is the fuel for learning.

Adrian P., the manager of two thriving car dealerships, describes it this way: "The hardest thing about being a manager is realizing that your people will not do things the way that you would. But get used to it. Because if you try to force them to, then two things happen. They become resentful—they don't want to do it. And they become dependent—they can't do it. Neither of these is terribly productive for the long haul."

In your attempts to get your people to perform, never try to perfect people. The temptation may be captivatingly strong, but you must resist it. It is a false god. What looks like a miraculous cure-all is actually a disease that diminishes the role, demeans the people, and weakens the organization.

Perhaps George Bernard Shaw was just in a particularly bad mood when he commented, "The road to hell is paved with good intentions." But when it comes to attempts to perfect people, he wasn't entirely off the mark.

TEMPTATION:
"MY PEOPLE DON'T HAVE ENOUGH TALENT"

As we discussed in the previous chapter, it is tempting to believe that some roles are so simple that they don't require talent. Hotel housekeepers, outbound telemarketers, and hospital service workers are all examples of roles that conventional wisdom suggests "anyone can do."

Misled by this wisdom, many managers don't bother selecting for people who have talent for these roles. They hire virtually anyone who applies. Consequently they end up with a hopelessly miscast work-force—thousands of employees who see their role as demeaning and who can think only of getting out of it as fast as possible. Thus cursed, their managers respond with strict legislation. They impose a Bible-thick procedure manual on their people in the hope that they can make the role "idiotproof." Their rationale: "If I give these people the chance to make choices, many of them will use that freedom to make the wrong choices."

Faced with this scenario, you can't really fault these managers their need for control. If you don't select for talent, then you *shouldn't* give people leeway. You *should* dot every "i" and cross every "t" and you *should* monitor every employee's performance to ensure that it meets the step-by-step guidelines. This is a time-consuming approach that, unfortunately, turns managers into policemen, but why leave anything to chance? Since your employees weren't carefully selected, who knows which way they would jump if the restraints were loosened?

Of course, a more productive solution would be to start by respecting the role enough to select for talent in the first place.

TEMPTATION:
"TRUST IS PRECIOUS—IT MUST BE EARNED"

Even when they have selected for talent, some managers are hamstrung by their fundamental mistrust of people. This mistrust might be a prod-uct of some deep-seated insecurity, or it might be couched as a rational conclusion—"I think the human race is basically driven by selfishness, and therefore most people will cut corners if they think they can get away with it." But whatever its source, their mistrust means that these managers are extremely reluctant to let each employee find his or her own route to performance.

Plagued by the nagging suspicion that someone, somewhere, is taking advantage of them, a mistrustful manager's only recourse is to impose rules. They spin a web of regulations over their world. Only through regulation, they believe, will they be able to protect themselves from people's inevitable misdeeds.

For a mistrustful person, the manager role is incredibly stressful. The ambiguity—"What might that employee be doing!?"—and the suspicion—"Whatever it is, I'm sure it's bad"—must be excruciating. Unfortunately for managers like this, the rules and regulations they impose rarely succeed in quelling their suspicions. They succeed merely in creating a culture of compliance that slowly strangles the organization of flexibility, responsiveness, and, perhaps most important, goodwill.

Consider this: If you are a teacher in Florida, it is illegal for you to use your judgment when assigning grades to your students. This is not an exaggeration. It is *illegal*. Driven by their mistrust and their desire to control, state legislators enacted a law defining percentages and grades. If a child scores above 94 percent, it is *illegal* for him to receive anything other than an A. If he scores between 85 percent and 93 percent, then he *must* receive a B. Arkansas is another state that saw fit to legislate away a teacher's judgment, although they were a little more lenient on the children—in Arkansas 90 percent or above gets an A, while anything over 80 percent warrants a B.

Great school superintendents say that there is nothing wrong with offering teachers a grading/percentage guideline. Most states do it, and it helps to ensure consistency across districts. But a law? No wonder so many teachers feel they have lost the trust and goodwill of the people.

And what of the notion that "trust must be earned"? Sensible though it may sound, great managers reject it. They know that if, fundamentally, you don't trust people, then there is no line, no point in time, beyond which people suddenly become trustworthy. Mistrust concerns the future. If you are innately skeptical of other people's motives, then no amount of good behavior in the past will ever truly convince you that they are not just about to disappoint you. Suspicion is a permanent condition.

Of course, occasionally a person will indeed let you down. But great managers, like Michael, the restaurant manager from the introduction, are wired to view this as the exception rather than the rule. They believe that if you expect the best from people, then more often than not the best is what you get.

Innate mistrust is probably vital for some roles—lawyering or investigative reporting, for example. But for a manager it is deadly.

TEMPTATION:
"SOME OUTCOMES DEFY DEFINITION"

Many managers say they would like to define the right outcomes and then let each person find his or her own route, but they can't. Some outcomes, they say, defy definition. And if you can't define the right outcomes then you have to try to define the right steps. It's the only way to avoid chaos, they say.

From some angles this perspective is actually quite sympathetic. First, some outcomes are indeed difficult to define. Sales, profit, or even student grades lend themselves to easy measurement. But customer satisfaction doesn't, nor does employee morale. Yet both of these are critical to excellent performance in many roles.

Second, if you do fail to define, in outcome terms, "customer satisfaction" or "employee morale," then you still have to find some way to encourage people to pay attention to their customers and to their employees. Defining the right steps would certainly be one such way.

This perspective may be sympathetic, but it is not wise. These managers have given up too quickly. Just because some outcomes are *difficult* to define does not mean that they defy definition. It simply means that the outcomes aren't obvious. Some thinking is required. If you do give it some thought, you find that even the most intangible aspects of performance can, in fact, be defined in terms of outcomes. And with these outcomes defined, you can then avoid the time-wasting futility of trying to force everyone to satisfy their customers or treat their employees in exactly the same way.

Let's look at the outcome "employee morale" in more detail (we will address customer satisfaction later in the chapter). As we described in chapter 1, many companies have realized that the strength of their culture is part of their competitive weaponry. If they can treat their people better than their competitors, they will be able to attract more talent, focus that talent, develop that talent, and ultimately dominate. In their view, culture—how managers treat their people—has become tremendously important. Too important, it appears, to be left to chance.

Rather than defining a strong culture in terms of the employees' *emotional outcomes*—"This is how we want our employees to feel"—many companies have chosen to break "culture" down into *steps*—"This is what all managers/leaders must do." As we described in chapter 2, these steps are usually called "competencies."

Once defined, competencies provide a common focus and a common language for a great deal of what happens within the company. New managers are required to learn them. Existing managers are rated against them, by peers, direct reports, and their superior. The picture of the perfect manager is he who possesses them all. Of course, everyone knows this person is a phantom, but that doesn't stop you from becoming concerned if your direct reports rate you low on competencies like "Compelling vision" or "Calm under fire." Nor does it stop your boss from telling you to improve your scores for the coming year if you are to earn 100 percent of your discretionary bonus. Yes, these competencies are quickly taken very seriously.

Not by great managers, fortunately. They know that you should not legislate in advance how a manager is to interact with his people, moment by moment. You should not try to script culture. First, it's distracting—it focuses the manager on compliance to a "standard" while she should be figuring out what style works best for her. Second, it's impossible—her innate talents, not her "competencies," drive the manager's moment-by-moment interactions, and talents cannot be taught.

But this does not mean that you should not hold your managers accountable for treating their employees well. You should. You just shouldn't legislate how to do it, step by step by step. It would be more effective to identify the few emotions you want your employees to feel and then to hold your managers accountable for creating these emotions. These emotions become your outcomes.

As an example, take those first six questions of the twelve that measure workplace strength:

1. Do I know what is expected of me at work?
2. Do I have the materials and equipment I need to do my work right?
3. At work, do I have the opportunity to do what I do best every day?
4. In the last seven days, have I received recognition or praise for good work?
5. Does my supervisor, or someone at work, seem to care about me as a person?
6. Is there someone at work who encourages my development?

These questions describe some of the most important emotional outcomes that you should expect your managers to create in their employees. You want their employees responding "Strongly Agree" to these questions by the end of the year, and you certainly want to hold your managers accountable for securing these 5's. But now that you've identified what you want their employees to feel, you are, happily, freed from forcing each manager to create these feelings in lockstep.

Take the emotion "trust," as measured by the question "Does my supervisor, or someone at work, seem to care about me?" One front-line supervisor has a quiet, caring relationship style. One supervisor builds relationships through his straightforwardness and his consistency. One supervisor uses his rah-rah passion and humor. But the great manager doesn't care one way or the other, as long as the supervisors' employees respond "5" to the question "Does my supervisor, or someone at work, seem to care about me as a person?" The great manager knows that he doesn't need to waste time and money sending the quiet one to public speaking class or the straightforward one to interpersonal sophistication class. (Of course, he may discover that a particular supervisor has no path of least resistance to building relationships with his people. For whatever reason, they just don't trust him. We'll describe how great managers handle this problem in chapter 6.)

As Gallup discovered, defining the right outcomes to measure "culture" can be quite a challenge. But it is worth the effort. If as much effort were spent identifying the right employee outcomes as has been spent trying to legislate the manager's style, then everyone would be better off. The company would be more efficient. The human resources department would be more popular. The employees would be more trusting. And the managers would be themselves. Finally.

Rules of Thumb

"When and how do great managers rely on steps?"

The best managers avoid all of these temptations. They know that the manager's challenge is not to perfect people, but to capitalize on each person's uniqueness. They select for talent, no matter how simple the role. Their first instinct is to trust the people they have selected. And they believe that, with enough thought, even intangibles like "customer satisfaction" and "employee morale" can be defined in terms of outcomes.

However, this does not mean they dismiss the need for steps. They don't. A manager's basic responsibility is to turn talent into performance. Certain required steps can often serve as the platform for that performance. In the course of Gallup's interviews, these managers described how and when they used required steps to drive performance. Here are the rules of thumb that guide them.

RULE OF THUMB #1: "DON'T BREAK THE BANK"

Employees must follow certain required steps for all aspects of their role that deal with accuracy or safety.

Take banking as an example. A bank performs many different functions, but in the long run it has value for its customers only if it handles their money accurately and safely. Therefore the foundation of every role within the bank, whether it be trader, investment adviser, or teller, is the need to do it accurately and safely. To show employees exactly what it means to be "accurate" or "safe," the banking industry has defined regulatory steps, and each bank has its own internal guidelines. The bank's employees *must* adhere to these. This isn't the only part of their job, but it is the foundational part. Any manager who forgets this, who gives his employees too much room to maneuver, runs the risk of destroying the bank's value.

The managers of Baring's bank, a two-hundred-year-old English banking institution, forgot.

In late 1994 Baring's general manager of futures trading in Singapore, twenty-eight-year-old Nicholas Leeson, began to invest heavily in the Japanese stock market, guessing that the market would rise. He guessed wrong. The market kept falling. And, naively, he kept increasing his bet, hoping against hope for an upswing. During November and December he lost a great deal of the bank's money.

This wasn't particularly unusual. Futures traders lose large sums of their company's money all the time. When this happens repeatedly, the company simply cuts off the money supply, fires the trader, absorbs the losses, and chalks it all up to the cost of doing business.

What was unusual was that, in Nick Leeson's case, it appears his superiors didn't know about the extent of the losses. In a bizarre example of empowerment run amuck, his manager had given him control of both the front and back office in Singapore—he was a fox in his own henhouse, policing his own trading. There was no system in place to ensure that Leeson was following the guidelines for "accurate" accounting and "safe" investing. This made it relatively easy to do what more than a few desperate twenty-eight-year-olds might do: set up dummy accounts to hide his mounting losses. Back in London, blithely unaware, his manager kept the money coming.

Leeson took his final gamble in January of 1995. He bet the farm that the Japanese Nikkei index would rise, finally. He must have done something spectacularly bad in a previous life, because on January 17 a violent earthquake pummeled the cities of Kobe and Osaka, driving the Nikkei index down through the floor. The bet had failed.

The next morning Baring's woke up to losses of over $1.3 billion, about $700 million more than they had in their cash reserves. A month later, on February 27, 1995, the bank collapsed. Leeson went to jail, and four thousand jobs were put in jeopardy. The two-hundred-year-old institution was destroyed.

This is a banking story, but it could just as well have been a story about jet engine manufacturing, theme park ride design, subway train operation, or scuba-diving instruction. All roles demand some level of accuracy or safety, and therefore all roles require employees to execute some standardized steps. Great managers know that it is their responsibility to ensure that their employees know these steps and can execute them perfectly. If that flies in the face of individuality, so be it.

Unrestrained empowerment can be a value killer.

RULE OF THUMB #2: "STANDARDS RULE"

Employees must follow required steps when those steps are part of a company or industry standard.

It would be hard to overestimate the importance of standards. And by "standards" we are not referring to moral or ethical standards. We mean languages, symbols, conventions, scales. These are the DNA of civilization. Without our ability to devise and then accept standards, we could never have developed such a complex society.

Standards enable us to communicate. Each language is simply a shared set of standards. If you don't share someone's grammatical standards, and if you cannot agree on what certain symbols mean, then you can't speak that person's language. All communication, no matter what its medium, demands shared standards—just ask a Windows user who has tried to download a document from his Mac-bound buddy.

Standards drive learning. The skill of arithmetic is teachable precisely because all the students and all the teachers know that they are adding and subtracting in "base ten." Shared standards make skills transferable.

Standards make comparison possible. For example, in order to function, market-driven economies needed a standard system for comparing the value of one company with that of another. Until the late fifteenth century no such system existed. But in 1494 a Venetian monk, Luca Pacioli, formalized that system and communicated it in the first book detailing the standards of double-entry bookkeeping. Wall Street still uses that system today.

Counterintuitively, standards fuel creativity. Take music as an example. There is no right way to structure sounds. But in Western Europe in the late sixteenth century, a structured scale gradually became standard. This scale, called a "chromatic scale," used twelve tones per octave, with each tone being one hundred cents apart in pitch—represented by the seven white keys and five black keys on a piano keyboard. On the surface this sounds as though it would restrict the composers' genius. But the opposite was true. Being limited to just twelve tones didn't dampen their creativity; it fostered their creativity. The chromatic scale, and its formal notation system, spawned two centuries of the most prolific and original composition. Composers as diverse as Vivaldi, Miles

Davis, Stravinsky, and Madonna all used the standard chromatic scale to give voice to the unique music playing in their minds.

Standards, then, are the code in which human collaboration and discovery is written. Great managers know that if they want to build a cooperative, creative organization, they will have to ensure that their employees use the relevant codes. Lawyers must study case law. Air traffic controllers have to learn the standard navigational protocols. Accountants have to learn the rules of double-entry bookkeeping. And engineers have to design products that will operate on the standard electrical frequency broadcast twenty-four hours a day from the National Bureau of Standards' radio station, WWVB.

If standards are important today, then that importance will surely multiply many times over in the coming decade. Here is how Kevin Kelly, writing in *Wired* magazine, describes this decade:

> The grand irony of our times is that the era of computers is over. All the major consequences of stand-alone computers have already taken place. Computers have speeded up our lives a bit, and that is it. In contrast, all the most promising technologies making their debut now are chiefly due to communication between computers—that is, to *connections* [italics added] rather than to computations.

Connections mean networks, and networks require standards. And as we speed into this networked world, the companies that define the new standards—the new languages, platforms, scales, conventions—will gain a huge advantage over latecomers. They will be the gatekeepers, perfectly positioned to meet the needs of the hungry new community they helped to create.

Making your standards *universal* is already a telling competitive advantage. This is how VHS beat Betamax. This is how Microsoft beat Apple. Over the next few years you will see more and more companies breaking all the rules of traditional business in order to build networks. This explains why Netscape gives away its browser; Sprint, MCI, and AT&T lure us with free cellular phones; and Sun Microsystems floods the market with Java. They are all trying to launch their standards toward the critical mass needed to become *the standard*.

Since building networks is so important, all employees will have to play their part. In the same way that Swiss clock makers were not encouraged to devise their own units of time, the employee of tomorrow will not be allowed to create his own standards. For example, given their intense competition with Sun Microsystems, Microsoft programmers will rarely be given the freedom to write new software using Sun's version of Java. Or, in a less high-tech setting, with the national focus on standard achievement tests, teachers will not be permitted to redesign their curricula based on their own preferences.

This doesn't mean that in the future management will be rigid and intrusive. It simply means that employees will have to express their creativity and individuality through a standard medium. Here again, unrestrained empowerment can kill a company's value.

RULE OF THUMB #3 : "DON'T LET THE CREED OVERSHADOW THE MESSAGE

Required steps are useful only if they do not obscure the desired outcome.

Mark B., a manager in a large consulting company, was taking the four P.M. flight from New York to Chicago. His plane had already left the gate and was lumbering over to its designated runway. Suddenly the captain's voice crackled over the intercom, announcing: "There is a weather ground stop at O'Hare. At this time, no planes are taking off or landing. Some delays may be possible. We'll let you know as soon as we hear anything."

As a passenger, this is a singularly depressing announcement. A ground stop is worse than a cancellation. At least with a cancellation you know for certain that you will have to make other arrangements. With a weather ground stop, who knows what you should do to take control of your situation. You might be delayed for five minutes or two hours. The weather gods are fickle.

So Mark pressed his call button and asked the flight attendant: "Please, do you think we could go back to the gate and deplane?"

The flight attendant had obviously heard this plea before and was already shaking her head. "I'm sorry, sir, but we don't want to miss our place in line. Besides, you never know when a ground stop will be lifted."

Mark smiled weakly and settled down to try to find something to do.

With no computers allowed and one hundred passengers battling for the three phone lines, he opted for a vacant stare out the window. He was still staring three hours later. He had seen squadrons of planes take off, but apparently none of them were destined for Chicago. Thinking that time might have softened her stance, he beckoned to the flight attendant and tried a more persuasive approach:

"Look, it's been all afternoon. Why don't you take us back to the gate? *We'd* all be happier. *You'd* be happier—you wouldn't have to deal with a planeload of short-tempered passengers. *The airport* would be happier—we'd be spending money in their stores and restaurants. Please take us back to the gate."

The flight attendant, perhaps feeling sympathetic, knelt down and whispered conspiratorially: "Sir, I'm afraid that the quality of this airline is partly measured by on-time departures. And unfortunately, on-time departures are measured by when we left the gate, not by wheels-up. So you see, sir, we really aren't encouraged to take passengers back to the gate in situations like this."

At this, Mark broke down and wept. Well, no, he didn't, but it's fair to say that he was less than pleased.

This is a classic example of where the very steps designed with a particular outcome in mind—in this case customer satisfaction—actually hindered the achievement of that outcome. And in fact, when you investigate this specific situation still further, you discover that there are other, even more compelling reasons not to return to the gate: flight and cabin crews are paid a higher wage, a command wage, when their plane leaves the gate.

Of course, many pilots will use their own judgment and decide that the present discomfort of the passengers is more important than the airline's future on-time departure rating or their own pay packet. But you can hardly blame the ones who choose to stay on the runway. All the signals are telling them to ignore the most important outcome—customer satisfaction.

As you look around, you can see many examples of steps hindering the very outcomes they were designed to facilitate. During the wave of quality initiatives, many hotel reservation centers decided that customers would want to have their call answered within three rings. Jobs were redefined, departments were reshuffled, and compensation systems were changed to ensure that the reservation agents would meet the three-ring goal. However, it gradually emerged that customers didn't really care about how quickly the phone was answered. They just wanted to have their questions, all of their questions, answered when they had the agent on the line. With agents hurrying to complete the call and move on to the next one, customers were feeling rushed. The steps were obscuring the outcome.

Perhaps the most obvious example, though, is scripting. Many managers seem to feel that the only way to ensure that employees deliver a consistent level of service is to put words in their mouth.

How many times have you heard a variation on this?

"Welcome to New York, where the local time is approximately 8:06 P.M. For your safety and for the safety of those around you, please remain in your seats until we reach the gate. Please be careful when you open the overhead bins, as contents may have shifted during flight. If New York is your final destination, welcome home. If not, we wish you a pleasant journey on to wherever your final destination may be. We know you have a choice of airline, and we hope that you will think of us again whenever your plans call for air travel."

You might think that the Federal Aviation Administration requires that flight attendants read this script. It doesn't. The FAA requires only that passengers be told about seat belts, oxygen masks, safety exit operations, and the water evacuation procedure if the flight is due to cross a large body of water. The rest of the script has been designed by managers to ensure consistency of service. Some airlines insist that their employees read it word for word. Others simply offer it, or some version of it, as a guideline. Although the level of enforcement may vary, most flight attendants are encouraged to use this script to show concern and warmth for their customers.

This is quite a trick. Concern and warmth, if you are going to attempt them, must be genuine emotions. And a script, even when designed with the best of intentions, makes it supremely difficult to convince a customer that you are genuine, even when you are. The problem here is not that managers provided their people with a script—all employees, particularly new hires, appreciate help in finding their feet. The problem here is that following the script, rather than showing genuine concern for the passengers, has become the definition of good performance. The creed has been allowed to overshadow the message.

Southwest Airlines, for the last six years winner of the Triple Crown

Award—fewest complaints, best baggage handling, best on-time performance—is one of the few airlines that has succeeded in maintaining its
focus on the message. Ellen P. is their director of in-flight training:

"Everything is focused on 'fun' here at Southwest. Obviously safety is
important—all our flight attendants must follow FAA regulations. But
the whole purpose of our company is to help the customers have fun.
How he or she makes that happen is up to each flight attendant. We
don't want them all sounding the same. In our training classes we will
give you ideas and tools, but you've got to use them in the way that fits
you. For example, we give every single flight attendant our Fun Book.
In the Fun Book we have a section on jokes, a section on five-minute
games, a section on twenty-minute games, a section on songs. There are
some great ideas in this little book for how you can entertain our customers. But you don't have to use them if that's not your style. It sounds
simple, really, but what we do here in my department is train you how to
be the best *You* possible for our customers. Because at Southwest, we
don't want clones."

Southwest Airlines, with their unabashed focus on fun for the customer, can then allow each flight attendant to find his or her own route
to that outcome. Ellen says it better:

"At Southwest, I think everyone is expected to color outside the
lines."

RULE OF THUMB #4: "THERE ARE NO STEPS LEADING TO CUSTOMER SATISFACTION"

*Required steps only prevent dissatisfaction. They cannot drive
customer satisfaction.*

In virtually every kind of business, customer satisfaction is paramount.
You, and every other employee worth his salt, want to do everything in
your power to build a growing number of loyal customers. You want to
take prospects, who have never tried your product or service before,
and turn them into advocates. Advocates are customers who are aggressively loyal. They will not only withstand temptations to defect, they will
actively sing your praises. These advocates are your largest unpaid sales
force. These advocates, more than marketing, more than promotions,
even more than price, are your fuel for sustained growth.

So how do you create them?

Over the last twenty years Gallup has interviewed over a billion customers, trying to identify what customers really want. As you would expect, we first discovered that customers' needs vary by industry.
Customers demand a different kind of relationship from their doctor
than they do from their cable repairman. They expect a more intimate
bond with their accountant than they do with their local grocery store.

Our second discovery was more surprising: Despite these differences, four customer expectations remain remarkably consistent across
various types of businesses and types of people. These four expectations
are hierarchical. This means that the lower-level expectations must be
met before the customer is ready to pay attention to the levels higher
up. These four expectations, in sequence, show companies what they
must do to turn prospects into advocates.

Level 1:   At the lowest level, customers expect *accuracy*. They expect
the hotel to give them the room they reserved. They expect their bank
statements to reflect their balance accurately. When they eat out, they
expect the waiter to serve what they ordered. It doesn't matter how
friendly the employees are, if the company consistently fails the accuracy test, then customers defect.

Level 2:   The next level is *availability*. Customers expect their preferred hotel chain to offer locations in a variety of different cities. They
expect their bank to be open when they can use it and to employ
enough tellers to keep the line moving. They expect their favorite
restaurant to be nearby, to have adequate parking, and to have waiters
who notice that distinctive "I need help now" look. Any company that
makes itself more accessible will obviously increase the number of customers who are willing to give it a try. Hence the proliferation of drive-
through windows, ATM machines, and, more recently, Web sites.

A couple of points about these two lower-level expectations: On the
one hand, they are, fortunately, quite easy to meet. Both lend themselves to technological or step-by-step solutions.

On the other hand, these solutions are, unfortunately, quite easy to
steal. Any restaurant succeeding because of its location soon finds itself
surrounded by competitors hoping to cash in on the prime real estate.
Federal Express's innovative package-tracking system is quickly repli-
cated by UPS, Airborne, and the post office. And, of course, ATM machines are now a dime a dozen. Any effort to meet these lower-level

expectations, no matter how unique, quickly shrivels from a competitive advantage to a commodity.

Finally, and most significant, both of these expectations, even if met successfully, can only prevent customer dissatisfaction. If the utility company manages to send an accurate bill, customers don't sit back and smile in admiration. The accuracy is demanded and expected. They react only if their bill seems to reflect the gas usage of the entire apartment complex next door. Similarly, if the cable company actually agrees to an appointment that is convenient, customers don't start calling all their friends with glee. They simply sigh with relief at being spared one of life's inevitable frustrations.

Accuracy and availability are undoubtedly very important expectations. Companies that consistently fail to meet them will wither. But accuracy and availability are insufficient. On their journey from prospect to advocate, your customers are only halfway there.

The next two expectations complete the journey. They don't just prevent negative feelings of dissatisfaction. Rather, when met consistently, these expectations create positive feelings of satisfaction. They transform a fickle customer into your most vocal advocate.

Level 3:   At this level customers expect *partnership*. They want you to listen to them, to be responsive to them, to make them feel they are on the same side of the fence as you.

Service businesses have long realized the importance of this partnership expectation. That's why Wal-Mart positions hearty senior citizens at their front door to smile a welcome and remember names. That's why all airlines create loyalty clubs offering special treatment to frequent fliers. And that's presumably why video stores offer a "staff picks" section: "We're like you. We watch videos, too."

But recently other businesses have zeroed in on the importance of looking at the world through the customers' eyes. For example, in the spirit of partnership, Levi's now offers you the chance to purchase made-to-order jeans. Furnished with your measurements, the retail store relays them to the manufacturing plant, which punches out a unique pair, for your size only.

Snapple has also cottoned on to the power of partnership. To urge its target market, college students, to drink more Snapple, it promises prizes if you are lucky enough to buy a bottle with the special code under its cap. Rather than offering hard cash, Snapple decided to position the prizes to coincide with the priorities of their young consumers. Thus the first prize is presented as "Let Snapple pay your rent for a year. 12 payments of $1,000." The second prize becomes "Let Snapple make your car payments for a year. 12 payments of $300." Even the smaller prizes, with onetime payments, are described by the way a young college student might spend them—thus a prize of $100 becomes "Let Snapple pay your phone bill for a month." Although few college students actually win, by presenting the prizes in this way, Snapple manages to communicate the same message to every young customer: "We understand what you are going through."

Most businesses, whether in the service, manufacturing, or packaged goods sectors, now realize that a customer who feels understood is a step closer to real satisfaction and genuine advocacy.

Level 4:   The most advanced level of customer expectation is *advice*. Customers feel the closest bond to organizations that have helped them learn. It's no coincidence, for example, that colleges and schools are blessed with the strongest alumni associations. But this love of learning applies across all businesses. The big public accounting firms now place a special emphasis on teaching their clients something that will help them manage their finances more effectively. Home Depot, the home improvement retailer, proudly advertises their on-site experts who offer training on everything from plant care to grouting. And Amazon.com, the on-line bookseller, continues to build a devoted following, at least in part, because they offer customers a recommended reading list based upon what other customers, who have purchased the same book, are also reading. Everywhere you look, companies are trying to transform their tellers/salespeople/clerks into "consultants." They have realized that learning always breeds loyalty.

Partnership and advice are the most advanced levels of customer expectation. If you can consistently meet these expectations, you will have successfully transformed prospects into advocates.

This is all well and good, but it does beg one question: How can you meet these higher-level expectations? The answer rarely lies with technology or steps. For example, customers will feel a sense of partnership only when employees are responsive. Therefore, to meet this expectation you need employees on the front line who are wired to find the right words and right tone for each specific customer. By its very definition, you cannot legislate this in advance. A sense of partnership develops in real time. It is in the hands of the employees.

The same goes for advice. Amazon.com may have found a technological solution, but they are the exception. Most teaching will occur between one employee and one customer. Realizing this, managers can certainly encourage their employees to help each customer learn something new, but teaching/learning is a very sensitive interaction. It requires a special kind of retail clerk or bank teller to find just the right time and just the right way to educate each customer. Technology can provide support. Suggested action steps can serve as guidelines. But the teaching/learning will happen, or fail to happen, based upon what transpires between each employee and each customer, moment by moment.

Gallup's research confirms what great managers know instinctively. Forcing your employees to follow required steps only prevents customer dissatisfaction. If your goal is truly to satisfy, to create advocates, then the step-by-step approach alone cannot get you there. Instead you must select employees who have the talent to listen and to teach, and then you must focus them toward simple emotional outcomes like partnership and advice. This is not easy to do, but it does have one decidedly appealing feature. If you can do it successfully, it is very hard to steal.

All of these rules of thumb help great managers decide how much of the role should be structured and how much should be left up to the employee's discretion. But even though some aspects of the role will indeed require conformity to steps or standards, great managers still place the premium on the role's *outcomes*. They use these outcomes to inspire, to orient, and to evaluate their employees. The outcomes are the point.

What Do You Get Paid to Do?

"How do you know if the outcomes are right?"

Getting focused on outcomes is one thing. Figuring out which outcomes are *right* is something else entirely. So how can you define the right outcomes? Of all the things your people *could* be doing, how can you know which are the few things they *should* be doing?

Well, as you would expect, we can't offer you a step-by-step solution. First, it takes a certain talent to hear the siren song through the clamor. Second, even if you have this talent, this talent to focus, to discriminate, then you will undoubtedly have your own way of deploying it. What we can offer you are some deceptively simple guidelines from some of the world's great managers.

#1: WHAT IS RIGHT FOR YOUR CUSTOMERS?

This is the first question you should ask. Whatever *you* happen to think, if the customer thinks that a particular outcome isn't valuable, it isn't. Since this is the basic tenet of capitalism, it is a rather straightforward guideline. Nonetheless, many companies, perhaps dazzled by their own habits and expertise, seem to have forgotten that the customer is the ultimate judge of value.

Not to pick on the airline industry, but they are as good an example as any. Most airlines ask their flight attendants to focus on safety first. Hence the captain's announcement "Please remember, the flight attendants are here primarily for your safety. If there is anything else they can do to make your flight more enjoyable, please don't hesitate to ask." Our flight attendants are professional safety experts, this announcement stresses, not glorified wait staff. Safety is paramount. Anything else, like friendly, attentive service, is an optional extra.

These airlines forget that customers don't usually choose one airline over another by comparing safety records. Whatever the airline, customers fully expect that they will arrive at their destination unharmed. They demand safety, but they are not impressed by it. It is the wrong outcome for airlines to emphasize.

Southwest Airlines again stands out as the exception. Their flight attendants are experts in all the required safety procedures, but safety is not the point of their work. Fun is the point. Their passionate CEO, Herb Kelleher, instinctively empathized with air travelers. He realized that air travel is inevitably stressful. He knew that he would never be able to remove everyone's fear and frustration. All he could do was encourage every one of his employees to make the flying experience as much fun as possible. Hence the songs, the jokes, the games, the "coloring outside the lines." Kelleher's intuition means that every Southwest employee is focused on the right outcome.

Intuitions like this can be powerful, but there are other, more practical ways to see the world through your customers' eyes. For example, Adrian P., the manager of two car dealerships, conducts focus groups with a selection of recent buyers every other month. The Walt Disney Company's Imagineers, the supremely creative individuals who design and build the theme parks, are constantly "on site," standing in the lines, mingling with guests, riding the rides.

Customer surveys are an even more sophisticated way to delve into the mind of your customers. If you have the time and the inclination, you can design a survey that includes questions on all possible aspects of the customers' experience. To identify the *most important aspects,* you must work out which questions show the strongest link to the customers' ratings of overall satisfaction, likelihood to recommend, and likelihood to repurchase. Using this technique, Gallup has been able to help many companies zero in on those few emotional outcomes that are truly important to their customers.

A large insurance company wanted to hold its doctors accountable for the quality of service they provided their patients. The insurance company was interested in doing this for all kinds of reasons, not least of which was the fact that unhappy patients tended to stay in the hospital longer, sue more readily, and die more often. For an insurance company these are rather important considerations. Thus you might have forgiven them if they had forced every doctor to run his or her practice according to a detailed procedures manual. But they resisted this tactic. Instead they asked Gallup to investigate which core emotional outcomes patients truly valued. We discovered that once you feel secure in your doctor's basic competence, there are only four things you really want from your doctor when you visit:

- You want to be kept waiting for no more than twenty minutes. (availability)
- You want to feel as though someone cared about you. It doesn't have to be the doctor. It might be the receptionist or the nurse. But someone has to care about you. (partnership)
- You want the doctor to explain what your condition is in words that you can understand. (partnership)
- You want the doctor to give you something that you can do for yourself at home to alleviate your condition. (advice)

If you can say "Yes" to all of these questions, you are much more likely to recommend and return and much less likely to sue or die. Using these four emotional *outcomes* as their measure of service, the insurance company could then hold each doctor accountable for quality of service without having to dictate how each doctor should run his or her practice.

#2: WHAT IS RIGHT FOR YOUR COMPANY?

Make sure that the outcomes you define for your people are in line with your company's current strategy. Again, this sounds like motherhood and apple pie. But with the dizzying pace of change in today's business world, it is sometimes hard for managers to keep track.

The key distinction here is between "mission" and "strategy." A company's mission should remain constant, providing meaning and focus for generations of employees. A company's strategy is simply the most effective way to execute that mission. It should change according to the demands of the contemporary business climate.

For example, the Walt Disney Company's mission has always been to release people's imagination by telling wonderful stories. In the past they relied on the twin strategies of movies and theme parks. Today, however, faced with increased competition, they have broadened their strategy to include cruise ships, Broadway shows, video games, and retail stores. As Bran Ferren, executive vice president of research and development at Walt Disney Imagineering, describes it: "Vibrant companies must put together five-year plans. But they must be willing to change these five-year plans every single year. It's the only way to stay alive."

Although this constant reassessment of strategy is vital to the health of the company, it does place managers in a rather difficult position. They are the intermediaries, charged with explaining the new strategy to the employees and then translating it into clearly defined performance outcomes.

Often this can be as simple as telling your salespeople that with the new company strategy focused on growing market share rather than profit, each salesperson will now be encouraged to focus on the outcome "sales volume," rather than the outcome "profit margin per sale."

However, sometimes the changes in strategy are more radical and the pressures on managers to refocus employees on different outcomes are more acute. For example, the most effective strategy for many high-tech companies used to be innovation. Hence the large R&D budgets, the hordes of disheveled but creative software designers, and the unpredictable, slightly unfocused work environments. Recently, though, the strategy of these high-tech companies has shifted focus. For the major players who dominate the marketplace, critical mass—getting your product to be accepted as *the standard*—is now more important than innovation. Innovation can be bought from the smaller boutique houses. Thus these larger companies need to change the way they operate to ensure that virtually everyone's efforts are focused on spreading the new language/platform/product into the marketplace. This means that managers in these companies will have to hustle to redefine the desired outcomes and find new definitions of success. Number of users, for example, may now be more important than revenue per user.

Of course, there are times when the change in strategy is so dramatic that no matter how clearly you redefine the desired outcomes, your current cadre of employees will be unable to achieve them. Faced with this situation, you can't rewire people's brains, as high-tech companies found when they tried to turn software designers into marketers, and as banks discovered when they tried to retrain tellers to become salespeople. All you can do is try to find roles within the new strategy that play to their talents. If no such roles exist, then you have no choice: these employees have to move on.

#3: WHAT IS RIGHT FOR THE INDIVIDUAL?

Dennis Rodman is arguably the best rebounder ever to play the game of basketball. He is certainly the most bizarre player. With hair that changes color every week, a fondness for women's clothing, and a persecution complex, he is an explosive, unpredictable man. How do you manage him so that he is motivated to use his talents and to limit his outbursts?

During the previous three seasons, the Chicago Bulls had lost Rodman to various infractions for at least twelve games per season, so for the 1997–98 season they opted for a different strategy. Keeping in mind Rodman's talents, and the challenges he presented, they drew up a contract built around some very specific outcomes. It was the most incentive-laden contract in the history of the NBA. Rodman was guaranteed $4.5 million. He would receive another $5 million if he stayed out of trouble for the duration of the season; another $500,000 for winning the rebounding title for the seventh time; and another $100,000 for having a positive assist-to-turnover ratio.

The numbers here are stratospheric, but the concept is applicable to every employee: Identify a person's strengths. Define outcomes that play to those strengths. Find a way to count, rate, or rank those outcomes. And then let the person run.

It worked for Rodman and the Chicago Bulls. By the end of the season Rodman had missed only one game for disciplinary reasons. He had won the rebounding title for the seventh time. He had 230 assists versus 147 turnovers. And the Bulls had won the championship.

Of course, if you are managing a large group of people who perform exactly the same role, it may be more difficult to tailor the outcomes to each individual. But if your team is small and variously talented, then you must take each person's unique talents into account when defining the right outcomes. Bud Grant, stone-faced Hall of Fame coach of the Minnesota Vikings, described it this way:

"You can't draw up plays and then just plug your players in. No matter how well you have designed your play book, it's useless if you don't know which plays your players can run. When I draw up my play book, I always go from the players to the plays."

When defining the right outcomes for their people, great managers do the same. They go from the players to the plays.

CHAPTER 5

The Third Key: Focus on Strengths

- Let Them Become More of Who They Already Are
- Tales of Transformation
- Casting Is Everything
- Manage by Exception
- Spend the Most Time with Your Best People
- How to Manage Around a Weakness

Let Them Become More of
Who They Already Are

"How do great managers release each person's potential?"

So, you have selected for talent and you have defined the right outcomes. You have your people, and they have their goals. What should you do now? What should you do to speed each person's progress toward performance?

Great managers would offer you this advice: Focus on each person's strengths and manage around his weaknesses. Don't try to fix the weaknesses. Don't try to perfect each person. Instead do everything you can to help each person cultivate his talents. Help each person become more of who he already is.

This radical approach is fueled by one simple insight: Each person is different. Each person has a unique set of talents, a unique pattern of behaviors, of passions, of yearnings. Each person's pattern of talents is enduring, resistant to change. Each person, therefore, has a unique destiny.

Sadly, this insight is lost on many managers. They are ill at ease with individual differences, preferring the blanket security of generalizations. When working with their people, they are guided by the sweep of their opinion—for example, "Most salespeople are ego driven" or "Most accountants are shy."

In contrast, great managers are impatient with the clumsiness of these generalizations. They know that generalizations obscure the truth: that all salespeople are different, that all accountants are different, that each individual, no matter what his chosen profession, is unique. Yes, the best salespeople share some of the same talents. But even among the elite, the Michael Jordans of salespeople, the differences will outweigh the similarities. Each salesperson will have her distinct sources of motivation and a style of persuasion all her own.

This rampant individuality fascinates great managers. They are drawn to the subtle but significant differences among people, even those engaged in the same line of work. They know that a person's identity, his uniqueness, lies not just in what he does—his profession—but in how he does it—his style. Peter L., the founder of a capital equipment rental company, describes two unit managers, one who is a terrific salesperson, networking the neighborhood, joining local business or community groups, literally wooing customers into the fold. The other is an extraordinary asset manager who squeezes life out of every piece of machinery by running the most efficient workshop in the company. Both of them excel at their roles.

Guy H., a school superintendent, manages two exemplary school principals. The first principal is what he calls a "reflective practitioner." He consumes libraries of journals, stays current with educational theory, and teaches others what he has learned. The second operates exclusively out of a sense of mission and a natural instinct for teaching. There is no educational jargon in her school, just boundless energy and a passion for learning, however it happens.

One of the signs of a great manager is the ability to describe, in detail, the unique talents of each of his or her people—what drives each one, how each one thinks, how each builds relationships. In a sense, great managers are akin to great novelists. Each of the "characters" they manage is vivid and distinct. Each has his own features and foibles. And their goal, with every employee, is to help each individual "character" play out his unique role to the fullest.

Their distrust of generalizations extends all the way to the broader categories of race and sex. Of course, cultural influences will shape some of your perspectives, giving you something in common with those who shared those influences. An affluent white female living in Greenwich, Connecticut, might have a more benign view of the world than, say, a young Hispanic male growing up in Compton, California. But these kinds of differences are too broad and too bland to be of much help. It would be more powerful to understand the striving talents of this *particular* white female or the relating talents of that *particular* Hispanic male. Only then could you know how to help each of them turn his talents into performance. Only then could you help each one live out her individual specialness.

For great managers, then, the most interesting and the most powerful differences are among people, not peoples.

This is a grand perspective, with far-reaching implications, but it's just common sense. Here's what Mandy M., a manager of a twenty-five-person design department, has to say on the subject:

"I want to find what is special and unique about each person. If I can find what special thing they have to offer, and if I can help them see it, then they will keep digging for more."

Gary S., a sales executive for a medical device company, describes it in even more pragmatic terms:

"I deliberately look for something to like about each of my people. In one, I might like his sense of humor. In another, I might like the way he talks about his kids. In another, I'll enjoy her patience, or the way she handles pressure. Of course, there's a bunch of stuff about each of them that can get on my nerves. If I'm not deliberate about looking for what I like, the bad stuff might start coming to mind first."

For Mandy, Gary, and other great managers, finding the strengths of each person and then focusing on these strengths is a conscious act. It is the most efficient way to help people achieve their goals. It is the best way to encourage people to take responsibility for who they really are. And it is the only way to show respect for each person. Focusing on strengths is the storyline that explains all their efforts as managers.

Tales of Transformation

"Why is it so tempting to try to fix people?"

As you might expect, conventional wisdom tells a rather different story. First, it spins us this tale: You can be anything you want to be if you hold on to your dreams and work hard. The person you feel yourself to be every day is not the real You. No, the real You is deep inside, hidden by your fears and discouragements. If you could free yourself of these fears, if you could truly believe in yourself, then the real You would be released. Your potential would burst out. The giant would awaken.

This is a tale of transformation, and we love it. It is just so uplifting and so hopeful, who wouldn't root for the hero who confronts his demons and transforms himself into everything he always knew he could be? Well, surely we all would. That's why we root for Michael J. Fox in *The Secret of My Success*, Melanie Griffith in *Working Girl*, and John Travolta in *Phenomenon*. We love all these stories of transformation, not least because they imply that all of us have the same potential and that all of us can access this unlimited potential through discipline, persistence, and perhaps some good luck along the way.

Softened by conventional wisdom's first installment, we are easily persuaded by the second: To access your unlimited potential, you must identify your weaknesses and then fix them. This remedial approach to self-perfection is drummed into you from your first performance appraisal. You are told that to advance your career, you must "broaden your skill set." You must become more "well-rounded." During each subsequent appraisal there may be a few words of congratulation for another year of excellent performance, but then it's into the nitty-gritty of the conversation—how to improve your "areas of opportunity." Your manager brings up, yet again, those few areas where you struggle—where you have always struggled—and you and she then cobble together another "developmental plan" to try to shore up your weaknesses once and for all. By the time you reach the end of your career, you have spent so much time fixing yourself that you must be well-nigh perfect.

The best managers dislike this story. Like all sentimental stories, it is comforting and familiar, but strangely unsatisfying. The hero, diligently shaving off his rough edges, seems sympathetic and noble, but some-how not . . . real. The more you ask these managers about this story, the more vivid their criticisms become. Listen to them long enough and they will peel back its cheery surface completely to reveal the rather sin-ister messages hidden beneath. This is what they told us:

First, its promise that each of us can "be anything we want to be if we just work hard" is actually quite a stark promise. Because if we can all "be anything we want to be," then we all have the same potential. And if we all have the same potential, then we lose our individuality. We are not uniquely talented, expressing ourselves through unique goals, unique capabilities, and unique accomplishments. We are all the same. We have no distinct identity, no distinct destiny. We are all blank sheets of canvas, ready, waiting, and willing, but featureless.

Second, there's the message that if you keep working away on your nontalents, your persistence will pay off in the end. On the surface this is a solid, if clichéd, morsel of advice: "If at first you don't succeed, try, try again." Yet the most effective managers reject it. Why? Because if the focus of your life is to turn your nontalents, such as empathy or strategic thinking or persuasiveness, into talents, then it will be a crush-ingly frustrating life.

Persistence is useful if you are trying to learn a new skill or to acquire particular knowledge. Persistence can even be appropriate if you are trying to cut a thin path through some of your mental wastelands, so that, for example, your nontalent for empathy doesn't permanently un-dermine your talents in other areas. But persistence directed primarily toward your nontalents is self-destructive—no amount of determination or good intentions will *ever* enable you to carve out a brand-new set of four-lane mental highways. You will reprimand yourself, berate yourself, and put yourself through all manner of contortions in an attempt to achieve the impossible.

From the vantage point of great managers, conventional wisdom's story, no matter how optimistic it may appear on the surface, is actually about fruitless self-denial and wasted persistence.

Third, this story describes a doomed relationship. The conventional manager genuinely wants to bring out the best in the employee, but she chooses to do so by focusing on fixing the employee's weaknesses. The employee probably possesses many strengths, but the manager ends up characterizing him by those few areas where he struggles. This is the same dynamic that often proves the undoing of other failed relationships.

Have you ever suffered through a bad relationship, the kind of relationship where the pressures of each day sapped your energy and made you a stranger to yourself? If you can stand to, think back to how you felt during that relationship and remember: A bad relationship is rarely one where your partner didn't know you very well. Most often, a bad relationship is one where your partner came to know you very well indeed . . . and wished you weren't that way. Perhaps your partner wanted to perfect you. Perhaps you were simply incompatible and your weaknesses grated on each other. Perhaps your partner was a person who simply enjoyed pointing out other people's failings. Whatever the cause, you ended up feeling as though you were being defined by those things you did not do rather than those things you did. And that felt awful.

This is the same feeling that many managers unwittingly create in their employees. Even when working with their most productive employees, they still spend most of their time talking about each person's few areas of nontalent and how to eradicate them. No matter how well intended, relationships preoccupied with weakness never end well.

Finally, at the heart of this story lurks its bleakest theme: The victim is to blame. Less effective managers cast themselves in the mentor role. Blind to the distinction between skills and knowledge—both of which can be acquired—and talents—which cannot—these managers relentlessly point out each employee's nontalents in the belief that he can fix them and become well-rounded. "You can become more persuasive, more strategic, or more empathic if you just work at it," or so their story goes. Their implicit message is that you, the employee, can control the outcome by "working at it." You can take classes, modify your reactions, censor yourself. The responsibility is yours. Therefore when you fail to achieve the impossible, to turn your nontalents into talents, the invisible finger of blame is left pointing at you. *You* weren't persistent enough. *You* didn't apply yourself. The fault is *yours*.

By telling you that you can transform nontalents into talents, these less effective managers are not only setting you up to fail, they are intrinsically blaming you for your inevitable failure. This is perverse.

For all of these reasons, great managers reject conventional wisdom's story. Their rejection does not mean that they think all persistence is wasted. It simply means that persistence focused primarily on nontalents is wasted. Nor does their rejection mean that they ignore a person's weaknesses. Each employee has areas where she struggles, and these areas must be dealt with—we will describe in more detail how great managers deal with a person's weaknesses later in this chapter.

But it *does* mean that great managers are aggressive in trying to identify each person's talents and help her to cultivate those talents.

This is how they do it: They believe that casting is everything. They manage by exception. And they spend the most time with their best people.

Casting Is Everything

"How do great managers cultivate excellent performance so consistently?"

As we have noted, everyone has talents—recurring patterns of thought, feeling, and behavior that can be applied productively. Simply put, everyone can probably do at least one thing better than ten thousand other people. However, each person is not necessarily in a position to use her talents. Even though she might initially have been selected for her talents, after a couple of reshuffles and lateral moves, she may now be miscast.

If you want to turn talent into performance, you have to position each person so that you are paying her to do what she is naturally wired to do. You have to cast her in the right role.

In sports this is relatively straightforward. Given his physical strength and combative personality, it's obvious that Rodman should be paid to crash the boards, not run the floor. In the performing arts, it is almost as clear cut. The original casting of *Butch Cassidy and the Sundance Kid* had Paul Newman playing Sundance and Robert Redford as Butch. After a few rehearsals it became apparent that the roles did not elicit the actors' strengths. The switch was made, and almost immediately both characters materialized. Newman reveled in the glib, self-confident persona of Butch Cassidy, while Redford captured perfectly the more brooding, almost deferential Sundance Kid. The strength of these performances gave this classic film an appeal it might otherwise have lacked.

In the working world casting becomes a little more challenging. First, what matters is what is inside the person, not physical prowess or appearance. Some managers find it hard to see beyond the physical to each person's true talents. Second, managers are often preoccupied with the person's skills or knowledge. Thus people with marketing degrees are inevitably cast into the marketing department and people with accounting backgrounds are siphoned off into the finance department. There is nothing wrong with including a person's skills and knowledge on your casting checklist. But if you do not place a person's talent at the top of that list, you will always run the risk of mediocre performance.

Casting for talent is one of the unwritten secrets to the success of great managers. On occasion it can be as simple as knowing that your aggressive, ego-driven salesperson should take on the territory that requires a fire to be lit beneath it. And, by contrast, your patient, relationship-building salesperson should be offered the territory that requires careful nurturing. However, most of the time casting for talent demands a subtler eye.

For example, imagine you have just been promoted to manage a team of people. You have no idea whether these people have talent or not. You didn't select them. But they have now been handed to you. Their performance is your responsibility. Some managers quickly split the team members into two groups: "losers" and "keepers." They keep the "keepers," clear the house of "losers," and recruit their "own people" to fill the gaps.

The best managers are more deliberate. They talk with each individual, asking about strengths, weaknesses, goals, and dreams. They work closely with each employee, taking note of the choices each makes, the way they all interact, who supports who, and why. They notice things. They take their time, because they know that the surest way to identify each person's talents is to watch his or her behavior over time.

And then, yes, they separate the team into those who should stay and those who should be encouraged to find other roles. But, significantly, they add a third category: "movers." These are individuals who have revealed some valuable talents but who, for whatever reason, are not in a position to use them. They are miscast. By repositioning each in a redesigned role, great managers are able to focus on each person's strengths and turn talent into performance.

Mandy M., the manager of the design team whom we met earlier, tells this story. Recently promoted to head up her company's design division, Mandy inherited an employee called John. He was positioned in a strategic role where he was being paid to offer conceptual advice to the client. The environment was intense and individualistic, with associates competing with each other to devise the cleverest solution for the client. And John was struggling. Everyone knew that John was smart enough to do the job. But the performance just wasn't there. He was emotionally disengaged and, according to most company sources, on his way out the door. If he didn't jump, he would soon be pushed.

But Mandy had seen something in John. A couple of months before being promoted, she had noticed that the only time he really blossomed was when he was working for a supervisor who paid attention to him. They developed a relationship, these two, and John began to shine. But then the supervisor moved on to a new role, and John's light dimmed.

Guided by that one glimpse, Mandy put John into the "movers" category. She guessed that he was a person who needed connections the way some people need recognition. So she took his thirst for relationships and applied it where it could be of great value to the company: business development.

John became a sales machine. He was naturally wired to reach out to people, to learn their names, to remember special things about them. He built genuine relationships with hundreds of individuals scattered among his company's clients and prospects. Bonded by these relationships, the clients stayed clients, and the prospects soon joined them. John was in his element, using his natural strengths to everyone's advantage.

When Mandy tells this story you can hear a little catch in her throat. Like many fine managers, she is overjoyed at the thought of someone using his talents to the fullest. She knows that it is a rare thing to be able to find a role that gives you a chance to express the specialness inside you, a role where what makes you You is also what makes you good. It is rare, not because there aren't enough interesting roles—virtually every role performed at excellence has the potential to interest somebody— but because so few individuals ever come to know their true talent and so many managers fail to notice the clues. Mandy knows that on another day, in another company, she might have missed that brief glimpse of John's talent. He would have failed, and he would have had little to learn from his failure.

But she didn't miss it. She noticed the sign of a latent strength. And through careful recasting she was able to focus on that strength and so turn John's talents into performance.

Everyone has the talent to be exceptional at something. The trick is to find that "something." The trick is in the casting.

Manage by Exception

"Why do great managers break the Golden Rule?"

"Everyone is exceptional" has a second meaning: Everyone should be treated as an exception. Each employee has his own filter, his own way of interpreting the world around him, and therefore each employee will demand different things of you, his manager.

Some want you to leave them alone from almost the first moment they are hired. Others feel slighted if you don't check in with them every day. Some want to be recognized by you, "the boss." Others see their peers as the truest source of recognition. Some crave their praise on a public stage. Others shun the glare of publicity, valuing only that quiet, private word of thanks. Each employee breathes different psychological oxygen.

Kirk D., a sales manager for a pharmaceutical company, learned this quickly. He tells of one particular salesperson, Mike, who was always in the top ten of the company's 150 salespeople, but who, Kirk felt, still had more to give.

"Initially I couldn't figure him out. I'm real competitive, and since he was a professional football player for eight years, a running back, I naturally assumed he must be as competitive as me. I would try to rile him up by telling him how much some of the other salespeople had done that month. But when I told him he just looked bored. No fire, no burn. Just bored. It turned out that, despite his background, Mike wasn't competitive at all. He was an achiever. He simply wanted to beat himself. He didn't care about anybody else. In his mind, they were irrelevant. So I started asking him what he was going to do this month to better himself. As soon as I asked him this he couldn't stop talking. Ideas poured out. And together we made them happen. He became the number one salesperson in the company for six straight years."

Remember the Golden Rule? "Treat people as you would like to be treated." The best managers break the Golden Rule every day. They would say *don't* treat people as *you* would like to be treated. This presupposes that everyone breathes the same psychological oxygen as you. For example, if you are competitive, everyone must be similarly competitive. If you like to be praised in public, everyone else must, too. Everyone must share your hatred of micromanagement.

This thinking is well intended but overly simplistic, reminiscent perhaps of the four-year-old who proudly presents his mother with a red truck for her birthday because that is the present *he* wants. So the best managers reject the Golden Rule. Instead, they say, treat each person as *he* would like to be treated, bearing in mind who he is. Of course, each employee must adhere to certain standards of behavior, certain rules. But within those rules, treat each one differently, each according to his needs.

Some managers will protest, "How can I possibly keep track of each employee's unique needs?" And who can blame them? It's hard to treat each employee differently, particularly since outward appearance offers few clues to an individual's particular needs. It's a little like being told to play chess without knowing how all the pieces move.

But the best managers have the solution: Ask. Ask your employee about her goals: What are you shooting for in your current role? Where do you see your career heading? What personal goals would you feel comfortable sharing with me? How often do you want to meet to talk about your progress?

Feel her out about her taste in praise: does she seem to like public recognition or private? Written or verbal? Who is her best audience? It can be very effective to ask her to tell you about the most meaningful recognition she has ever received. Find out what made it so memorable. Also ask her about her relationship with you. Can she tell you how she learns? You might inquire whether she has ever had any mentors or partners who have helped her. How did they help?

With such a bulk of information to remember about each employee, managers often find that it helps to jot it all down. Some design organized filing systems, where each employee has his own folder, flecked with ticklers that remind the manager when each employee's check-in cycle has come full circle. Others just scribble the details down on scruffy little note cards and carry them around in their pocket—employee "cheat sheets," they call them.

Obviously there is no right way to capture this information. Just capture it. Without it you are functionally blind, flailing around with stereotypes, generalizations, and misguided notions that "fairness" means "sameness." But armed with it you are focused. You can focus on each person's strengths and turn talents into performance. You can "manage by exception."

Spend the Most Time with Your Best People

"Why do great managers play favorites?"

If you are a manager, you may want to try this exercise. On the left-hand side of a blank sheet of paper write down the names of the people who report to you in descending order of productivity, the most productive at the top, the least productive at the bottom. On the right-hand side, write down the same names, but this time in descending order of "time you spend with them," the most time at the top, the least time at the bottom. Now draw straight lines joining the names on the left with the appropriate names on the right.

Do your lines cross? They often do. Many managers find themselves spending the most time with their least productive people and the least time with their most productive people. On the surface this would appear to be an eminently safe way for a manager to invest his time. After all, your best employees can already do the job. They don't need you. But those few employees who are struggling? They need all the help you can give them. Without your support they might not only fail as individuals, they might also drag down the entire team.

Investing in your strugglers appears shrewd, yet the most effective managers do the opposite. When they join the names, their lines are horizontal. They spend the *most* time with their *most* productive employees. They invest in their best. Why?

Because at heart they see their role very differently from the way most managers do. Most managers assume that the point of their role is either to control or to instruct. And, yes, if you see "control" as the core of the manager role, then it would certainly be productive to spend more time with your strugglers because they still need to be controlled. Likewise if you think "instructing" is the essence of management, investing most in your strugglers makes similarly good sense because they still have so much to learn.

But great managers do not place a premium on either control or instruction. Both have their place, particularly with novice employees, but they are not the core: they are too elementary, too static.

For great managers, the core of their role is the catalyst role: turning talent into performance. So when they spend time with an employee, they are not fixing or correcting or instructing. Instead they are racking their brains, trying to figure out better and better ways to unleash that employee's distinct talents:

- They strive to carve out *a unique set of expectations* that will stretch and focus each particular individual; think back to detail and the uniqueness of Rodman's contract, and remember that every other Bulls player will demand a similarly detailed and similarly unique set of expectations.
- They try to *highlight and perfect each person's unique style*. They draw his attention to it. They help him understand why it works for him and how to perfect it. That's what Mandy was doing with John; it's what she has to do for all of her direct reports.
- And they plot how they, the manager, can *run interference* for each employee, so that each can exercise his or her talents even more freely. As Robert T., a branch manager for a large brokerage house, explains: "My brokers don't work for me. I work for them. If I can't think up any new ideas to help my superstars, the least I can do is grease the administrative wheels so that nothing gets in their way."

If this is how you see your role, if this is what you are doing when you spend time with your people—setting unique expectations, highlighting and perfecting individual styles, running interference—you cannot help but be drawn toward your most talented employees. Talent is the multiplier. The more energy and attention you invest in it, the greater the yield. The time you spend with your best is, quite simply, your most productive time.

"NO NEWS" KILLS BEHAVIOR

Conversely, time away from your best is alarmingly destructive. Graduates from the machismo school of management, with its steely-eyed motto "No news is good news," would be surprised by just how destructive it is.

At its simplest, a manager's job is to encourage people to do more of certain productive behaviors and less of other, unproductive behaviors.

Machismo managers have forgotten that their reactions can significantly affect which behaviors are multiplied and which gradually die out. They have forgotten that they are on stage every day and that, whether they like it or not, they are sending signals that every employee hears.

Great managers haven't forgotten. They remember that they are permanently center stage. In particular they remember that the less attention they pay to the productive behaviors of their superstars, the less of those behaviors they will get. Since human beings are wired to need attention of some kind, if they are not getting attention, they will tend, either subconsciously or consciously, to alter their behavior until they do.

Therefore, as a manager, if you pay the most attention to your strugglers and ignore your stars, you can inadvertently alter the behaviors of your stars. Guided by your apparent indifference, your stars may start to do less of what made them stars in the first place and more of other kinds of behaviors that might net them some kind of reaction from you, good or bad. When you see your stars acting up, it is a sure sign that you have been paying attention to the wrong people and the wrong behaviors.

So try to keep this in mind: You are always on stage. Your misplaced time and attention is not a neutral act. No news is never good news. No news kills the very behaviors you want to multiply.

In practical terms, then, great managers invest in their best because it is extremely productive to do so and actively destructive to do otherwise. However, during our interviews great managers were happy to explain the benefits in more conceptual terms. They told us that investing in their best was, first, *the fairest thing to do;* second, *the best way to learn;* and, third, *the only way to stay focused on excellence.*

INVESTING IN YOUR BEST IS . . .
THE FAIREST THING TO DO

Although great managers are committed to the concept of "fairness," they define it rather differently from most people. In their mind "fairness" does not mean treating everyone the same. They would say that the only way to treat someone fairly is to treat them as they deserve to be treated, bearing in mind what they have accomplished. Jimmy Johnson, the coach who led the Dallas Cowboys to two Super Bowl rings and who now manages the Miami Dolphins, captures their attitude toward "fairness." He made this point in a speech to the Miami players immediately after taking the reins from Don Shula:

"I am going to be very consistent with every one of you because I'll treat every one of you differently. That's the way it is. The harder a guy works, the better he performs, and the more he meets my guidelines, the more leeway he is going to have with me. By the same token, if a guy doesn't work very hard or if he's not a good player, he's not going to be around for very long."

That language might seem a little blunt for the corporate environment, but the concept rings true with great managers. Quite simply, they choose to invest more time with their best because their best are more deserving of it.

They know that human beings crave attention. Each individual might value different kinds of attention, but, to a person, we all hate to be ignored. If love is not the opposite of hate, then surely indifference is the opposite of both. If you spend the most time with your worst performers, then the message you are sending to your employees is that "the better your performance becomes, the less time and attention you will receive from me, your manager." From any angle, this is an odd message.

So spend the most time with your top performers. Pay attention to them. Be fair to the right people.

One of the most powerful things you can do after reading this book is to go back and "rehire" your best people—that is, go back and tell them why they are so good. Tell them why they are one of the cornerstones of the team's success. Choose a style that fits you, and don't allow the conversation to slip into promises about promotion in the future—that's a different conversation, for a different time. Simply tell them why their contribution is so valued today. Don't assume your best know.

INVESTING IN YOUR BEST IS . . .
THE BEST WAY TO LEARN

There's a great deal you can learn from spending time with your strugglers. You can learn why certain systems are hard to operate. You can learn why initiatives are poorly designed. You can learn why clients become unhappy. And over time, you can become, as some managers are, highly articulate in describing the anatomy of failure and its various cures.

Ironically, none of this is going to help you understand what excellence looks like. You cannot learn very much about excellence from studying failure. Of all the infinite number of ways to perform a certain task, most of them are wrong. There are only a few right ways. Unfortunately you don't come any closer to identifying those right ways by eliminating the wrong ways. Excellence is not the opposite of failure. It is just different. It has its own configuration, which sometimes includes behaviors that look surprisingly similar to the behaviors of your strugglers.

For example, if you spent most of your time investigating failure, you would never discover that great housekeepers lie on the guests' bed and turn on the ceiling fan, or that great table servers offer clear opinions, or that great salespeople feel call reluctance on almost every call they make, or that great nurses form strong emotional attachments with their patients. Instead, having found some of the very same behaviors among the very worst housekeepers, the worst table servers, salespeople, and nurses, you might have actually devised regulations or policies to prevent these behaviors from happening.

Gallup worked with one of the largest health care providers in Europe to help them find more nurses similar to their best. As part of our research we identified, using supervisor ratings, one hundred excellent nurses and one hundred average nurses. We then interviewed each individual, searching for those few talents that the excellent nurses shared.

Among the many talents common to great nurses, we discovered one called "patient response." Great nurses *need* to care. They cannot not care. Their filter sifts through life and automatically highlights opportunities to care. But if the caring itself is a need, the *joy* of caring comes when they see the patient start to respond. Each little increment of improvement is fuel for them. It is their psychological payoff. This love of seeing the patient respond is the talent that prevents great nurses from feeling beaten down by the sadness and suffering inherent in their role. It is the talent that enables them to find strength and satisfaction in their work.

When we told their managers this, they replied: "We're not organized that way, because we don't want our nurses getting too close to their patients." They said that patients were moved around all of the time. That it was usual for a nurse to return after a weekend or a day off and find his patients gone, moved to a different ward, transferred to a different hospital, or simply discharged. "There's a great deal of pressure to make beds available," they said. "And there's no way we can organize ourselves to keep a nurse and a patient together for very long at all. Some of our nurses got upset when they found their patients gone. Consequently we now tell our nurses to keep their distance. We don't want them feeling any loss when the patient is moved."

Despite these worthy intentions, their arrangement caused suffering all around. The nurses suffered—the whole setup denied them one of their most potent sources of satisfaction. The patients suffered—many studies have shown that patients will recover faster if they are cared for by a nurse with whom they have established a relationship. And the managers suffered—they had to cope with patients feeling isolated and nurses feeling demoralized.

How should the hospitals have been organized? This is a difficult question. There's no getting past the fact that in order to keep health care costs down, every hospital feels pressure to "turn" patients quickly so that the beds can be made available. However, although Gallup couldn't offer them a quick-fix answer to their predicament, we could highlight the best route to that answer: Sit down with your best nurses and ask them to describe how *they* would balance the needs of patients, nurses, and number crunchers. Whatever solution they came up with, they couldn't do worse than the assembly-line system that demeans patients and cuts great nurses off from their oxygen supply.

Unfortunately this organization chose to ignore the voices of their best. They could not find the reasons, or perhaps the will, to alter their flawed but superficially efficient system. They are now struggling more than ever with patient dissatisfaction, nurse morale, and rising costs.

Fortunately many other companies have started to realize the wisdom of studying excellence to learn about excellence. Organized business tours of such "gold standard" companies as Southwest Airlines, GE, and Ritz-Carlton have year-long waiting lists, and the Walt Disney Company even packages the secrets of "the Disney Way" as a seminar series.

Doubtless managers can learn something useful from investigating the practices of these companies, but even when focused on external best practices, they often miss the most important lesson: Go back and study your *own* top performers. That's what Disney, Southwest Airlines, GE, and Ritz-Carlton did. To generate the material for their tours and seminars, they interviewed, shadowed, filmed, and highlighted their best practitioners. They studied excellence as it was happening every day within their world. They learned from their best.

Every manager should do the same. Spend time with your best. Watch them. Learn from them. Become as articulate about describing excellence as you are about describing failure. Studying external best practices has its merits. But studying *internal* best practices is the regimen that makes the difference.

How can you do it? The best way to investigate excellence is simply to spend a great deal of time with your top performers. You might start by asking them to explain their secret—although most of them are so close to their own success that it often proves difficult for them to describe exactly what they do that makes them so good.

Instead, many of the great managers we interviewed said they spend a lot of time just observing their best. Sales managers discipline themselves to travel with one or two of their sales stars every month. School principals observe a couple of their best teachers' classes. Customer service supervisors regularly listen in on their top customer service reps' calls. The point of this time and attention is not to evaluate or monitor. The point is, as one sales manager put it, "to run a tape recorder in my head, so that back in my office I can replay it, dissect it, understand what happened and why it worked." Like other great managers, you need to keep that tape recorder running.

INVESTING IN YOUR BEST IS . . .
THE ONLY WAY TO REACH EXCELLENCE

The language of "average" is pervasive. Reservation centers calculate the "average" number of calls a customer service representative can handle in an hour. Restaurant chains project staffing needs by estimating how many servers are needed to staff the "average" restaurant. In sales organizations, territories are divided up based on how many prospects the "average" salesperson can handle. "Average" is everywhere.

The best managers wouldn't necessarily disagree with this kind of "average thinking." They would admit that the effective management of a company requires some way of approximating what is going on every day within the company. However, they disagree vehemently when this "average thinking" bleeds into the management of people. Unfortunately it happens all the time.

They might not be aware of it, but many managers are fixated on "average." In their mind they have a clear idea of what they would consider to be an acceptable level of performance; what sales organizations often call a "quota." This quota, this performance "average," serves as the barometer against which each individual's performance is assessed. So, for example, a manager may give her employees a rating based upon how far above or below "average" their performance lies. She may calculate her employees' bonuses by figuring out the correct proportion of the "average" bonus each should receive. And, probably the most obvious symptom of "average thinking," she may well spend most of her time trying to help her strugglers inch their performance up above "average," while leaving her above average performers to their own devices.

This kind of "average thinking" is very tempting. It seems so safe and so practical—by focusing on your strugglers you are protecting yourself, and the company, from their inevitable mistakes. Nonetheless, great managers reject it.

Here are a couple of reasons why. First, they don't use average performance as the barometer against which each person's performance is judged. They use excellence. From their perspective, average is irrelevant to excellence.

Second, they know that the only people who are ever going to reach excellence are those employees who are already above average. These employees have already shown some natural ability to perform the role. These employees have talent. Counterintuitively, employees who are already performing above average have the greatest room for growth. Great managers also know that it is hard work helping a talented person hone his talents. If a manager is preoccupied by the burden of transforming strugglers into survivors by helping them squeak above "average," he will have little time left for the truly difficult work of guiding the good toward the great.

Jean P.'s story illustrates both the irrelevance of average and the growth potential of talent.

For data entry roles, the national performance average is 380,000 keypunches per month, or 19,000 per day. Many companies use an average performance measure like this to determine how many data entry employees they need to hire. Upon hiring these data entry folk, a good manager should probably be able to raise his employees' performance higher than this national average. How much higher? Using this average as your measure, what should a good manager's goal be—25 percent higher? 35 percent higher? 50 percent higher? Fifty percent higher would put you over 500,000 keypunches per month. In fact, the top-performing data entry employees make a mockery of the national average. They outperform it almost tenfold.

Jean P. is one such employee. When she was first measured, she averaged 560,000 punches per month, already 50 percent above the national average. She was recognized for her performance, then she and her manager set out some individual goals that could help her improve and track her performance. Three months later she hit a million keypunches. A couple of weeks after that milestone, Jean checked her total at the end of the day and saw that she had managed 112,000 keypunches in one day. She approached her manager and said, "You know what? If I average over 110,000 for the whole month, then I'll hit the 2 million mark." They put a plan together, and six months later she soared past 2 million.

Jean became a model for the role. Her manager spent time watching her, asking her why she loved her work so much—"I'm real competitive; I love counting"—and why she seemed to make fewer mistakes the more keys she punched—"I have more practice." He designed a talent profile to find more like her and a compensation plan to reward her excellence. Today Jean's personal best is 3,526,000 keypunches in a month, and the average of all the data entry employees working around her is over a million.

The lessons from Jean's story are applicable to almost any role. Don't use average to estimate the limits of excellence. You will drastically *underestimate* what is possible. Focus on your best performers and keep pushing them toward the right-hand edge of the bell curve. It is counterintuitive, but top performers, like Jean P., have the *most* potential for growth.

BREAKING THROUGH THE CEILING

"Average thinking" not only leads managers away from excellence and away from their top performers. There is one final, and perhaps most damaging, way in which it harms a manager's best efforts. "Average thinking" actively limits performance. Jeff H., a sales manager for a computer software company, describes this debilitating effect:

"I work for a company with one goal: 20 percent annual growth in revenue and profits. We have it drummed into us from day one that 20 percent growth is how we will judge our success as a company. We've hit it for twelve years straight, and Wall Street loves us. I can see why the company needs to shoot for that number every year. I can see why Wall Street likes that predictability. But as an individual manager of people, it's hard.

"Put yourself in my shoes. We've been the number one region for the last four years. Every year I get to the end of the third quarter and all my people have hit their 20 percent growth targets. They have a whole quarter to go, but they've already reached their target. You try motivating this group to give it all they've got for the final three months. To them, it makes much more sense to save all their sales for next year, so that, come January, they've got themselves off to a rolling start. You can't blame them for slowing down. The quota system encourages it. Every year I have to fight against the very system that was designed to help us all excel. I have to hunt for other ways to keep everybody fired up."

How does he do it? Jeff happens to have an intense and conceptual style, so he resorts to writing thoughtful letters to all of his people, cajoling them to look inside themselves and deliver one last ounce of effort. Here's an example:

October 29
People:
With only two months remaining it is imperative that you stay focused on your goals for this year. It has been a long, well-run race so far this year, and for many of you you could just coast the rest of the year and still make quota. That decision is yours; I can't make that for you—and I will not pound or threaten for more.
However, if we want and you want to be the best you are capable of being and you want to develop your abilities to their maximum, that goal is a never-ending one. You must understand that success is achieved through a never-ending pursuit of improvement—personally, professionally, financially, and spiritually. Like it or not, that is what is involved, and that is the commitment you made to yourself when you accepted the challenge to be the best.

Remember, stay focused. Never lose your commitment to your own standard of excellence. Push a little every day, and a lot over time.
Sincerely,
Jeff
P.S. You are the best the company has and the best I have ever had the privilege of managing.

Jeff is fortunate. With his sincere personal appeals and his mantra that each person should "push a little every day, and a lot over time," Jeff has managed to break through the restraints of the quota system. He has found a way to keep everyone focused on excellence. Despite the limits imposed by quotas, Jeff has now led his region to the company's top spot four years in a row.

Other great managers, with their unique talents and styles, will have devised their own routes to excellence. But despite their success, it is still a shame that they have had to waste so much creativity maneuvering around performance evaluation schemes that unwittingly place a ceiling on performance. It is still a shame that they have had to exert so much energy railing against "average thinking." This energy and creativity would be much more valuable in the unfettered pursuit of excellence.

However, if you face the same "average thinking," you should rail against it just as energetically. Define excellence vividly, quantitatively. Paint a picture for your most talented employees of what excellence looks like. Keep everyone pushing and pushing toward that right-hand edge of the bell curve. It's fairer. It's more productive. And, most of all, it's much more fun.

How to Manage Around a Weakness

"How do great managers turn a harmful weakness into an irrelevant nontalent?"

Of course, none of this means that great managers ignore nonperformance. They don't. Focus on strengths is not another name for the power of positive thinking. Bad things happen. Some people fail. Some people struggle. And even your star performers have their faults. Poor performance must be confronted head-on, if it is not to degenerate into a dangerously unproductive situation. And it must be confronted quickly—as with all degenerative diseases, procrastination in the face of poor performance is a fool's remedy.

The most straightforward causes of an employee's poor performance are the "mechanical" causes—perhaps the company is not providing him with the tools or the information he needs; and the "personal" causes—perhaps she is still grieving from a recent death in the family. As a manager, if you are confronted with poor performance, look first to these two causes. Both are relatively easy to identify. Both also happen to be rather difficult to solve—the former will almost certainly require some careful job redesign and better cooperation between individuals or departments; the latter will demand understanding and patience. But at least you will know what is causing the performance problems.

However, many performance problems have subtler causes. Causes like this are more difficult to identify, but fortunately, with the right mind-set, their solutions are all within a manager's control.

The great manager begins by asking two questions.

First, is the poor performance trainable? If the employee is struggling because he doesn't have the necessary skills or knowledge, then it almost certainly *is* trainable. Jan B., a manager in an advertising agency, gives us a simple example:

"One associate was supposed to turn all of my handwritten notes into killer presentations. But it wasn't happening. Her turnaround was slow, and the finished product wasn't that great. I sat her down and subjected her to one of my heart-to-hearts, during which she confessed that she had never learned PowerPoint properly. She was a brilliant art student, but no one had taught her the detailed mechanics of putting that brilliance onto a computer. Well, that's easy. I just set her up with some intensive PowerPoint training and now she's a star."

Laurie T., a manager in a petrochemical company, describes a slightly more subtle approach to imparting knowledge:

"Jim was a young man, very talented, who always used to come in late. We talked about it, and he said that he was just terrible at organizing himself to arrive on time. Every morning something would happen to throw him off. He said I shouldn't worry because he always stayed late and completed his assignments. I told him that I *was* worried. I was worried about how others were perceiving him. I asked him what he imagined other people's perceptions of him were. He confessed that they probably associated his lateness with laziness, a lack of responsibility, a poor team player. 'But that's not me,' he said. 'I know that's not you,' I replied. 'But *they* don't. I'm not saying that you must come in on time from now on. I *am* saying that you must manage your teammates' perceptions better. Otherwise they won't trust you, you'll drag the team down, and I'll have to ask you to leave.'

"Jim now comes in on time 95 percent of the time. *I* didn't change his behavior. What changed his behavior was his knowledge of how negatively others were perceiving him and his awareness that he didn't like that."

These examples are probably familiar to you. You may have faced the salesperson who didn't know the product well enough. Or the secretary who didn't know how to process expenses. Or the recently hired business school graduate who hadn't yet learned how to prepare a report for the real business world. All of these cases of nonperformance can be traced to the employee's lack of certain skills or knowledge. Whether it's as simple as teaching someone a computer program, or as delicate as helping someone gain a perspective on himself, all of these skills and knowledge can and should be trained.

The second question great managers ask is this: Is the nonperformance caused by the manager himself tripping the wrong trigger? Each employee is motivated differently. If the manager forgets this, if he is trying to motivate a noncompetitive person with contests, or a shy person with public praise, then the solution to the nonperformance might well lie in *his* hands. If he can find the right trigger and trip it, perhaps the employee's true talent will burst out.

John F., a general insurance agent, needed a very public misstep to help him understand this. His most productive agent was an individual called Mark D. A repeat winner of the Agent of the Year award, Mark let it be known that he hated the banal plaques that accompanied the award. If he was going to be recognized, he said, he would prefer something other than another meaningless plaque to shove in a drawer along with the others. John listened patiently, but believed he knew better. All salespeople love plaques, he thought.

At the awards banquet, John announced Mark as the winner yet again, ushered him up onto the stage, and proudly presented him with his plaque. Mark took one look at it, turned to the audience, made an obscene gesture, and stalked off the stage, vowing to leave the company. The banquet was a disaster.

John F. spoke to some of Mark's colleagues to see if he could learn anything that would help recover the situation. Apparently on car journeys, in the hallways, and over lunches, or whenever the conversation inched toward life outside the office, Mark would bring up his two daughters. He and his wife thought they could never have children, so these two little girls were a particularly precious gift. Mark would describe their exploits and their triumphs and the funny little things they would say to him. He was so proud of them. They were his life.

As quick as he could, John called up Mark's wife and explained the situation. Mark's wife had an idea. She brought the two girls into a photographic studio. A beautiful portrait was taken of them and mounted in a frame. Mark's plaque was embossed on the frame.

Two weeks later John held a luncheon. In front of all his agents and the guests of honor, Mark's wife and daughters, John unveiled the portrait and presented it to Mark. The same prima donna who had flipped off the crowd now started to cry. Mark's trigger was his two daughters.

This would not have worked if Mark had felt that John didn't genuinely care about him. But fortunately, over the years, trust had developed between the two of them. The only aspect that had been missing from their relationship was a full understanding, on John's part, of what was truly important to Mark. Guided by the clues from Mark's colleagues, John filled that gap. From now on he would respect, and play to, Mark's unique motivational trigger.

All managers can learn from John's example. If an employee's performance goes awry, perhaps you have misread what motivates him.

Perhaps if you tripped a different trigger, the employee's true talents would reengage. Perhaps you are to blame for his poor performance. Before you do anything else, consider this possibility.

However, if you can genuinely answer "No" to both of these initial questions—"No," it's not a skills/knowledge issue, and "No," it's not a trigger issue—then by default the nonperformance is probably a talent issue. The person is struggling because she doesn't have the specific talents needed to perform. In this case, training is not an option. Given the enduring nature of talent, it is highly unlikely that the person will ever be able to acquire the necessary talent. She is who she is, and left to her own devices, she will always be hamstrung by those few areas where she lacks talent.

This situation seems bleak. But it's actually rather commonplace. After all, no one's perfect. No one possesses all of the talents needed to excel in a particular role. Each of us is a couple of talent cards short of a full deck.

THE DIFFERENCE BETWEEN A NONTALENT AND A WEAKNESS

As you might expect, great managers take a welcomingly pragmatic view of our innate imperfection. They begin with an important distinction, a distinction between weaknesses and nontalents. A nontalent is a mental wasteland. It is a behavior that always seems to be a struggle. It is a thrill that is never felt. It is an insight recurrently missed. In isolation, nontalents are harmless. You might have a nontalent for remembering names, being empathetic, or thinking strategically. Who cares? You have many more nontalents than you do talents, but most of them are irrelevant. You should ignore them.

However, a nontalent can mutate into a weakness. A nontalent becomes a weakness when you find yourself in a role where success depends on your excelling in an area that is a nontalent. If you are a server in a restaurant, your nontalent for remembering names becomes a weakness because regulars want you to recognize them. If you are a salesperson, your nontalent for empathy becomes a weakness because your prospects need to feel understood. If you are an executive, your nontalent for strategic thinking becomes a weakness because your company needs to know what traps or opportunities lie hidden over the horizon. You would be wise not to ignore your weaknesses.

Great managers don't. As soon as they realize that a weakness is causing the poor performance, they switch their approach. They know that there are only three possible routes to helping the person succeed. *Devise a support system. Find a complementary partner. Or find an alternative role.* Great managers quickly bear down, weigh these options, and choose the best route.

DEVISE A SUPPORT SYSTEM

Approximately 147 million Americans are incapable of seeing with twenty-twenty vision. Seven hundred years ago anyone cursed with farsightedness, shortsightedness, or astigmatism would have been seriously handicapped. But as the science of optics developed, it became possible to grind lenses that could correct for these conditions. These lenses were then mounted in frames to make spectacles or glasses. And with this one invention, the weakness of imperfect vision was reduced to an irrelevant nontalent. Millions of Americans still suffer from imperfect vision, but armed with the support system of glasses or contact lenses, nobody cares.

The speediest cure for a debilitating weakness is a support system. If one employee finds it difficult to remember names, buy him a Rolodex. If another is an appalling speller, make sure she always runs spell check before she prints. Mandy M., the manager of the design department, describes one effective consultant who undermined her own credibility by always wearing trendy coveralls. Mandy took her shopping and made sure she had at least one presentable business suit that could be worn in front of clients. Jeff B., the sales manager for the computer software company, saw one of his salespeople's performance slipping because of pressures at home—the salesperson's wife was upset that he was receiving so many business calls on their personal line. Jeff bought him a second line and told him to designate one room in his house as an office, to define set hours when the office door would be shut, and to turn off the ringer during those hours.

Marie S., a general insurance agent, had to contend with a superbly productive agent who not only wielded a huge ego, but also spread negativity around him every time he was back in the office. Her solution?

Cut a new door in his office wall that opened directly onto the elevator hallway and then mount a plaque over the door announcing the agent's name in classic gold lettering. With one stroke she not only fulfilled his ego needs, she also diverted him directly into his office and away from his negative wanderings.

This solution may seem a little extreme, but whether they are cutting holes in walls or simply buying Rolodexes, these managers are all doing the same thing: they are managing around the employee's weakness so that they can spend time focusing on his strengths. As with all focus on strength strategies, devising a support system is more productive and more fun than trying to fix the weakness.

Occasionally a support system can serve a different purpose. A large restaurant chain had made a commitment to hiring a certain number of mentally retarded employees, believing that they could find these individuals some simple yet meaningful work. Their altruism occasionally proved rather difficult to execute in the real world. The president describes one individual, Janice, who was employed to unpack chicken, place each piece carefully in the fryer, and then lift them all out once the timer had sounded. Janice was fully capable of understanding the responsibilities of the role and performed its mechanics perfectly. But she couldn't count. And unfortunately the fryer could hold only six pieces of chicken. More often than not Janice would overfill the fryer, leaving each piece of chicken dangerously undercooked.

The company could have easily given up on Janice because of her inability to count. But they chose not to. Instead they devised a simple support system to manage around her weakness: they asked their chicken supplier to send the chicken in packages of six. This way Janice wouldn't have to count. She could just empty each packet into the fryer, and the chicken would be cooked to perfection every time. The supplier refused the request. "It will be too much work on our end," they complained.

So the company fired the supplier and engaged another that was willing to ship chicken in packets of six. Now nobody cares that Janice can't count. Her weakness is irrelevant; it is now a nontalent.

FIND A COMPLEMENTARY PARTNER

Each year, buoyed by the hope that leaders are made, not born, tens of thousands of budding executives traipse off to leadership development courses. Here they discover the many different traits and competencies that constitute the model leader. They receive feedback from their peers and direct reports, feedback that reveals the peaks and valleys of their unique leadership profile. Finally, after all the learning and reflection is complete, the hard work begins. Each willing participant is asked to craft a plan to fill in those valleys, so that he can reshape himself into the model leader, smooth and well-rounded.

That last step, according to great managers, is an unfortunate mistake. They agree that leaders should know all the roles that need to be played. They agree that leaders should look in the mirror and learn how they come across to peers and direct reports. But that last step, crafting a plan to become more well-rounded, is in their view woefully naive. If the individual comes to the training class a poor public speaker, he will leave a poor public speaker. If he is nonconfrontational, he will always be tempted to shy away from battle. If he is impractical, he will forever struggle with bringing his ideas down to land. A training class might help him learn why certain talents are important and how they work. But no matter how earnest he is, a training class will not help him acquire them.

This isn't a depressing revelation. The most renowned leaders in the history of corporate America have always known it. As they struggled to carve out their success, the last thing on their mind was to become well-rounded. They may have been aware of their own shortcomings, but none of them worked at turning these shortcomings into strengths. They knew what a hopeless waste of time that would be. So they did something else instead: they looked for a partner.

Walt Disney didn't have to look far to find his brother, Roy. Through the good graces of their Stanford professor, William Hewlett found David Packard. Bill Gates and Paul Allen were fortunate enough to bump into each other in their high school computer club. None of these extraordinarily successful leaders were well-rounded. They may have had a broad knowledge of their respective businesses, but in terms of talent, each one was sharp in one or two key areas and blunt in many others. Each partnership was effective precisely because where one partner was blunt, the other was sharp. The partnerships were well-rounded, not the individuals.

Even leaders who appeared to stand alone usually balanced their act with a complementary partner. At Disney the massively intelligent, insatiably competitive Michael Eisner benefited from the more practical, down-to-earth Frank Wells. And at Electronic Data Systems, behind the impetuous, inspirational Ross Perot you would have found the wise, guiding hand of the president, Mitch Hart.

The lesson from these leaders is quite clear. You succeed by finding ways to capitalize on who you are, not by trying to fix who you aren't. If you are blunt in one or two important areas, try to find a partner whose peaks match your valleys. Balanced by this partner, you are then free to hone your talents to a sharper point.

This lesson is applicable across virtually all roles and professions. Since few people are a perfect fit for their role, the great manager will always be looking for ways to match up one person's valleys with another person's peaks.

Jan B. had a highly creative researcher, Diane, who seemed to be congenitally incapable of turning in her expense reports on time. Instead of wasting time berating her for her constant failure, Jan simply told her: "Every time you get back from a trip, drop your expenses into an envelope and hand them to Larry. He'll figure them out." Larry isn't an assistant; he's a researcher like Diane. But he's the most organized person on the small team, so he gets to handle his peer's expenses. It may be unconventional. It certainly requires trust and respect between Larry and Diane. But in Jan's mind, it is the only way to capitalize on Larry's talent and simultaneously release Diane from her weakness.

Jeff B., the software sales manager, is not only a sincere, passionate, and conceptual man, he is also, it turns out, a rotten planner. "I've never been good at tactics," he confesses. "I am excellent at ground zero, building trust face-to-face. And I am excellent at twenty thousand feet, finding patterns, playing out scenarios. But I'm terrible in between. That's where Tony's so good. When we look at a situation he asks different questions than me. I'll ask, 'What if?' or, 'Why not?' He'll ask, 'How many?' or, 'When?' or, 'Prove it.' If I went to the board with my half-baked ideas, I'd get shot down every time. But with the two of us working on the same idea, our case ends up looking so convincing, they haven't been able to turn us down once. As I say to Tony, individually we're not much, but together we have a brain."

When you interview great managers, you are bombarded with examples like these. After a while the partnerships they describe begin to seem almost archetypal. Of course the creative but impractical thinker wound up partnered with the streetwise, business-savvy operator. Of course the administratively impaired salesperson teamed up with the "no detail too small" office manager. And of course the cocky, needy highflier found a mentor in the tough-loving veteran. It was inevitable. These things just happen.

But they don't. The partnerships great managers describe are not archetypes. There is nothing inevitable about them at all. Each partnership is, in fact, an anomaly, a surprisingly rare example of one manager bucking the system and figuring out how to make the most of uniquely imperfect people. Great managers talk about these partnerships so nonchalantly, it is easy to forget just how difficult they are to forge in the real world.

HOW COMPANIES PREVENT PARTNERSHIPS

A healthy partnership is based on one crucial understanding: Neither partner is perfect. If potential partners are afraid to admit their imperfections, or are trying diligently to correct them, or are reluctant to ask for help, neither will be on the lookout for a productive partnership. They will be nervous of confessing to too many faults and suspicious of anyone who offers.

Strangely, most companies actively encourage this kind of behavior. Job descriptions, for even the simplest roles, run to two or three pages, presumably in hopes of capturing every minute task that the perfect incumbent should be able to perform. Training classes and development plans target those few behaviors where you consistently struggle. Everyone talks of the need to "broaden your skill set."

Perhaps the most pervasive example of "partnership prevention," however, can be found in the conventional wisdom on teams and teamwork. Conventional wisdom's most frequently quoted line on teams is "There is no 'I' in team." The point here seems to be that teams are built on collaboration and mutual support. The whole is, apparently, more important than its individual parts.

On the surface this appears to be eminently right-minded. Taking these sentiments as their starting point, many companies have dedicated themselves to creating self-managed teams. Here team members are encouraged to rotate into different roles on the team. The more roles they learn, the more they are paid. And everyone is supposed to focus on the team's goals and performance, not his own.

However, conventional wisdom's view of teamwork is dangerously misleading. Great managers do not believe that a productive team has camaraderie as its cornerstone and team members who can play all roles equally well. On the contrary, they define a productive team as one where each person knows which role he plays best and where he is cast in that role most of the time.

The founding principle here is that excellent teams are built around *individual excellence*. Therefore the manager's first responsibility is to make sure each person is positioned in the right role. Her second responsibility is to balance the strengths and weaknesses of each individual so that they complement one another. Then, and only then, should she turn her attention to broader issues like "camaraderie" or "team spirit." One team member might occasionally have to step out of his role to support another, but this kind of pinch-hitting should be a rarity on great teams, not their very essence.

Jim K., a full bird colonel in the army—an organization that might be forgiven for emphasizing flexibility and camaraderie over individual excellence—gives this description of team building:

"When I first assemble the platoon I ask each person to tell me what activities he is mostly drawn to. One will say sharpshooting. One will say radio. One will say explosives. And so on. I'll go around the whole group, taking notes. Then, when I build each squad, I try to assign each person to the role he said he was drawn to. Obviously you won't get a perfect match. And obviously every soldier will be required to learn every role on the platoon—we might lose a man in battle, and every soldier must be able to step in. But you've got to start by assigning the right duties to the right soldier. If you get that wrong, your platoon will falter in combat."

Whereas conventional wisdom views individual specialization as the antithesis of teamwork, great managers see it as the founding principle.

If individual positioning is so important, then at the heart of a great team there must be an I. There must be lots of strong, distinct I's. There must be individuals who know themselves well enough to pick the right roles and to feel comfortable in them most of the time. If one individual joins the team with little understanding of his own strengths and weaknesses, then he will drag the entire team down with his poor performance and his vague yearnings to switch roles. Self-aware individuals—strong I's—are the building blocks of great teams.

FIND AN ALTERNATIVE ROLE

There are some people for whom nothing works. You trip every trigger imaginable. You train. You find partners. You buy Rolodexes, teach spell check, and cut through office walls. But nothing works.

Faced with this situation, you have little choice. You have to find this employee an alternative role. You have to move him out. Sometimes the only way to cure a bad relationship is to get out of it. Similarly, sometimes the only way to cure poor performance is to get the performer out of that role.

How do you know if you are at that point? You will never know for sure. But the best managers offer this advice:

You will have to manage around the weaknesses of each and every employee. But if, with one particular employee, you find yourself spending *most* of your time managing around weaknesses, then know that you have made a *casting error.* At this point it is time to fix the casting error and to stop trying to fix the person.

CHAPTER 6

The Fourth Key:
Find the Right Fit

- The Blind, Breathless Climb
- One Rung Doesn't Necessarily Lead to Another
- Create Heroes in Every Role
- Three Stories and a New Career
- The Art of Tough Love

The Blind, Breathless Climb

"What's wrong with the old career path?"

Sooner or later every manager is asked the question "Where do I go from here?" The employee wants to grow. He wants to earn more money, to gain more prestige. He is bored, underutilized, deserves more responsibility. Whatever his reasons, the employee wants to move up and wants you to help.

What should you tell him? Should you help him get promoted? Should you tell him to talk to Human Resources? Should you say that all you can do is put in a good word for him? What is the right answer?

There is no *right* answer—any one of these answers might be the right one, depending on the situation. However, there is a *right way* to approach this question—namely, *help each person find the right fit.* Help each person find roles that ask him to do more and more of what he is naturally wired to do. Help each person find roles where her unique combination of strengths—her skills, knowledge *and* talents— match the distinct demands of the role.

For one employee, this might mean promotion to a supervisor role. For another employee, this might mean termination. For another, it might mean encouraging him to grow within his current role. For yet another, it might mean moving her back into her previous role. These are very different answers, some of which might be decidedly unpopular with the employee. Nonetheless, no matter how bitter the pill, great managers stick to their goal: Regardless of what the employee wants, the manager's responsibility is to steer the employee toward roles where the employee has the greatest chance of success.

On paper this sounds straightforward; but as you can imagine, it proves to be a great deal more challenging in the real world. This is primarily because, in the real world, conventional wisdom persuades most of us that the right answer to the question "Where do I go from here?" is "Up."

Careers, conventional wisdom advises, should follow a prescribed path: You begin in a lowly individual contributor role. You gain some expertise and so are promoted to a slightly more stretching, slightly less menial individual contributor role. Next you are promoted to supervise other individual contributors. Then, blessed with good performance, good fortune, and good contacts, you climb up and up, until you can barely remember what the individual contributors do at all.

In 1969, in his book, *The Peter Principle,* Laurence Peter warned us that if we followed this path without question, we would wind up promoting each person to his level of incompetence. It was true then. It is true now. Unfortunately, in the intervening years we haven't succeeded in changing very much. We still think that the most creative way to reward excellence in a role is to promote the person out of it. We still tie pay, perks, and titles to a rung on the ladder: the higher the rung, the greater the pay, the better the perks, the grander the title. Every signal we send tells the employee to look onward and upward. "Don't stay in your current role for too long," we advise. "It looks bad on the résumé. Keep pressing, pushing, stretching to take that next step. It's the only way to get ahead. It's the only way to get respect."

These signals, although well intended, place every employee in an extremely precarious position. To earn respect, he knows he must climb. And as he takes each step, he sees that the company is burning the rungs behind him. He cannot retrace his steps, not without being tarred with the failure brush. So he continues his blind, breathless climb to the top, and sooner or later he overreaches. Sooner or later he steps into the wrong role. And there he is trapped. Unwilling to go back, unable to climb up, he clings to his rung until, finally, the company pushes him off.

A RUNG TOO FAR

Marc C. was pushed. He was pushed off, down, and out. Standing on Pennsylvania Avenue, Marc gazed up at the White House and tried to piece together what had happened.

Two years earlier he had still been living out of his suitcase. As the leading foreign correspondent for a European television station, one week he would find himself in Zaire covering the fall of a dictator, and the next week he would turn up in Chechnya to record the retreat of rebel insurgents. Wherever he went, everyone acknowledged Marc as the master. Somehow he was able to find the center of all the anger and the confusion and extract some meaning from the madness. When armies shelled marketplaces, or snipers picked off civilians on their walk to work, Marc would be found at the scene explaining what happened, why it happened, and what it all meant. To his viewers he was a calming, authoritative presence. They trusted him. So no one was surprised when he was posted to Jerusalem.

On the foreign correspondents' ladder, Washington is the top rung. It has the most prestige, the most money, and, important, the most air-time. It is the posting everyone wants. But if Washington is number one, then Jerusalem runs a close second. More interesting than the European parliament in Brussels, more important than post–cold war Moscow, Jerusalem is one of the few places where local clashes have such global significance. It is a foreign correspondent's dream.

In Jerusalem Marc refined his talents. Israel is a small country, and Marc was able to report live from the scene no matter where the action erupted. Israeli settlers protesting the latest peace accords? Marc would be in their midst, marching with them, shouting his report over the noise of the crowd. Palestinian youths hurling paving stones at Israeli troops? Marc would be filmed in one of the narrow side streets, explaining the reasons for their anger simply and clearly. In the overheated climate of the Middle East, Marc became the cool voice of reason.

A year later his European managers offered him the top rung. They offered him the money, the prestige, and the exposure of Washington. Marc loved what he was doing, but there was no way he was going to turn this down. It was the plum job of all reporting assignments. He willingly unpacked his suitcases for the last time and settled in to become the newest, best Washington bureau chief. And very quickly things started to fall apart.

Outside of the occasional titillating scandal, not much happens in Washington—at least not during his tenure. Yes, there might be a presidential veto one week and a filibuster the next, but back in Europe few understand these events and even fewer care. Most of the action is dry and repetitious, important but uninteresting. The Washington bureau chief's role is to take the tedious business of politics and inject it with heroes and villains, daring triumphs and crushing defeats. His job is to spice things up.

And Marc couldn't do it. He was brilliant at giving real-life drama a political context. But he was terrible at giving politics the sheen of real-life drama. Marc was surefooted in the aftermath of a mortar attack. But in a town where a State of the Union address was big news, he didn't know what to do. The stories went begging. His reporting became bland. He was lost.

Back in Europe, his audience turned away. His European managers couldn't put their finger on it, but they noticed the difference. They stuck with him for a while—he deserved that much—and then they pulled the plug. In six months the hero of Jerusalem had shriveled into the embarrassment in Washington. He was removed.

Marc's role might seem quite exotic, but his fate is commonplace. In his desire to grow and to please his managers, he kept climbing the ladder until, one day, he climbed one rung too far. Sadly, this happens all the time. In order to gain money, title, and respect, teachers must become administrators. Managers must reach for leadership. Nurses must aspire to be nurse supervisors. Craftsmen must yearn to be managers of other craftsmen. And reporters must yearn to be bureau chiefs. In most companies Marc's fate awaits us all.

Laurence Peter was right. Most employees *are* promoted to their level of incompetence. It's inevitable. It's built into the system.

IT DOESN'T HAVE TO BE THIS WAY

This system is flawed, for it is built on three false assumptions.

The first fallacy is that each rung on the ladder represents a slightly more complex version of the previous rung. Consequently, if a person excelled on one rung on the ladder, it is a sure sign that with just a little more training, he will be able to repeat his success on the rung above. The best managers reject this. They know that *one rung doesn't necessarily lead to another.*

Second, the conventional career path is condemned to create conflict. By limiting prestige to those few rungs high up on the ladder, it tempts every employee, even the most self-aware, to try to clamber onto the next rung. Each rung is a competition, and since there are fewer rungs than there are employees, each competition generates many more losers than winners. Great managers have a better idea. Why not resolve the conflict by making prestige more available? Why not carve out alternative career paths by conveying meaningful prestige on every role performed at excellence? *Why not create heroes in every role?*

The third, and most devastating, flaw in the system is its assumption that varied experiences make the employee more attractive. This assumption focuses the employee on hunting for marketable skills and experiences. With these skills and experiences proudly displayed on his résumé, the employee then meekly waits—or aggressively lobbies—to be chosen for the next rung. In this scenario the employee is the supplicant. The manager is the gatekeeper, pushing back the hordes and selecting the attractive ones—the ones with the most skills and the best experiences—for advancement. Great managers know that this whole scenario is awry. In their view the hunt for marketable skills and experiences should not be the force driving the employee's career. They envision a different driving force. They have *a new career* in mind.

One Rung Doesn't Necessarily Lead to Another

"Why do we keep promoting people to their level of incompetence?"

Why do we continue to assume that a person's success on one rung will have any relevance to his or her likelihood to succeed on the rung above? More than likely we have been confused about what is trainable and what is not. We have made no distinction among skills, knowledge, and talents, and this clumsy language has made it easier for us to say, "If John has shown himself to be a good salesperson, then I am sure we can just train him to be a good manager." Or, "Since Jan has proven herself a solid manager, I am confident that we can teach her the strategic thinking and the vision needed to be a great leader."

As we noted earlier, we now know that excellence in every role requires distinct talents, and that these talents, unlike skills and knowledge, are extraordinarily difficult to train. Armed with this knowledge, we can dismantle some long-standing career paths. We know that the talents needed to sell and the talents needed to manage, while not mutually exclusive, *are* different—if you excel at one, it does not tell us very much about whether you will excel at the other. We can say the same about the talents needed to manage, as compared to the talents needed to lead. In fact, we can say the same about all roles—even roles that, at first glance, seem to be very similar.

Consider, for example, the conventional information technology career path. If you work in information technology, you will tend to begin your career as a computer programmer—writing code—and then progress to a systems analyst role—designing integrated systems. Programmer to systems analyst: these are the first two rungs on the conventional IT career path. And given their superficial similarity, this would seem to be a sensible way to structure things.

In fact, these two roles are quite different. Great programmers possess a thinking talent called problem solving. The best programmers want to be given *all of the pieces* to the puzzle. Once they are armed with all the pieces, their particular talent is the ability to rearrange the pieces so that they all fit together perfectly. In their personal life this talent often draws them toward crossword puzzles or brainteasers, like the ones in chapter 3. In their professional life this talent enables them to write thousands of lines of computer code and arrange them in the most effective and efficient order.

While this talent is nice for a systems analyst to possess, it is not particularly relevant to success on the job. By contrast, their most important thinking talent is called formulation. They revel in situations where they are faced with *incomplete data*. Lacking some of the most important facts, they can then do what they love: play out alternative scenarios, hypothesize, test out their theories. On the job this talent enables them to construct highly intricate systems and then test these systems for bugs. If one system has a glitch, they then play out different scenarios, narrowing the range of possible solutions until they have identified exactly what needs to be changed and where and why.

The talents of problem solving and formulation are not mutually exclusive. It is entirely possible for an employee to possess both. But if you are blessed with problem solving, it does not *necessarily* mean that you are similarly blessed with formulation. To promote programmers to systems analysts simply because the conventional career path dictates that you should is to take a blind roll of the dice. You are just as likely to wind up with a team of misfits as you are a team of talented systems analysts.

Before you promote someone, look closely at the talents needed to excel in the role—the striving, thinking, and relating talents necessary for success. After scrutinizing the person and the role, you may still choose promotion. And since each person is highly complex, you may still end up promoting your employee into a position where he struggles—no manager finds the perfect fit every time. But at least you will have taken the time to weigh the fit between the demands of the role and the talent of the person.

If Marc's managers had bothered to think this through, perhaps they would have seen the poor fit between the Washington job, which required a reporter who loved to spice things up, and Marc, whose dominant talent was an ability to calm things down.

Create Heroes in Every Role

"How to solve the shortage of respect."

Even if you thoughtfully examine the match between the employee and the role, you've still got a problem. No matter what conclusion *you* come to, the employee will invariably want to move up. The employee will want to be promoted. Every signal sent by the company tells him that higher is better. A larger salary, a more impressive title, more generous stock options, a roomier office with a couch and a coffee table, all this and more awaits the lucky employee on the next rung on the ladder. No wonder he wants to move up.

These blazing neon lights are a damaging distraction. They not only tempt employees to jump from excellence on one rung to mediocrity on another, they also create a bottleneck—legions of employees all trying to scramble onto increasingly fewer rungs. Conflict and disappointment are inevitable. There has to be a way to redirect employees' driving ambition and to channel it more productively.

There is. *Create heroes in every role.* Make every role, performed at excellence, a respected profession. Many employees will still choose to climb the conventional ladder, and for those with the talent to manage others or to lead, this will be the right choice. However, guided by meaty incentives, many other employees will decide to redirect their energies toward growth within their current role. Great managers envision a company where there are multiple routes toward respect and prestige, a company where the best secretaries carry a vice president title, where the best housekeepers earn twice as much as their supervisors, and where anyone performing at excellence is recognized publicly.

If this sounds fanciful, here are a few techniques that great managers are already using to build such a company.

LEVELS OF ACHIEVEMENT

How long does it take to become excellent in a chosen field? In a study called the Development of Talent Project, Dr. Benjamin Bloom of

Northwestern University scrutinized the careers of world-class sculptors, pianists, chess masters, tennis players, swimmers, mathematicians, and neurologists. He discovered that across these diverse professions, it takes between ten and eighteen years before world-class competency is reached. If you show some interest, he becomes even more specific. He will tell you, for example, that it takes 17.14 years from your first piano lessons to your victory at the Van Cliburn, Tchaikovsky or Chopin piano competitions. While figures like this can feel a little too precise, Dr. Bloom's general point is nevertheless well taken: The exact length of time will vary by person and profession, but whether you are a teacher, a nurse, a salesperson, an engineer, a pilot, a waiter, or a neurosurgeon, it still takes years to become the world's best. As Hippocrates, the philosopher and founder of modern medicine, observed: "Life is short. The art is long."

If a company wants some employees in every role to approach world-class performance, it *must* find ways to encourage them to stay focused on developing their expertise. Defining graded levels of achievement, for every role, is an extremely effective way of doing just that.

Lawyers figured this out a long time ago. The young lawyer, fresh out of law school, selects his field of expertise—corporate law, criminal law, tax law—is hired into that field by a law firm and joins as a junior associate. Over the next four or five years he will be promoted to associate and then to senior associate. As a senior associate he will still be practicing law in his chosen field. He will simply be more accomplished. Over the next five years he will, hopefully, be promoted to some kind of equity position within the firm, where he will start as a junior partner, move up to partner, and then be promoted to senior partner. As a senior partner in the firm he will garner a tremendous amount of respect and earn a very generous salary, yet he will still be practicing the same kind of law as he was back in his junior associate days. The work will be more complex, and he will have his pick of the most interesting and most lucrative work. The only difference is that, by now, he will be one of the world experts in his chosen field.

Law firms are rarely considered cutting-edge organizations, but with their use of graded levels of achievement, they are far ahead of most companies. Although all lawyers are free to choose more conventional career paths—moving into the management of other lawyers, perhaps, or becoming a legal generalist for a corporation—these levels of achievement provide lawyers with an alternative, but equally respected, path to growth. It is a path that offers them both the opportunity to become experts and a simple way to track their progress.

Lawyers aren't the only ones to realize the power of these levels of achievement. In medicine the levels build from intern all the way to senior consultant over a period of, at minimum, fifteen years. In professional sports you can measure your expertise as you progress from rookie to second string to starter to all-star. In sales the entry grade might be the Million Dollar Roundtable, an important first step for the fledgling salesperson, but the pinnacle is the Presidents Club, where the criteria for membership are ten million dollars in sales and perfect client-service scores. And in music you track your progress not by whether you are promoted from the violin to the conductor, but rather by your journey from the most junior third-chair violinist to concertmaster or first-chair associate.

In fact, anywhere individual excellence is revered, you will find these graded levels of achievement. Conversely, if you cannot find them, it means that, either overtly or accidentally, the company does not value excellence in that role. And by this standard, companies don't value excellence in most roles.

As we stated earlier, great managers rebel against this. They believe instead that every role performed at a level of excellence is valuable, that there is virtuosity in every role. So no matter how menial the role appears, they work hard to define meaningful criteria that can help a dedicated employee track his or her progress toward world-class performance.

- AT&T provides help desk solutions to hundreds of companies. AT&T managers decided to organize each help desk according to the complexity of the client's question. Level one deals with simple queries like "How can I turn on my computer?" Level two addresses slightly more difficult issues. Level three handles the panicked "What do I do? I think I've just crashed our entire intranet!" inquiries. These three distinct levels are not only the most efficient way to structure the operation—each level has a different pace, a different call volume, and so on—but they also provide a genuine career path for employees who want to grow into superior technicians rather than into supervisors.

- At Phillips Petroleum, managers provide employees with a well-respected engineer career track. If the employee can show proficiency in the required procedures, then she can gradually progress through the different levels of this career path, all the way up to a director-level position, where she will be recognized as one of the most accomplished engineers in the firm.
- In the mid-eighties Gallup worked with Allied Breweries to measure the performance of bartenders in pubs. One of the signs of greatness in bartending is an ability to remember not only the names of regulars, but also the drinks that go with them. We devised a program called the One Hundred Club. Any bartender who could prove that he knew one hundred names, and the drinks to match, would be awarded a button and a cash prize. The levels progressed up to the world-class Five Hundred Club, which brought better prizes and bigger bonuses.

    When we started the One Hundred Club with Allied Breweries, few managers believed that any bartender would ever reach the Five Hundred Club level. But by 1990 Janice K., a bartender in a pub in the north of England, became the first member of the Three Thousand Club. She knew the names of three thousand regulars *and* their favorite beverage. From this angle Janice was the best bartender in the world.

    It just goes to show: In most cases, no matter what it is, if you measure it and reward it, people will try to excel at it.

These are just a few examples of managers guiding employees with a series of levels that lead to world-class performance. Levels of achievement like these are invaluable for a manager. When confronted by that thorny question "Where do I go from here?" the manager is now able to offer a specific and respected alternative to the blind, breathless climb up.

BROADBANDING

These levels of achievement will certainly help redirect an employee's focus toward becoming world class. However, the manager's efforts at career redirection will be forever hindered if all of the *pay* signals are telling the employee to look upward.

Although each of us is motivated by money in different ways, the fact of the matter is that few of us are repelled by money. All of us may not hunger for it, but only a tiny minority of us find money positively distasteful. Therefore the simple truth is that it will be much easier for managers to redirect employees toward alternative career paths if some of those paths involve a raise in pay.

The ideal pay plan would allow the company to compensate the person in direct proportion to the amount of expertise she showed in her current role—the more she excelled, the more she would earn. In practice this ideal plan is complicated by the fact that some roles are simply more valuable than others. On balance, a pilot is probably more valuable than a flight attendant. A principal is more valuable than a teacher. A restaurant manager is more valuable than a waiter. Any pay plan must take these value differentials into account.

But before we design our plan, there is one final twist to consider. Some roles performed excellently are more valuable than roles higher up the ladder performed averagely. An excellent flight attendant is probably more valuable than an average pilot. A brilliant teacher is more valuable than a novice principal. A superstar waiter is more valuable than a mediocre restaurant manager. The perfect pay plan must be sophisticated enough to reflect this overlap.

Simple and effective, it is called broadbanding. For each role, you define pay in broad bands, or ranges, with the top end of the lower-level role overlapping the bottom end of the role above.

For example, at Merrill Lynch the top end of the pay band for financial consultants is over $500,000 a year. In contrast, the bottom end of the branch manager pay band is $150,000 a year. This means that if you are a successful financial consultant and you want to move into a manager role, you might have to endure a 70 percent pay cut. The upside for the novice manager is that the top end of the manager pay band runs into the millions. So while you may have to stomach the 70 percent pay cut initially, if you prove yourself to be excellent at managing others, then in the end you will reap significant financial rewards.

The Walt Disney Company takes a similar approach. As a brilliant server in one of their fine-dining restaurants, you might earn over $60,000 a year. If you choose to climb onto the manager career path, your starting salary will be $25,000 a year. Again, once you start to excel as a manager and are promoted up and through the various supervisory levels, your total compensation package can take you far above $60,000. But, initially, your pay packet will be sliced in half.

Even traditional, hierarchical organizations are starting to experiment with broadbanding. Martin P., the chief of police for a state capital in the Midwest, describes the conventional career path from police officer to police sergeant—the front-line supervisor role—to police captain (he removed the lieutenant role a couple of years ago) to assistant chief to police chief. "Time was," he says, "when the only way to earn more money was to move into management—to go from officer to sergeant. Now all my pay grades overlap. If you are a superb police officer, you don't need to get promoted to sergeant to earn more. The fact is, my very best police officers earn more than their captain does."

On the surface, broadbanding appears disorienting. Front-line employees earning two or three times what their managers earn? This is a world turned upside-down. On closer scrutiny, however, broadbanding makes sense.

First, with its *broad* bands of pay, it provides a way to value world-class performance in a particular role very differently from average performance in that role. As with levels of achievement, wherever individual excellence is revered, we see broadbanding. In professional sports, no matter what the position, the superstars at that position earn multiples greater than the average players in the same position. This also applies to actors, musicians, artists, singers, and writers. In all of these professions the broad range in pay encourages the person to refine his talents and so become world class. Great managers advise us to apply the same logic to all roles.

Second, with its *overlapping* bands of pay, broadbanding slows the blind, breathless climb up. It forces the employee to open her eyes and ask, "Why am I angling for this next promotion? Why am I pushing so hard to climb onto the next rung?" Without broadbanding, the answer to these questions is clouded by her knowledge that the next rung brings more money. With broadbanding the employee can answer only by examining the *content* of the role and weighing the match between its responsibilities and her strengths. Her answers will be more honest and more accurate. She will make her career choices based at least as much upon fit as upon finances.

Some companies take broadbanding to its limits. At Stryker, a $2 billion medical device manufacturer, the pay band for salespeople ranges from $40,000 for a novice to $250,000 for the best of the best. If you decide to move into the manager ranks, you have to take a 60 percent pay cut—the starting salary for a new regional manager is just under $100,000 a year. What is intriguing is that the top end of the manager band—about $200,000 in total compensation—is lower than the top end for salespeople. The best regional manager in the company can never earn as much as the best salesperson. Why would Stryker choose to do this? All manner of reasons: They value their best salespeople very highly; they want to entice their best salespeople to stay close to the customer for as long as possible; they want each employee to think long and hard before climbing onto the manager ladder. Whatever their reasons, their pay plan has proven very successful. Powered by the best salespeople and the best managers in the business, Stryker has achieved 20 percent annual growth in sales and profit for the last twenty years.

Broadbanding is a vital weapon in the arsenal of great managers. It gives teeth to their commitment that every role, performed at excellence, will be valued. And if the Stryker example appears a little extreme, remember this: During Gallup's interviews with great managers, we found a consistent willingness to hire employees who, the managers knew, might soon earn significantly more than they did.

CREATIVE ACTS OF REVOLT

Great managers have to survive in a hostile world. Most companies do not value excellence in every role. They do not provide alternative career paths for their employees. And they do not give their managers the leeway to design graded levels of achievement or broadbanded pay plans. If you find yourself living in this restricted world, what can you do?

Brian J. can tell you. His advice: Revolt, quietly and creatively. Brian manages artists in a large media company. His company has seen fit to construct an intricate hierarchy comprising over thirty distinct pay grades, each with clearly defined benefits and perks. One of the rules within this elaborate structure is that you cannot be promoted to a director-level position unless you manage other people. Another rule is that only directors are granted such perks as stock options and first-class seating when traveling.

"I was caught between a rock and a hard place," Brian says. "I wanted to show some of my best graphic artists how valuable they were, but rules are rules. I couldn't reward them with a director-level promotion without promoting them to a manager role. But I didn't want to promote them to a manager role because that's not their talent. So instead I asked each of them to become mentors for junior graphic artists—they wouldn't manage these people, they would just be expected to pass on their expertise. I then went to Human Resources and said that, as far as I was concerned, a mentor was the equivalent of a manager and so I had a right to promote them to a director-level position. HR took some convincing, but I got my way in the end."

Garth P. tells a similar story. Garth runs an applied technology division in an aeronautics company. In his production facilities he employs hundreds of technical specialists.

"The best engineer I had was a guy called Michael B. We've got a pretty rigid structure here, so whenever we wanted to reward Michael we had to promote him up the ladder. After ten years of promotions, he found himself doing less and less of the engineering he loved and more and more people management, which, to be frank, he struggled at. So together we decided to create a new position: master engineer. Michael would be a roving genius, getting involved in only the most complex projects. He would also be the main resource, and the last word, on all engineering problems any of the other teams faced. *And* he would be freed from any manager responsibilities at all. I decreed that this was a vice president–level job, got the okay from personnel, and then promoted him. I can't think of when I've made an employee happier."

Laura T., an executive in a Texas-based petrochemical company, faced a similar situation but solved it in a slightly different way:

"I have lots of people who want to grow and who deserve to be recognized, but since we aren't growing right now, new positions aren't opening up. So I take my top performers and assign them to special projects. These projects are ad hoc. They have a specific objective, with a specific timeline. Once the objective is met, the project team disbands. Special projects like this work really well for me, because they give my talented employees a chance to grow, and at the same time they give me a chance to recognize each of them for excellent work—I got permission from HR to reward each successful team member with a gift certificate for a weekend in Dallas and seats to a Cowboys game. Recognition like that might not sound like a big deal to you, but for a traditional petro-chemical company like ours, it's a whole new way of thinking."

Each of these managers, in his or her own way, is providing alternative routes toward growth *and* prestige. Each of them, maneuvering within a restricted world, is devising innovative ways to reward employees for excellent performance, without necessarily promoting these employees out of their current role. Each of them is trying to create heroes in every role.

Three Stories and a New Career

"What is the force driving the New Career?"

Today's unpredictable business climate has undoubtedly caused a shift in the employer-employee relationship. Employers, acutely aware of the need to be nimble, can no longer guarantee lifelong employment. All they are willing to offer the employee is lifelong employability: "We will provide you with marketable experiences that will make you attractive to other employers, should we ever need to cut back our labor costs." This is certainly a shift from twenty years ago, but great managers contend it is merely a superficial shift. Very little of substance has changed. Conventional wisdom's core assumption about careers remains the same, and it remains wrong.

It assumes that the energy for a career should emanate from the employee's desire to better herself, to fill herself out with attractive experiences. She should not linger long in one particular role. Instead she should skip from one role to the next every couple of years so that, over time, her résumé becomes impressively varied. Under the terms of lifelong employment, the employees with the most impressive résumés were the most likely to be selected for the next rung on the internal ladder. Under the terms of lifelong employability, the employees with these attractive résumés are the most likely to be snapped up, externally, by a new company. The location may be different, but the assumption is the same: Varied experiences make an employee attractive. Therefore, from conventional wisdom's perspective, a career can be best understood as the employee's focused search for interesting and marketable experiences.

Great managers disagree. Acquiring varied experiences is important but peripheral to a healthy career. It is an accessory, not the driving force. The true source of energy for a healthy career, they say, is generated elsewhere. Listen to enough of their stories and you can start to figure out where. They tell stories of people who took a step, looked in the mirror, and discovered something about themselves. In some cases the person looked in the mirror spontaneously. In others he had to be coaxed to turn his head before seeing himself clearly. There are stories where the discovery was a confirmation to stay the course. There are stories, like the three that follow, where the discovery prompts a change in direction. But whatever the details of the story, it is always the same story.

Their recurring story reveals that *self-discovery is the driving, guiding force for a healthy career.* The energy for a healthy career is generated from discovering the talents that are already there, not from filling oneself up with marketable experiences. Self-discovery is a long process, never fully achieved. Nonetheless, great managers know that it is this search for a full understanding of your talents and nontalents that serves as the source of energy powering your career.

#1: Dr. No's Story

George H. was the vice president of development in a large real estate development company. He had risen through the ranks as a project manager, and now, midway through his career, he found himself second in command to a creative, articulate risk taker called Howard P. George was perfectly suited to his role. While Howard dreamed up wildly elaborate and expensive schemes, George identified all of the impediments, all of the pitfalls, that could derail Howard's plan. George called this his "parade of horribles." Everyone called George "Dr. No."

Dr. No was respected and admired. He was honorable and courageous and detail oriented. And the whole company knew that every plan was strengthened by exposure to Dr. No's refining fire. He was a most valuable executive.

Then Howard left, and Dr. No was promoted, and quite soon he lost the admiration of his colleagues. You see, Dr. No's particular talent was to make small things out of big things. This talent had enabled him to take Howard's crazy ideas and break them down into manageable projects, each of which could then be analyzed for costs, benefits, and risks. But this talent was rendered useless without raw material, without a dreamer to dream up the humongous, outrageous idea. And the dreamer had moved on.

There were others within the company who would now present Dr. No with an Everest of an idea, but he would immediately slice it up into a series of middling hillocks, small projects, low risk. And, thus dismantled, the idea lost its impact. It was no longer worth the effort. By the middle of his first year Dr. No had red-lighted every single project.

Dr. No knew what he was doing, but, strangely, he couldn't prevent it. When he imagined the sheer size of the risk, so many variables, all out of his control, he would feel his throat begin to constrict. As he played out the project in greater and greater detail, his throat would close so tightly that he could barely breathe. It happened every time and a little worse each time. At work he now felt physical pain and the attack of panic.

Panicky feelings like this can sometimes bring clarity. As the year progressed, Dr. No came to understand what everyone else already knew: He would *never* get anything going. The talents that had served him so well as the dreamer's partner would forever strangle the organization. Left to his own devices, he would always kill big ideas.

So Dr. No removed himself from the position. He set himself up as an independent contractor, where he would be paid to conceive, design, and execute lots and lots of small ideas. He can breathe more easily now.

#2: A Touching Story

Mary G. has fingers that are as strong and as firm as they appear, and powerful forearms. Standing up straight above you, she has shoulders that seem to stretch from wall to wall, and as she reaches back to twist her hair out of the way, you notice that her elbows are surprisingly rounded. Later, when she bears down on them, they feel as though they must be six inches across. It is a good feeling.

Mary is a massage therapist, and she was born to touch. "Other people's bodies fascinate me. When someone is lying in front of me, it's like their skin is transparent. I can see the bands of muscle stretched up and around their shoulder blades, across their back, and down their legs. I can see where the muscles are pulled taut and where they are all scrunched up in an angry little knot. I can almost see the nerves, too. I sense that with one person they might like long strokes that pump the muscle and get the blood going. With someone else they might prefer shiatsu. That's a technique where you use pressure points on the body to stimulate the nerve endings and open up the whole nervous system. Everyone is different."

Three years after finishing her training, Mary found herself the most sought-after therapist at the exclusive Arizona health spa where she worked. The word had spread. If you want a massage that pummels and loosens and opens you up, but with no pain, you must schedule with Mary.

Soon her employer decided to promote her to manage all of the massage therapists at the resort. This meant more money, more security, better benefits, and fewer appointments of her own. And she was miserable.

"I missed the intimacy. As a massage therapist, I stand in a room with another person for an hour or more, in silence, and look through their skin and see their pain and ease their pain. I come to love each one, just a little bit. I love the immediate gratification of releasing someone's stress. They look different afterward, immediately afterward. Their skin looks brighter, their eyes are clearer. And I know it will last. It is a great feeling for me and, I hope, for them."

Mary wanted to get that feeling back. So she quit her job, moved to Los Angeles, and set up her own practice. Her appointment book is filled up, and once again Mary gets to touch people every single day.

#3: Mandy's Designer Story

We met Mandy back in chapter 5. She is the manager of a department that designs logos and other images to drive a product's brand identity. She tells this story:

"I inherited this woman, a design consultant, called Janet. A design consultant has two responsibilities—first, to interact with the clients and find out their needs; and second, to manage the designers so that they deliver what the client wanted. Janet was very ambitious, very talented, but she wasn't performing either of these roles very well. She wasn't failing, but she wasn't a star, either. And she was the kind of person who needed to be a star.

"She realized pretty quickly that I thought she was mediocre, so her attitude took a dive. She wouldn't tell me directly, but I got word from her best friend in the office that she wanted me to fire her so that she could collect unemployment. It pissed me off that she wouldn't come clean with me, but I was damned if I was going to let her manipulate me into firing her. I wanted her to be honest with herself about her feelings and her intentions. I wanted her to understand that, in the end, she would be rewarded for her honesty.

"So I waited her out. And over a period of about four months, we started to talk. We discussed her performance, her strengths, her weaknesses, likes, dislikes, that kind of thing. I told her that it wasn't her fault she wasn't excelling in this role, but that, together, we would have to find a solution.

"Then one day it occurred to me that she should go back to school and become a designer herself. She was very curious about the business, very creative, and much preferred to do a job by herself. She played with the idea for a while, and then she acted on it. She enrolled at New York University, got her degree, and is now at a large advertising agency as a designer. And very successful.

"Janet wasn't a bad person. She had just picked the wrong career, and having started it, she didn't want to admit to herself that she had made a mistake. I helped her."

With self-discovery as its energy source, great managers now paint this picture of a healthy career. Guided perhaps by her choice of college major, perhaps by her family, perhaps by necessity, the employee selects her first role and jumps into the fray. In this first role she is unsure of herself. She is unsure of her ability to perform, unsure of her talents and her nontalents. As she achieves certain levels of performance, she might then move into different roles, or she might simply grow within that first role. Either way it is now her responsibility to look in the mirror and ask, "Do I thrill to this role? Did I seem to learn this role quickly? Am I good in this role? Does this role bring me strength and satisfaction?" It is her responsibility to listen for the clues that this role plays to her talents.

She might have started in sales, then moved into marketing—in this new role does she like being further removed from the customer? Does she love dealing with the patterns and concepts inherent in marketing, or does she miss the direct interaction and the knowledge that she, and she alone, made that sale? She might have started as a flight attendant and then moved into the training department—does she like helping novice flight attendants grow, or does she yearn for the drama and the challenge of winning over tired, nervous passengers?

As she looks in the mirror, she learns. Each step is the chance to discover a little more about her talents and her nontalents. These discoveries guide her next step and her next and her next. Her career is no longer a blind hunt for marketable experiences and a breathless climb upward. It has become an increasingly refined series of choices, as she narrows her focus toward that role, or roles, where her strengths—her skills, her knowledge, and her talents—converge and resound.

Deep down, most people probably know that self-discovery is important to the building of a healthy career. The difference lies in the way great managers use self-discovery.

First, they give self-discovery a central role, making it an explicit expectation for each employee. Mike C., a manager in a courier company, describes how he turns self-discovery from a theoretical concept into a simple, practical demand:

"When someone joins the team, I tell him that one of our major goals in working together is to help him figure out who he is. I tell him to look in the mirror. And if he doesn't know how to do that, I tell him to use the Sunday night blues test. If he doesn't feel that little stab of depression on Sunday night, if he actually finds himself looking forward to the week, then he should stop and ask himself, 'Why?' What is it about the role that he loves so much? Whatever he answers, he should scribble it down and make sure that he keeps it in mind when he chooses another role.

"If he does feel those Sunday night blues coming on every weekend, then it's not necessarily his fault. It's not some failing in him. But he does need to ask the same question, 'Why?' What does he need that his current role is not giving him? Again, he should bear his answer in mind as he looks for other places to work."

Managers like Mike C. aren't suggesting that gaining varied experiences is a bad idea, simply that it is insufficient. They know that an employee will fail to find the roles that fit him if he spends his career gorging himself on skills and experiences, while neglecting to look in the mirror—an approach to career building that is as likely to succeed as is trying to build a healthy body by popping vitamins and diet pills while neglecting to exercise.

Second, these exemplary managers emphasize that the point of self-discovery is not to fix your nontalents. The point is not to "identify and then fill in your skill gaps," as many human resources departments euphemistically describe it. In the spirit of the insight that "you cannot put in what was left out, you can only draw out what was left in," the point of self-discovery is to learn about yourself so that you can capitalize on who you are. The point is to take control of your career, to make more informed decisions, and to gradually select roles that represent an increasingly good fit for your natural talents.

THE MANAGER AND THE NEW CAREER

How can the manager help? In the new career, the employee is the star. It is his responsibility to take control of his career. It is his responsibility to look in the mirror and make sound choices based upon what he discovers. But what role should the manager play? She is no longer the gatekeeper, picking and choosing from among the most attractive, the most skilled, the most experienced supplicants. What is her role?

One could make a case for saying that since the employee is the star and since companies can no longer guarantee lifelong employment, the manager's role has become less significant. She should focus her people on performance today, but not concern herself with where they are headed tomorrow. The employee should figure that out for himself. Besides, if the manager invests too much in her people, she might soon be disappointed. Given the speed of change today, she might well end up having to terminate the people she has nurtured so carefully.

The best managers reject this perspective. They know that in this new career they can play some significant roles. They can *level the playing field*. They can be the ones to *hold up the mirror*. And they can *create a safety net*.

GREAT MANAGERS LEVEL THE PLAYING FIELD

This is why creating new heroes, designing graded levels of achievement, and establishing broadbanded pay plans are all so important. These techniques provide an environment where money and prestige are spread throughout the organization. Since the employee now knows he can acquire them through a variety of different paths, money and prestige become less of a factor in his decision making. He is free to choose his path based upon his current understanding of his talents and nontalents. He may still make the occasional misstep, but he is much more likely to focus not only toward roles where he excels, but toward roles that bring him lasting satisfaction and roles that he yearns to play for a very long time.

On this leveled playing field, you hear conversations that you never thought you would hear. Conversations like the one Jeff H., the computer software sales manager, had with his supervisor:

"I love my role. I'm the best in the company at it. I am making a lot of money doing it. And I am having more of an impact than I ever thought was possible in my life. So I said to my boss, I said, 'Your one objective with me is to see to it that I am never promoted again. If you can do that, you have me for life.'"

GREAT MANAGERS HOLD UP THE MIRROR

Great managers excel at "holding up the mirror." They excel at giving performance feedback. Don't confuse this with the once-a-year performance appraisal chore, with its labyrinthine form filling and remedial focus; or with the empty, arbitrary employee-of-the-month feedback. The feedback given by great managers is quite different.

It is the kind of feedback that Laura T., the petrochemical executive, gives to her people. She describes a program called Excel, where she meets with each of her twenty-two direct reports once every quarter. "In these meetings we quickly review the last three months. And then it's on to the good stuff—the next three months. What are their plans, their goals, what measurements will we use? With each of them, we talk about what they enjoy doing and how we can structure things so that they get to do more of that."

Martin P., the police chief, is less structured but has the same kinds of conversations. "I have sixteen direct reports, and with each of them I probably spend about twenty minutes each week talking about their performance, the project they are working on, how they can improve, and what I can do to help. These discussions happen all the time. With one of my guys, we went to a convention together last month. We accomplished nothing at the convention. But we did on the plane, and in the rental car, and over dinner, and in the lobby of the hotel."

Jeff H. simply schedules time to travel on sales calls with each of his salespeople once or twice a quarter. "I try to not play the role of the knight on the white horse, riding in and saving the day. Instead I just travel with them, listen to their challenges, watch them with clients. I need to get a granular look at them at work. Back at the office, I replay what I saw for them. We then talk about plans and goals, and together we figure out the best way forward. My role isn't to correct or fix. My role is to keep them aware of their style and to keep them realistic about what is possible, given that style."

Other great managers make use of 360-degree feedback techniques or psychological profiles or employee opinion surveys or customer comment cards. Whatever their style, whatever their tools of choice, they are all trying to do the same thing: to hold up the mirror so that the employee has a chance to discover a little more about who he is, how he works, and the footprint he leaves on the world.

Although each manager employed his or her own approach to feedback, in the study of great managers Gallup found that their approaches did share three characteristics.

First, *their feedback was constant.* They varied the frequency according to the preferences or the needs of the individual employee. But whether the meetings happened for twenty minutes every month or for an hour every quarter, these performance feedback meetings were, nonetheless, a constant part of their interaction with each employee throughout the year. How much of a time commitment did this represent? According to the managers in Gallup's study, the total time spent discussing each employee's style and performance was roughly four hours per employee per year. And as one front-line supervisor said, "If you can't spend four hours a year with each of your people, then you've either got too many people, or you shouldn't be a manager."

Second, *each session began with a brief review of past performance.* The purpose of this was not to evaluate, "You should do less of that. You should fix this." Rather, the purpose was to help the employee think in detail about her style and to spark a conversation about the talents and nontalents that created this style. After this review, *the focus always shifted to the future and how the employee could use her style to be productive.* Sometimes they would work together to identify the employee's path of least resistance toward her goals, but often the discussion would revolve around partnership. What talents did the manager bring that could complement the nontalents of the employee?

During that convention trip, most of Martin P.'s conversations dealt with partnership. "This guy is incredibly driven, incredibly goal oriented, but he lacks strategic thinking—he has a hard time imagining what obstacles might get in his way as he plows ahead. I can help him here. I can

play out alternative scenarios for him, and then we can put together con-
tingency plans should any of these scenarios actually happen."

Jeff H. gives a similar description. "One of my salespeople knows all
the tricks for getting her foot in the door and asking the right questions,
but lacks creativity when it comes to pricing the deal. I'm pretty good at
that. So when we meet, she tells me the players and the situation, and I
tell her whether she should present a leasing option, a buy-back option,
a volume discount deal, or whatever."

Third, *great managers made a point of giving their feedback in private, one on one.* The purpose of feedback is to help each individual to
understand and build upon his natural strengths. You cannot do this in a
group setting.

This sounds obvious, but given today's preoccupation with teamwork,
it is surprising how many managers forget the importance of spending
time *alone* with each of their people. As Phil Jackson, the extraordinarily
successful coach of the Chicago Bulls, observes:

"I prefer to deal with [the players] on an individual basis. This helps
strengthen my one-on-one connection with the players, who sometimes
get neglected because we spend so much of our time together en masse.
Meeting with players privately helps me stay in touch with who they are
out of uniform. During the 1995 playoffs, for instance, Toni Kukoc was
troubled by reports that Split, Croatia, where his parents live, had been
hit by a barrage of artillery fire. It took several days for him to get
through on the phone and learn that his family was all right. The war in
his homeland is a painful reality of Toni's life. If I ignored that, I probably wouldn't be able to relate to him on any but the most superficial
level."

GETTING TO KNOW YOU

With descriptions like this, Phil helps provide an answer to the
manager's age-old question "Should you build close personal relationships with your employees, or does familiarity breed contempt?" The
most effective managers say yes, you should build personal relationships
with your people, and no, familiarity does not breed contempt.

This does not mean that you should necessarily become best friends
with those who report to you—although if that is your style, and if you

keep them focused on performance outcomes, there is nothing wrong with doing so. The same applies to socializing with your people—if that is not your style, don't do it. If it is your style, then there is nothing damaging about having dinner or a drink with them, as long as you still evaluate them on performance outcomes.

When great managers like Phil Jackson say they build close relationships with their people, when they say that familiarity does not breed contempt, they simply mean that a great manager must get to know his employees. And "getting to know someone" extends beyond a detailed understanding of an employee's talents and nontalents. It extends all the way to the practicalities and dramas of his personal life. The great manager does not necessarily have to intervene in the employee's life—although some do—but she does have to know about it. And she does have to care about it.

During Gallup's eighty thousand manager interviews we asked this question: "You have a talented employee who consistently shows up late for work. What would you say to this employee?" The answers ranged from the authoritarian to the laissez-faire:

"I would fire him; we don't tolerate lateness here."

"I would give him a verbal warning, then a written warning, then fire him."

"I would lock the door to the office and tell him that, from now on, even if you are two seconds late, you won't be allowed in."

"That's fine. I don't care what time they come in as long as they stay late and get their work done."

Each of these responses is defensible. Each has its merits. But these were not the answers of great managers. When told that an employee was consistently showing up late for work, the great managers gave this one reply, which sums up their attitude toward manager-employee relationships:

"I would ask why."

Maybe it has something to do with a bus schedule. Maybe he has to wait for a nanny to arrive. Maybe there is trouble at home. Once they had understood the employee's personal situation, they might take any number of different actions—ranging from changing the employee's hours to ten to six to telling him to get the situation sorted out, fast. But no matter what the next step, their *first* step was always to get to know the employee: "Ask why."

Phil Jackson's comments about personal relationships ends with this line:

"Athletes are not the most verbal breed. That's why bare attention and listening without judgment are so important."

GREAT MANAGERS CREATE A SAFETY NET

The conventional career path lacks forgiveness. As the employee climbs from rung to rung, the rungs are burned behind him. If he climbs onto a rung and struggles, he knows that his reputation will suffer and his job will be in jeopardy. There is no turning back. By punishing career missteps so severely, this path discourages everyone from taking bold career steps. In conventional wisdom's world, taking bold career steps in order to discover a latent talent or to refine an existing one is almost as foolhardy as volunteering to learn the trapeze without a safety net. No wonder people are so protective of their careers, so closed to their own feedback, so reluctant to change their career track based upon what they have discovered about themselves. This career path kills learning.

Great managers want to encourage career learning. They want to promote active self-discovery. So they have devised their own makeshift career safety net: trial periods.

Ellen P., the manager of in-flight training at Southwest Airlines, describes the safety net she built:

"It is a big step for a flight attendant to move out of the planes and into the training room. Some people want to become a trainer because they will get to travel less—we knock those people out right away. But others talk about wanting to teach, wanting to pass on the tradition of Southwest. If we think they have the talent, and if we think they are seeking the job for the right reasons, then we bring them in for a six-month trial period.

"We are very explicit that this is a time for them, and for us, to decide if this is really something that they will love to do, for a long time. People don't realize that teaching is hard. We do teach ideas for having fun with the guests and playing games and telling jokes. But there is a lot of boring detail to communicate and a lot of rules for the students to learn. This trial period is a way for them to get a sense of how they like this kind of work.

"During the trial period, we sit down with them once a month and discuss their performance, what they are really enjoying, where they are struggling. We send other trainers in to evaluate them and give them feedback. And at the end of the six months they have to pass certain tests to show that they have learned all the necessary information.

"Most do exactly that—and we now have a really talented group of trainers. But all of our trainees knew that if, during the trial period, either they or the company felt that they were not a fit, they would have been able to go back to the planes and resume their flight attendant role. And that's happened a couple of times over the last few years. There was no shame in that, no failure. These people wanted to experiment, to learn if they could be a trainer. They took the step and learned that teaching was not for them.

"It worked out great for us, too. They are back on the planes now, focused on our guests, and undistracted by vague thoughts of moving into training. They have closed that door. They can move on."

Trial periods are tricky. You must not use them as a substitute for selection. Like Ellen, you should use them only with people who have already shown some talent and some genuine interest in the role. After all, your main focus as a manager is not to help every employee play around within the company in the hope of finding something they like to do. Your main focus is to drive performance by matching the talent to the role. Even if an employee begs and pleads for a chance to discover a new talent, if you know he doesn't have it, don't offer him the trial period.

Furthermore, if you use trial periods, then, like Ellen, you must be very clear about the details. How long will it last? What criteria will you use to assess fit? How often, if at all, will you meet during the trial period to discuss performance? Where will the employee go if she does not stay in the new role? You must answer all of these questions explicitly if the trial period is to be a success.

Finally, and most significant, you must make it clear that the employee will be moved back into his previous role *if either you or he* is unhappy with the fit. This will avoid any unfortunate misunderstandings. The trial period is not just for his benefit; it is also for yours. If, after the trial period is over, *he* loves the role but *you* perceive a misfit, your assessment wins. He may not be happy with this, but at least he will not feel ambushed.

The Art of Tough Love

"How do great managers terminate someone and still keep the relationship intact?"

Whether the employee is at the end of a trial period, or whether he is just struggling along in his current role, it is still difficult to bring him bad news. It is still difficult to tell him that he needs to move out of his role. During Gallup's interviews, many managers, both great and average, confessed that they were physically sick before each conversation of this kind. No matter how you approach it, no matter how accomplished you are as a manager, removing someone from his role is never easy.

Here we are not referring to situations where the employee has committed some heinous or unethical act—with their quasi-legal or legal nature, these dramas are more clear-cut. Rather, we are referring to those unfortunate times when it becomes obvious that a particular employee is consistently failing to perform.

Situations like this are much less well defined. As a manager, you have many decisions to make: What level of performance is unacceptable? How long is too long at that level? Have you done enough to help, with training, motivation, support systems, or complementary partnering? Should you break the news all at once, or should you give them a probationary period? When the final conversation happens, what words will you use?

Some managers are so overwhelmed by these questions that they avoid the issue altogether. They take the easy way out and "layer over" the problem employee with a new hire. In the short run this can appear to be a painless and convenient solution. But in the long run, like wrapping pristine bandages around an infected wound, it is deadly for the company.

Some managers solve the problem by deciding to keep all their employees at arm's length. With this neat trick they hope to diminish the tension and the pain inherent in giving bad news to a friend. Unfortunately, as Phil Jackson pointed out, by refusing to get to know their employees, they also diminish the likelihood that they will ever be able to help any of these employees excel.

The best managers do not resort to either of these evasive maneuvers. They don't have to. They employ tough love, which is not a technique, or sequence of action steps, but a mind-set, one that reconciles an uncompromising focus on excellence with a genuine need to care. It is a mind-set that forces great managers to confront poor performance early and directly. Yet it allows them to keep their relationship with the employee intact.

So what is tough love? How does it work?

The "tough" part is easy to explain. Because great managers use excellence as their frame of reference when assessing performance, *Tough* love simply implies that they do not compromise on this standard. So in answer to the question "What level of performance is unacceptable?" these managers reply, "Any level that hovers around average with no trend upward." In answer to the question "How long at that level is too long?" Great managers reply, "Not very long."

It was this uncompromising standard of excellence that drove Harry D., a successful manager of two car dealerships. "We opened a second car dealership, much larger than the first. I wanted to create what I called a total service culture, where the customers received a seamless quality experience whether they were dealing with the sales department, the financing department, or the service department. I was looking for total integration of systems and total cooperation from my department heads. Big plans, right? It got off to a rocky start, let me tell you.

"My biggest mistake was the guy I promoted to head up the sales department, Simon. He came from my smaller dealership, where he was sales manager, very successful. But when he moved into the new spot, he couldn't get into the cooperation thing at all. He wouldn't communicate with the other department heads. He wouldn't show up for meetings. He wouldn't sit down with the other department heads and work out how to integrate the systems and ease the interdepartmental hand-offs so that the customer wouldn't feel a jolt. He was just interested in *his* guys and *his* numbers.

"At the same time, back at the other dealership, I had stupidly promoted one of the salespeople to sales manager, and he was struggling, too. So I had grown from one success to two failures. Not bad going.

"I knew I had to move quickly. I had talked with Simon about my concerns a couple of times but saw no improvement at all. So, five months in, I pulled him into my office and told him that I wanted him back in the other dealership. I told him that in this new dealership I was not interested simply in sales numbers, that I wanted to build this integrated, total service experience, and that he wasn't helping. I told him that he was a loner and that, back in the other dealership, he could narrow his focus all he wanted, but here, in the new world, it wouldn't fly. I'm sending you back, I said.

"He was so pissed off, he looked like he was going to punch me. 'You haven't given me enough time. You got to let me have another shot.' All that kind of stuff. But I know my people, sometimes better than they know themselves. I knew that Simon wasn't a team person. I knew that he would never be able to build the total experience I wanted. Better to pull the trigger now, I thought, rather than letting things drag on, with him beginning to feel more invested and me getting more disappointed.

"Now he's doing extremely well back at the smaller place, and I managed to find a collaborative sales manager for this place. My brave new world is coming along nicely."

Harry is universally loved by his employees. He is a pushover when employees need to change their hours, take a day off, or short-cut a process for the sake of the customer. But he is rock solid when it comes to excellence. As he says, "Excellence is my thing. If you don't like it, that's fine. Just don't come to work here."

The "love" element of tough love is a little subtler. This element still forces managers to confront poor performance early but allows them to do so in such a way that much of the bitterness and the ill will disappear. And it all springs from the concept of talent. An understanding of talent, an understanding that each person possesses enduring patterns of thought, feeling, and behavior, is incredibly liberating when managers have to confront poor performance. Why? Because *it frees the manager from blaming the employee.*

Consider the manager who believes that with enough willpower and determination, virtually all behaviors can be changed. For this manager, every case of poor performance is the employee's fault. The employee has been warned, repeatedly, and still he has not improved his performance. If he had more drive, more spirit, more willingness to learn, he would have changed his behavior as required, and the poor performance would have disappeared. But it hasn't disappeared. He must not be trying hard enough. It is his fault.

This seductive logic puts this manager in a very awkward position.

Since she told the employee what to do, and since it wasn't done, then the employee must be weak-willed, stupid, disobedient, or disrespectful.

How can you have a constructive conversation with someone when beneath the surface politeness this is what you are compelled to think of him? It's hard. If you are, by nature, an emotional manager, you fear you might lose your temper and let your anger show. If you are, by nature, a caring and supportive manager, you worry that he might see through your soothing words and realize how deeply disappointed you are in him. Whatever your style, a conversation where you have to mask your true feelings is a stressful conversation, particularly when your feelings are so negative. No wonder so many managers try to avoid it.

But great managers don't have to hide their true feelings. They understand that a person's talent and nontalent constitute an enduring pattern. They know that if, after pulling out all the stops to manage around his nontalents, an employee still underperforms, the most likely explanation is that his talents do not match his role. In the minds of great managers, consistent poor performance is not primarily a matter of weakness, stupidity, disobedience, or disrespect. It is a matter of miscasting.

If there is blame here, it is evenly spread. Perhaps the employee should have been more self-aware. Perhaps the manager should have been more perceptive. Perhaps. But this is just hindsight pointing the finger. No employee will ever be completely self-aware. No manager will ever know each of his people perfectly, even if he has selected very carefully for talent. So casting errors are not cause for anger or recrimination. Casting errors are inevitable.

When an employee is obviously miscast, great managers hold up the mirror. They encourage the employee to use this misstep to learn a little more about his unique combination of talents and nontalents. They use language like "This isn't a fit for you, let's talk about why" or "You need to find a role that plays more to your natural strengths. What do you think that role might be?" They use this language not because it is polite, not because it softens the bad news, but because it is true.

This is the "love" element of tough love. The most effective managers do genuinely care about each of their people. But they imbue "care" with a distinct meaning. In their minds, to "care" means to *set the person up for success*. They truly want each person to find roles where he has a chance to excel, and they know that this is possible only in roles that play to his talents.

By this definition, if the person is struggling, it is actively uncaring to allow him to keep playing a part that doesn't fit. By this definition, firing the person is a caring act. This definition explains not only why great managers move fast to confront poor performance, but also why they are adept at keeping the relationship intact while doing so.

All in all, the tough love mind-set enables a great manager to keep two contradictory thoughts in mind at the same time—the need to maintain high performance standards and the need to care—and still function effectively. Tough love enables Mike H., an IT executive, to say in the same breath, "I've never fired someone too early," and, "I truly care about helping my people be successful."

Tough love allows John F., a manufacturing supervisor, to reminisce, "I have fired a few people in my time. But I've stayed close to them. Now that I think about it, each of the best men at my two weddings was someone I had previously fired."

Tough love explains the incongruous nature of Gary L.'s conversation. Gary, an enormously successful entrepreneur, six-time winner of the Queens Award for Industry, brought in one of his factory managers one evening and told him, "Come in, sit down, I love you; you're fired; I still love you. Now, get a drink and let's talk this through."

"MANAGER-ASSISTED CAREER SUICIDE"

Tough love is a powerful mind-set, providing a coherent rationale and a simple language for handling a delicate situation. But if you choose to incorporate it into your own management style, remember: Counseling a person out of a role is, and will always be, a delicate situation. Tough love is helpful but will never make it easy.

Harry D., the car dealer, captures one of the constant difficulties perfectly with his comment "But I know my people, sometimes better than they know themselves." In the tough love approach, the manager often has to confront the employee with truths that the employee may not be ready to hear. This will always be a subtle negotiation. That is why you need to get to know your people so well, why you need to meet with them so regularly, why your rationale needs to be clear and your language consistent.

Some may complain that even if you do all of these things, you still don't have the right to believe that you know the person better than he does himself. Great managers disagree. When Gallup asked, "Would you rather get employees what they want, or would you rather get them what is right for them?" the great managers consistently replied, "Get them what is right for them."

This sounds authoritarian, even arrogant, but Martin P., the police chief, makes a compelling point:

"I believe that, deep down, the poor performer knows he is struggling before you do. Maybe he can't find the words, or maybe his pride won't let him say it, but he knows. On some level he wants your help. And so, subconsciously, he puts himself in situations where his weaknesses are exposed. He is daring you, pushing you to fire him. I call this manager-assisted career suicide. If you suspect that this is happening, the best thing you can do is help put him out of his misery.

"I had one police officer, Max, who couldn't handle confrontation. Imagine, as an officer you meet the worst people, and you meet the best people on their worst days. You get shouted at, verbally, and sometimes physically abused. You have to keep your cool under all of these conditions.

"Max couldn't. He would become frustrated, angry, rude. We had reports of an occasional use of profanity. These are low-level disciplinary matters that are brought before a tribunal. I would sit in on these meetings and read the reports and Max would deny them, vigorously. Very vigorously. I saw exactly the kinds of behaviors in these meetings that citizens were complaining about.

"We gave him behavioral counseling, and he worked on it. But it was such a basic part of his personality. He kept going out on patrol, he kept losing his cool, and he kept denying it in the tribunals. He was committing manager-assisted career suicide. He *wanted* me to fire him. It was his only way out.

"So I did. I removed him from the department. He was a good person with the wrong demeanor for a police officer. Through our outplacement service he found a role as a claims adjuster for an insurance agency here in town, which fits his character so much better. I am still in touch with him, still friendly, and more important, he is doing very well."

Many of the great managers we interviewed echoed the themes in Martin's story: The employee refused to confront the truth of his situation and so was angry at the time, but months, and sometimes years later, the employee would make a call, or write a letter, or walk up to the manager in an airport, to tell him, "Thank you. I didn't realize it then, but moving me out of that job was one of the best things anyone has ever done for me."

It doesn't always happen this way. Some employees remain bitter to the end. But tough love does provide a way for the manager and the employee to handle this delicate situation with dignity. Tough love keeps everyone whole.

Turning the Keys:
A Practical Guide

- **The Art of Interviewing for Talent**
- **Performance Management**
- **Keys of Your Own**
- **Master Keys**

Every great manager has his or her own style. But every great manager shares the same goal: to turn each employee's talent into performance. The Four Keys, *select for talent, define the right outcomes, focus on strengths, find the right fit,* reveal how they attack this goal.

In the previous four chapters we described the Four Keys, how each works, and why each is important to the challenge of turning talent into performance. Now, in this chapter, we will describe what *you* can do to turn each of these Keys. Bear in mind that these Keys are not steps. They are not a structured series of actions intruding on your natural style. Rather, each Key is simply a way of thinking, a new perspective on a familiar set of challenges. As we mentioned in the introduction, our purpose is to help you capitalize on *your* style by showing you how great managers think, not to replace your style with a standardized version of theirs.

We are not suggesting that you incorporate every single one of these actions into your style. These techniques simply represent a cross sec-

tion of ideas gleaned from thousands of different managers. No one
manager embodies them all. We suggest you pick and choose from
these actions, refine them, improve them, and fashion them into a form
that fits you.

The Art of Interviewing for Talent

"Which are the right questions to ask?"

1. MAKE SURE THE TALENT INTERVIEW STANDS ALONE

Recruiting can be a complicated process. The candidate has to learn about you, the company, the role, and the details of his compensation. You have to check his résumé, make him an offer; he may counter, you then resubmit your offer; and so the negotiating continues until finally you both feel comfortable enough to commit. This process is important, but all of it should be handled separately from the talent interview.

The talent interview should stand alone. It has but one purpose: to discover whether the candidate's recurring patterns of thought, feeling, or behavior match the job. This is difficult enough without trying to accomplish everything else simultaneously. So set aside a defined amount of time where both you and the candidate know that the exclusive goal is to learn about his talents. Let him know that the interview will be a little different from other interviews. It will be more structured, more focused; less banter, more questions.

2. ASK A FEW OPEN-ENDED QUESTIONS AND THEN TRY TO KEEP QUIET

The best way to discover a person's talents in an interview is to allow him to reveal himself by the choices he makes. In a sense, the talent interview should mirror verbally what will face him on the job behaviorally. On the job, he will face thousands of situations every day to which he could respond in any number of ways. How he *consistently* responds will be his performance.

So in the interview, ask *open-ended* questions that offer many potential directions and do not telegraph the "right" direction—questions such as "How closely do you think people should be supervised?" or "What do you enjoy most about selling?"

The direction he takes, spontaneously, will be most predictive of his future behaviors.

When you have asked a question it is best to pause and remain silent. If he asks you to explain what you mean, deflect his question. Tell him that you are really more interested in what *he* means. Say that it is *his* interpretation that is important. Let him answer your questions as *his* filter dictates. Let him reveal himself to you.

Most important, when he answers, believe him. No matter how much you might like his first impression, if you ask him how important it is to be the best and he replies, "Well, I like to be the best, but mostly I just try to be the best I can be," believe him. If you ask him what he likes about selling and he keeps talking about how quickly he wants to move into management, believe him. If you ask him what he loves about teaching and he never mentions children, believe him. Whatever he says, believe him. A person's unaided response to an open-ended question is powerfully predictive. Trust it, no matter how much you might want to hear something else.

3. LISTEN FOR SPECIFICS

Past behavior is a good predictor of future behavior. Therefore questions like "Tell me about a time when you . . ." can serve you well.

But be careful with these "Tell me about a time" questions. First, you should always be listening for a specific example. And by "specific" we mean specific by time, by person, or by event. In this way you will avoid giving credit to the person who rattles off a whole paragraph of theory about how important something is but who never actually recounts a specific time when she did it.

Second, give credit only to the person's top-of-mind response. Past behavior is predictive of future behavior only if the past behavior is *recurring*. If the behavior does indeed happen a lot, then the person should be able to come up with a specific example with only one prompt. If he can, then it gives you a clue that this behavior is a recurring part of his life.

For example, let's say you are selecting for a sales position and you have decided to include the relating talent assertiveness in your talent profile. You might ask a question like "Tell me about a time when you overcame resistance to your ideas." Notice that you haven't asked for a specific—you have simply asked the individual to tell you about a time when it happened. However, *you are now listening for a specific.*

Here are two, of the infinite number of possible answers:

1. "I think it is very important to be persistent, particularly if you really believe in your ideas. We really encourage that kind of candor here. With my team, if I have a suggestion that others disagree with, I know they will expect me to keep supporting my idea until somebody comes up with a better one. In fact, it happens all the time."

2. "It happened yesterday."

Which is the better answer? Well, it is hard to say which is "better." But 2 is certainly the more *predictive* answer. Here the candidate spontaneously gave you an example that was specific by time, "yesterday." You don't know exactly what happened, but who cares? The details are less important than the top-of-mind specificity. You didn't ask for a specific, but with only one prompt, "Tell me about a time . . ." he gave you a specific. Although you must ask many more questions to gain a fuller picture of his talent, his answer here is a first clue that this behavior, supporting his ideas in the face of resistance, is a *recurring* part of his life.

By contrast, in 1, the candidate gave you a nice little description of why she thought it was important to be candid and then claimed that "it happens all the time." There is nothing wrong with this answer. But, lacking any specifics, there is nothing predictive about it, either. Faced with answers like 1, some managers are tempted to probe, "Can you tell me more about that? Can you tell me what happened?" They then judge the answer on the quality of the person's example: How much detail did she provide? How articulate was she? Do I agree with what she said she did?

This is a cardinal sin of interviewing. Regardless of the detail the candidate eventually provided, if she needed two or three probes to describe a specific example, then the chances are that the behavior in question is not a recurring part of her life. When you ask "Tell me about a time" questions, don't judge the response on the quality of its detail. If you do, you will end up evaluating whether the person is articulate or whether the person has a good memory, rather than whether he or she has the particular recurring talent you want.

Instead, judge the response on whether it was specific *and* top of mind.

(Of course, with either 1 or 2, if you want to ask more questions to satisfy your own curiosity, go ahead. But remember, even if she eventually provides you with a detailed example, the fact that she required two or three probes to dredge it up tells you that the behavior is not a recurring part of her life.)

4. CLUES TO TALENT

Aside from specific examples of past behavior, what else should you be listening for? Are there any other signs that can tip you off that the candidate does indeed possess the talents you are looking for?

Over the years we have found many small clues to a person's talent: a sudden glimpse of excellence at the role, a yearning toward certain activities, a feeling of flow while performing the activity. Of all these clues, two might be useful to you during the talent interview. Each person is so complex that no interviewing or testing system will ever be able to define his profile of talents perfectly. However, if you focus your questions toward these clues, then, like an image on a fresh Polaroid, the person's most dominant talents should gradually emerge. You can then compare his talents to those in your desired profile and assess the match.

a. Rapid Learning

When you learn a new role, you tend to learn it in terms of steps. Sometimes the steps stay with you no matter how hard you practice. For example, you may have been giving presentations for years, but you still struggle. Every time you have to present you revert back to the three basic steps you remember from public speaking class: "Okay, first I must tell them what I am going to tell them; then I must tell them; then I must tell them what I just told them."

But with other activities, the steps just seem to fall away. You feel a sense of gliding, of smoothness. For example, after a couple of months as a salesperson you may have begun to feel this smoothness. All of a sudden you seemed to be able to see inside the mind of the prospect and you knew almost instinctively what words to say next. Or perhaps as a student teacher, after your initial nervousness had faded, the names of the children came easily and you found yourself walking up and down the rows of desks as if you had been teaching all of your life.

When you have this feeling it is as if the steps of the new role are simply giving form to a mental pattern already grooved within you—which, if you think about it, they are.

Rapid learning is an important clue to a person's talent. Ask the candidate what kinds of roles she has been able to learn quickly. Ask her what activities come easily to her now. She will give you more clues to her talent.

b. Satisfactions

Everyone breathes different psychological oxygen. What is fulfilling for one person is asphyxiating for another.

Great accountants love the fact that two plus two equals four every time they do it. Great salespeople get a kick out of turning a no into a yes. Great flight attendants gravitate toward the tired, angry business traveler or the boisterous school sports team at the back, because they enjoy turning around the tough customers.

A person's sources of satisfaction are clues to his talent. So ask him what his greatest personal satisfaction is. Ask him what kinds of situations give him strength. Ask him what he finds fulfilling. His answers will help you know what he will be able to keep doing week after week after week.

5. KNOW WHAT TO LISTEN FOR

Many managers have a list of favorite questions they resort to every time they interview someone. So do great managers, but with one important distinction. They ask only questions where they know how top performers respond.

In their mind, the question is not nearly as important as knowing how the best answer.

For example, here is a question that can identify the different striving talents of salespeople and teachers: "How do you feel when someone doubts what you have to say?" You might think that the best salespeople would say they like a little doubting, that it would give them a chance to show just how persuasive they could be. Surprisingly, they don't. They report that they hate it. It upsets them to be doubted (although they may not show it) because, as we described earlier, great salespeople are selling *themselves*. To doubt them is to question their personal integrity. Disagree with them, argue with them, choose not to buy from them. But don't doubt them.

Average salespeople are not personally invested. They don't mind being doubted, so this question doesn't strike any emotional chord with them at all.

For sales managers, then, this has proved to be a good question, because what they listen for is, "Upset." (Of course, this isn't the only question great sales managers ask. As we described earlier, the worst salespeople are also upset by rejection. Managers must ask further questions—"how" questions and "who" questions—to discover whether the candidate possesses other vital sales talents, like innate assertiveness or a love of breaking the ice with people.)

By contrast, it turns out that great teachers say they *love* being doubted. They cherish those moments. Great teachers instinctively interpret the "doubters" as students, and they see this doubting as a sign of an active, inquisitive mind. For great teachers, then, doubting means learning. Conversely, average teachers say they don't like to be doubted. Their first point of reference is their own competence, not the students' learning. Being doubted means having their competence challenged, and for them there is nothing worse.

This question works well for selecting teachers, then, but only if the desired response is, "I love it."

The question doesn't work at all if you are selecting nurses. Why? Because the best nurses do not answer in a way that is consistent with each other and different from their less successful colleagues. When you think about it, this is hardly surprising. After all, on those rare occasions when a nurse is doubted, how she reacts to the doubting probably has little to do with how good a nurse she is overall.

How can you develop these question/listen-for combinations? First, you can try out a question on a few of your best employees and a few of the "rest" and then see if the best answer differently, consistently. If they do, the question/listen-for combination is a good one. If they don't, as with nurses and the "doubting" question, then the question might not be worth asking.

Second, you can ask the question of all new applicants. Write down what they say and keep a record of it. After they have been hired, check back to see if the people who subsequently performed well answered your question in a consistent way.

This takes time and focus, but, as with any art, time and focus are required to cultivate the art of interviewing for talent.

The concept of talent applies to all that great managers do. However, the *activity* of selecting for talent is separate. It occurs at the time that you make the hiring decision. The activities of the other three Keys—define the right outcomes, focus on strengths, and find the right fit—cannot be separated so easily. How you set expectations for someone is interwoven with the way you motivate him to achieve those expectations. How you motivate and encourage him is often part of a broader conversation where you are also helping him find the right fit. The day-to-day challenge of turning talent into performance involves the turning of all three Keys, all at once, all the time.

Performance Management

"How do great managers turn the last three Keys every day, with every employee?"

The exemplary managers Gallup interviewed described a variety of ideas for turning the final three Keys. But their real challenge lay in disciplining themselves to implement these ideas with each of their people, despite the day-to-day pressures of getting the actual work done. They met this challenge by following a routine, a "performance management" routine. This routine, of meetings and conversations, forced them to keep focused on the progress of each person's performance, even though many other business demands were competing for their attention.

Each manager's routine was different, reflecting his or her unique style. Nonetheless, hidden within this diversity we found four characteristics common to the "performance management" routines of great managers.

First, the routine is *simple*. Great managers dislike the complexity of most company-sponsored performance appraisal schemes. They don't want to waste their time trying to decipher the alien terms and to fill out bureaucratic forms. Instead they prefer a simple format that allows them to concentrate on the truly difficult work: what to say to each employee and how to say it.

Second, the routine forces *frequent interaction* between the manager and the employee. It is no good meeting once a year, or even twice a year, to discuss an employee's performance, style, and goals. The secret to helping an employee excel lies in the details: the details of his particular recognition needs, of his relationship needs, of his goals, and of his talents/nontalents. A yearly meeting misses these details. It degenerates into a bland discussion about "potential" and "opportunities for improvement." The only way to capture the details is to meet at a minimum once a quarter, sometimes even more frequently. At these meetings the specifics of a success or a disappointment are fresh in the memory. The employee can talk about how a particular meeting or interaction made him "feel." The manager can recall the same meeting and suggest subtle changes in approach or a different way of interpreting the same event. The conversation can be vivid, the advice practical. Furthermore, in the intervening weeks between meetings the manager and the employee are motivated to concentrate on events as they occur, because each knows that a forum for discussing these events will soon arise. Frequent performance meetings force both manager and employee to pay attention. (If you are worried about the time drain inherent in frequent performance meetings, remember that the best managers spend, on average, only one hour per quarter per person discussing performance.)

Furthermore, frequent performance meetings make it so much easier to raise the always sensitive subject of the employee's areas of poor performance. If you meet only once or twice a year, you are forced to drop your criticisms on the employee all at once, like a bomb. When the employee inevitably recoils, you then have to dredge your memory for examples to support your argument. But by meeting frequently, you can avoid this battle of wills. You can introduce areas of poor performance little by little over time, and each time you raise the subject, you can refer to recent, vivid examples. Your criticisms will be easier to swallow and the conversation more productive.

Third, the routine is *focused on the future*. Great managers do use a review of past performance to highlight discoveries about the person's style or needs. However, their natural inclination is to focus on the future. They want to discuss what "could be," rather than allowing the conversation to descend into recriminations and postmortems that lead nowhere. Therefore, while the first ten minutes of the meeting may be used for review, the rest of the time is devoted to the truly creative work: "What do you want to accomplish in the next few months? What measuring sticks will we use? What is your most efficient route toward those goals? How can I help?" In their view, these kinds of conversations are more energetic, more productive, and more satisfying.

Last, the routine asks the employee to *keep track of his own performance and learnings*. In many companies "performance appraisal" is something that happens to an employee. She is a passive observer, waiting to receive the judgment of her manager. If she is lucky, she may be asked to rate herself before she sees how the company rates her. But even here she is still reactive. She knows that the purpose of her self-assessment is to serve as a counterpoint or comparison with the assessment of her manager. So her self-assessment becomes a negotiating tool—"I'll pitch mine high and we'll probably end up somewhere in the middle"—rather than an honest evaluation of her own performance.

The best managers reject this. They want a routine that asks each employee to keep track of her own performance and learnings. They want her to write down her goals, her successes, and her discoveries. This record is not designed to be evaluated or critiqued by her manager. Rather, its purpose is to help each employee take responsibility for her performance. It serves as her mirror. It is a way to step outside herself. Using this record, she can see how she plans to affect the world. She can weigh the effectiveness of those plans. She can be accountable to herself.

Naturally, great managers want to discuss and agree to each employee's short-term performance goals, but the rest of the record—her discoveries about herself, the descriptions of new skills she has learned, the letters of recognition she may have received—are part of a private document. If the employee is fortunate enough to have a trusting relationship with her manager, she may feel comfortable sharing the whole record—successes, failures, perceived strengths. But this is not the point of it. The point is to encourage the employee to keep track of her own performance and learnings. The point is self-discovery.

Recent research into adult learning reveals that students stay in school longer and learn more if they are expected to direct and record their progress. Great managers realized this long ago and now apply it with their employees.

These four characteristics—simplicity, frequent interaction, focus on the future, and self-tracking—are the foundation for a successful "performance management" routine. In the basic routine below we describe some of the questions many great managers ask to learn about their employees and the format they usually follow. Our purpose is not to tell you exactly what to say, or how to say it, or to whom, because that would be cumbersome and artificial—you will of course want to adapt the questions and tools to your own talent and experience.

However, if you follow this basic routine and incorporate it successfully into your own style, you will give yourself the best chance possible to *define the right outcomes,* to *focus on strengths,* and to help each person *find the right fit.*

THE BASIC ROUTINE

The Strengths Interview

At the beginning of each year, or a week or two after the person has been hired, spend about an hour with him asking the following ten questions:

- Q.1 What did you enjoy most about your previous work experience?
       What brought you here?
       (If an existing employee) What keeps you here?
- Q.2 What do you think your strengths are? (skills, knowledge, talent)
- Q.3 What about your weaknesses?
- Q.4 What are your goals for your current role? (Ask for scores and timelines)
- Q.5 How often do you like to meet with me to discuss your progress?
       Are you the kind of person who will tell me how you are feeling, or will I have to ask?
- Q.6 Do you have any personal goals or commitment you would like to tell me about?
- Q.7 What is the best praise you have ever received?
       What made it so good?
- Q.8 Have you had any really productive partnerships or mentors?
       Why do you think these relationships worked so well for you?
- Q.9 What are your future growth goals, your career goals?
       Are there any particular skills you want to learn?
       Are there some specific challenges you want to experience?
       How can I help?
- Q.10 Is there anything else you want to talk about that might help us work well together?

The main purpose of this session is to learn about his strengths, his goals, and his needs, *as he perceives them.* Whatever he says, even if you disagree with him, jot it down. If you want to help him be productive, you have to know where *he* is starting from. His answers will tell you where *he* thinks he is. During the course of the year it may be appropriate to help him change his opinions, but initially you are interested in seeing *his* world through *his* eyes.

During the course of the strengths interview he will tell you how often he wants to meet to discuss his progress with you (Q.5) Schedule the first performance planning meeting of the year at the interval he indicated. For the purposes of this description, we will assume he said, "Once every three months."

The Performance Planning Meetings

To help him prepare, ask him to write down answers to these three questions before each meeting:

A. **What actions have you taken?** These should be the details of his performance over the last three months. He should include scores, rankings, ratings, and timelines, if available.

B. **What discoveries have you made?** These discoveries might be in the form of training classes he attended, or they might simply be new insights derived from an internal presentation he made, or a job-shadowing session in which he participated, or even a book that he read. Wherever they came from, encourage him to keep track of his own learning.

C. **What partnerships have you built?** These partnerships are the relationships he has formed. They might be new relationships or the strengthening of existing relationships. They might be relationships with colleagues or clients, professional relationships or personal ones. It is up to him to decide. Whatever he decides, it is important that he take responsibility for building his constituency, inside and outside the company.

At the beginning of the meeting ask him A, B, and C. Jot down his answers and keep a copy. He should keep his written copy. If he wants to share all of his written answers with you, wonderful, but don't demand it. Either way, use his answers as a jumping-off point to discuss his performance over the last three months.

After about ten minutes direct the conversation toward the future, drawing on the following questions:

D. **What is your main focus?** What is his primary goal(s) for the next three months?
E. **What new discoveries are you planning?** What specific discoveries is he hoping to make over the next three months?
F. **What new partnerships are you hoping to build?** How is he planning to grow his constituency over the next three months?

Terms such as "discovery" or "partnership" may not fit your style or your company's culture. You will know the right words to choose. But whatever your word choices, make sure that your conversation about his next three months extends beyond simple achievement goals. Suggest that he write down his answers. You should discuss his answers, agree to them, and then keep your copy. His answers will now serve as your specific expectations of him for the next three months.

After another three months have elapsed, ask him to write down his answers to A, B, and C, and once again, at your second performance planning meeting, ask him these three questions and use his answers to spur discussion about his performance. Then quickly move into a discussion about the future and ask him D, E, and F—once again, it will be helpful if you and he write down what he says and keep copies. As you talk through his successes, his struggles, and his goals, try to keep focusing on his strengths by setting expectations that are right for him, by helping him to perfect his style, and by discussing how you can run interference for him.

Repeat this routine at the next three-month interval, and the next, until the year cycle is complete.

By the end of the year you will have met at least four times. You will have reviewed his past and planned in detail his future progress. You will have learned more about his idiosyncrasies and, perhaps, have used what you learned to help him identify his true strengths and weaknesses more accurately. Perhaps he will have changed his mind about some of his opinions and some of his needs. You will have been close to him through some difficult times and through some successes. You will have disagreed on some things and agreed on much. But whatever happens, you will now be stronger partners. By meeting frequently, by listening, by paying attention, by advising, and by planning in detail, you will have developed a shared and realistic interest in his success. And, important, he will have a record of it all.

Career Discovery Questions

At some point during your performance planning meetings, the employee may want to talk about his career options. He may want to know where you think he should go next. A healthy career discussion rarely happens all at once. Instead it is a product of many different conversations, at many different times. However you choose to handle these conversations—and each will be unique, according to the potential and the performance of the individual employee—you need to ensure that, over time, two things happen. First, the employee needs to become increasingly clear about his skills, knowledge, and talents. Lacking this kind of clarity, he will be a poor partner as you and he together plan out his next career steps. Second, he needs to understand, in detail, what this next step would entail and why he thinks he would excel at it.

He must come to these understandings by himself. But you can help. You can use these five career discovery questions, at different times, to prompt his thinking:

Q.1 How would you describe success in your current role?
Can you measure it?
Here is what I think. (Add your own comments.)

Q.2 What do you actually do that makes you as good as you are?
What does this tell you about your skills, knowledge, and talents?
Here is what I think. (Add your own comments.)

Q.3 Which part of your current role do you enjoy the most?
Why?

Q.4 Which part of your current role are you struggling with?
What does this tell you about your skills, knowledge, and talent?
What can we do to manage around this?
Training? Positioning? Support system? Partnering?

Q.5 What would be the perfect role for you?
Imagine you are in that role. It's three P.M. on a Thursday. What are you doing?
Why would you like it so much?
Here is what I think. (Add your own comments.)

These questions, scattered throughout the year, will function as cues to get the employee thinking in detail about his performance. Does he want to build his career by growing within his current role? Does he want to move into a new role? If so, what strength and satisfaction would he derive from it? These five questions won't necessarily provide the answers. But, asked in the right way, at the right time, they will help the employee focus his thoughts, and he will come to know your thoughts. Together you will form a few firm conclusions about his present performance and his potential. Together you will now make better decisions about his future.

Keys of Your Own

"Can an employee turn these Keys?"

No manager can *make* an employee productive. Managers are catalysts. They can speed up the reaction between the talent of the employee and the needs of the customer/company. They can help the employee find his path of least resistance toward his goals. They can help the employee plan his career. But they cannot do any of these without a major effort from the employee. In the world according to great managers, the employee is the star. The manager is the agent. And, as in the world of performing arts, the agent expects a great deal from his stars.

This is what great managers expect of every talented employee:

- **Look in the mirror any chance you get.** Use any feedback tools provided by the company to increase your understanding of who you are and how others perceive you.
- **Muse.** Sit down for twenty or thirty minutes each month and play the last few weeks back in your mind. What did you accomplish? What did you learn? What did you hate? What did you love? What does all of this say about you and your talents?
- **Discover yourself.** Over time become more detailed in your description of your skills, knowledge, and talents. Use this increasingly deep understanding to volunteer for the right roles, to be a better partner, to guide your training and development choices.
- **Build your constituency.** Over time, identify which kinds of relationships tend to work well for you. Seek them out.
- **Keep track.** Build your own record of your learnings and discoveries.
- **Catch your peers doing something right.** When you enter your place of work, you never leave it at zero. You either make it a little better or a little worse. Make it a little better.

SO YOU WORK FOR A DISCIPLE OF "CONVENTIONAL WISDOM" . . . OR WORSE

Great managers are still a minority. Few employees are lucky enough to work for "supersupervisor": the perfect balancer of warmth and drive, support and authority, a manager who understands them, accepts them in all of their imperfection, and knows just how to energize them on even the most sluggish of mornings.

Instead most employees work for a supervisory "work in progress": a manager who genuinely wants to treat his people well, who genuinely wants them to excel, but who is still struggling to get it right. Maybe he spends too much time telling his people what to do and not enough time listening to the unique needs of each person. Maybe he wants to perfect his people by making them learn *his* way of doing things. Maybe he naively treats everyone the way *he* would like to be treated. Maybe he is well intentioned but too busy to find the time to talk with all employees about their performance. Or maybe he is less well intentioned. Maybe he dislikes people, distrusts them, takes credit for their successes, and blames them for his failures.

If you work for any one of these managers, what can you do? What can you do to help him or her make the most of you? While we cannot offer you a surefire solution, we can give you a few pointers for managing your manager.

A. If your manager is just too busy to talk with you about your performance or your goals . . . schedule a performance planning meeting with him. Remove the planning burden from his shoulders and tell him that you will provide the structure for the meeting in advance so that you can use your time together most efficiently. You will prepare a short review of the last three months, the actions you took, the discoveries you made, the new partnerships you built. You will then want to discuss with him the next three months—specifically, your main focus, the new discoveries you want to make, and the new relationships you want to build. All he has to do is show up to the meeting and focus on you for forty-five minutes.

If he consistently cancels the scheduled meeting, or has nothing to say to you during the meeting, then your problem is not that he is too busy. Your problem is that he is a poor manager. Faced with this problem, you are limited in your options. If you love the job itself and feel you are doing well, you may simply have to put up with him. The alternative is to make a move, which we will discuss in item E.

B. If your manager forces you to do things her way . . . she is probably focusing on process too much. Pick your moment, perhaps during your performance planning meeting, and tell her that you want to define your role more by its outcomes than by its steps. Ask her which outcomes she would use to measure your success. As you discuss this, describe for her how your style, although different from hers, will still enable you to achieve the outcomes expected of you. Your point here is not to persuade her that your style is better than hers. Your point is simply that your style is the most efficient way for *you* to reach the outcomes on which you and she have agreed. When viewed through this lens, *her* style, no matter how sensible it might seem to her, really does not apply.

Of course, a misfocus on steps rather than outcomes may not be the problem. She may be forcing you to do things her way because she likes this feeling of power and control. If you can adapt to her style without compromising your integrity, fine; otherwise you may wish to make a move to another job.

C. If your manager praises you inappropriately or at inappropriate times . . . you can suggest alternatives. This isn't always an easy conversation. In fact, telling your manager that you much prefer to be praised in private rather than in public, can sometimes feel arrogant and presumptuous. Once again, you have to pick your moment. It would probably be neither wise nor sensitive to correct him immediately after he had the whole team stand up and cheer your success—Mark D., the insurance agent from chapter 5, certainly woke his manager up by storming off the stage, but we wouldn't recommend this approach. Instead make your comments at a time when you are discussing *all* aspects of your performance, perhaps during the structured, dispassionate setting of a performance planning meeting, (and it would not hurt to thank him for his good intentions). This will show him that you have thought carefully about what you need from him and will give him a chance to assimilate what you told him into the way he manages you.

If the problem is less that he gives you the wrong kind of praise, and more that he gives you no praise at all, you will need to survive for as long as possible on your own reserves. If you are a natural self-starter, you may find that you can survive adequately for quite a while without any recognition at all. Most people, though, will soon feel a drain on their energy. Faced with the prospect of a recognitionless environment, you may wish to consider a move.

D. If your manager constantly asks you questions about how you are doing and feeling, or otherwise intrudes . . . suggest that you don't find this helpful. It is a delicate matter because you don't want to seem insubordinate or as if you are *his* manager. But ask if it would be okay if you "check in" with him less frequently than he obviously wants to check in with you. Tell him that it is no reflection on him. Say that you are hoping to function a little more independently, and that if you can schedule a "check-in" meeting on *your* cycle rather than his, then you will probably be able to be a great deal more productive. Obviously it is a sensitive situation, but if you use unambiguous, unemotional terminology like "I like to check in every couple of weeks rather than every couple of days," you should be able to handle it and come to some practical arrangements that work for both of you.

If your manager is intruding because he is suspicious of you, the most unambiguous, unemotional terminology will be of little help. You will have to resort to a different strategy—a move.

E. If the problems we have discussed are of an altogether different nature, which is to say, if your manager *consistently* ignores you, distrusts you, takes credit for your work, blames you for his mistakes, or disrespects you . . . then get out from under him. You might look for a lateral move or another position within the company, or you might simply leave. Yes, you might decide to stick it out for six months in the hope that he will leave. Yes, the generous company benefits might dull your pain enough to make your situation tolerable. Yes, you might be able to find a sympathetic ear with your manager's boss or with the human resources department. But don't fool yourself. If his behavior has been consistent over time, he is not going to change that much. Some managers simply should not be managers. Their misbehavior is not a func-

tion of misunderstandings or misdirected good intentions. It is a function of lack of talent (or sometime neurosis). Lacking the appropriate
four-lane highways in their mind, they will forever make poor decisions.
They will forever mistrust, overshadow, abandon, intrude, and stifle.
They have to. It's in their nature. Neither you nor this book nor weeks of
sensitivity training will give them the strengths, the self-esteem, and the
security they need to be a great manager.

We would like to be able to tell you, "Don't worry. Soldier on. Rely on
the strength of your own talent and you will still excel." But we cannot.
You might be able to survive your predicament for a while in the hope
that the manager will prove his own undoing and get fired. But, lacking
a good manager, you won't be able to last long. As this book has shown,
in your struggle to turn all of your talents into performance, your immediate manager is a very important partner. If you are cursed with a truly
bad one, then you will never see the best of you. No matter how much
you enjoy the job itself, get out, fast. You deserve better.

Master Keys

*"What can the company do to create a friendly climate
for great managers?"*

We have said that an employee may join a company because of its prestige and reputation, but that his relationship with his immediate manager determines how long he stays and how productive he is while he is
there. We have said that the manager is the critical player in turning
each employee's talent into performance. We have said that managers
trump companies.

All this is true. From the employees' perspective, the manager is indeed more influential than the company. However, the company still
wields enormous power. By themselves, great managers can offer limited local resistance to conventional wisdom. Only a total *company* effort can dislodge it completely.

In most companies conventional wisdom remains deeply entrenched.
Even though many managers might disagree with some of its central
tenets—each person has unlimited potential; help each person to overcome his weaknesses; treat others as you would like to be treated—still
these tenets survive. They are held firmly in place by a network of policies, practices, and languages. This network pervades the company, af-
fecting the way employees are selected, trained, paid, punished, and
promoted. By themselves, great managers can make small advances in
the opposite direction, but they can never break all the way through to
the other side. No matter which route they try, sooner or later they open
a door and find convention standing there with some policy or rule or
system that stops the great manager in his tracks:

"You can't pay people that way."

"You can't promote him if he doesn't have more than three years' experience."

"You're not treating every employee the same. That's unfair."

"Here's our new performance management system. Make sure every
employee is trained on every one of these competencies."

"You can't give her that title. She doesn't have anyone reporting to
her."

Conventional wisdom is barricaded behind a wall of selection, training, compensation, and performance management systems. The only way to dislodge it completely is to replace these systems. And only the *company* can replace these systems.

Using the Four Keys as our guide, here are some of the master keys that the senior management of a company can use to break through conventional wisdom's barricades.

A. Keep the focus on outcomes: The role of the company is to identify the desired end. The role of the individual is to find the best means possible to achieve that end. Therefore strong companies become experts in the destination and give the individual the thrill of the journey.

- As much as is possible, define every role using outcome terms.
- Find a way to rate, rank, or count as many of those outcomes as possible. Measurement always improves performance.
- The four most important emotional outcomes for a customer are accuracy, availability, partnership, and advice. Examine each role within the company and identify what actually needs to happen to create these outcomes. In training classes, explain how the standardized steps of the role lead to one or more of these emotional outcomes. Also explain where, how, and why employees are expected to use their discretion to create these outcomes.
- Hold managers accountable for their employees' responses to the twelve questions presented in chapter 1. These twelve questions are a very important outcome measure. Although we would not advise paying managers on their employees' responses, managers *should* use the twelve questions as part of their overall performance scorecard.

B. Value world-class performance in every role: At strong companies every role, performed at excellence, is respected. If you want to understand the culture of a company, look first to its heroes.

- Within as many roles as possible, set up different levels of achievement. Identify specific criteria for moving up from one level to the next. Reward progress with plaques, certificates, and diplomas. Take every level seriously.

- Within as many roles as possible, set up broadbanded compensation plans. Identify specific criteria for moving up within each band. Explain clearly the reason for the pay cut when shifting from one band to another.
- Celebrate "personal bests." Many people like to compete with themselves. Design a system so that each person can keep track of his or her performance monthly or quarterly. Use this system to celebrate monthly or quarterly "personal bests," as and when they occur. A growing number of "personal bests" means a growing company.

C. Study your best: Strong companies learn from their very best. Internal best practice discovery is one of their most important rituals.

- Start with your most significant roles and study your best practitioners. Build a talent profile for each role. This will help you select more people like your best.
- Revise all training to incorporate what you have learned about excellence in each role.
- Set up an internal "university." The main function of this "university" should be to provide a forum for showcasing how your best, in every role, do what they do. As far as is possible, every employee should be exposed to the thinking, the actions, and the satisfactions of your best, in every role. Your employees can learn many other things at this "university"—policies, rules, techniques—but the main focus should be a presentation of internal best practices. Remember, this "university" can be as flexible, informal, and brief as the size and complexity of your organization requires—the important thing is to learn from your best in a disciplined way.

D. Teach the language of great managers: Language affects thinking. Thinking affects behavior. Companies must change how people speak if they are to change how people behave. Strong companies turn the language of great managers into the common language.

- Teach the Four Keys of great managers. In particular emphasize the difference among skills, knowledge, and talents. Make sure people know that all roles, performed at excellence, require talent, that a talent is *any* recurring pattern of thought, feeling, or behavior, and that talents are extraordinarily difficult to teach.

- Change recruiting practices, job descriptions, and résumé qualifications to reflect the critical importance and the broader definition of talent.
- Revise all training content to reflect the differences among skills, knowledge, and talents. A great company is clear about what can be trained and what cannot.
- Remove the remedial element from training. Send your most talented people to learn new skills and knowledge that can complement their talents. Stop sending less talented people to training classes to be "fixed."
- Give every employee the benefit of feedback. Know that 360-degree surveys, personality profiles, and performance appraisal systems are all useful as long as they are focused on helping the person understand himself better and build upon his strengths. Stop using them if they are focused on identifying what needs to be fixed.
- Start the great managers' "performance management" routine.

These master keys, although not a substitute for great managers, are a valuable companion. Left unturned, they allow conventional wisdom to create a climate hostile to great managers. With every policy, system, and language built around its core assumptions, conventional wisdom drowns out the small voices of dissent and forces each great manager to question even her most fervently held beliefs. In a climate like this, great managers cannot grow. They cannot refine their intuitions with practice. They are too busy trying to stay clearheaded and to survive.

However, when turned successfully, these master keys alter the whole company climate. The climate becomes supportive to great managers, reinforcing their insights and pushing them to practice and to experiment and to refine. In *this* climate great managers will thrive. Employees will excel. The company will sustain its growth. And conventional wisdom will be uprooted once and for all.

Gathering Force

Great managers make it all seem so simple. Just select for talent, define the right outcomes, focus on strengths, and then, as each person grows, encourage him or her to find the right fit. Complete these few steps with every single employee, and your department, division, or company will yield perennial excellence. It sounds almost inevitable.

We know, just as you do, that it isn't. It is very hard to manage others well. The essence of the role is the struggle to balance the competing interests of the company, the customers, the employees, and even your own. You attend to one, and you invariably upset the others. If you have just intervened between a rude customer and a stammering employee, it is hard to find the right words to placate the customer and yet save face for the employee. If you have just assumed responsibility for a team of thirty jaded veterans, it is hard to know how to gain their trust while still pushing them to perform. If you have just realized that the new employee, whom you so carefully selected, does not, in fact, have the talent to perform, it is hard to know how to break the news without demoralizing him and alarming his colleagues. No matter which way you spin it, it's hard being the middleman.

This book doesn't offer to make your role easy. It simply offers you a vantage point. It offers you a way to gain a clearer perspective on what you are doing, why you are doing it, and how to do it better. This perspective won't tell you what to do in every situation. But it *will* guide you toward sound action. It *will* help you know how to start laying the foundations for an enduringly strong workplace.

We cannot promise miracles overnight. And you wouldn't believe us if we did. You know that at work tomorrow you are going to see a lot of people cast in the wrong roles. You know that you are going to see many managers marching in lockstep with conventional wisdom. And you know the limits of what you can change on your own. You know that you will only be able to change things one employee at a time, conversation by conversation. Like all great managers, you are at the start of a long journey.

We can only promise that these Four Keys are an extraordinarily powerful beginning.

• • •

On your journey, take strength from this: As you chip away at conventional wisdom, you are being aided by the gathering of two powerful forces. The needs of the company and the needs of the employee, misaligned since the birth of the "corporation" 150 years ago, are slowly beginning to converge. Today you, the manager, find yourself at their meeting point. . . .

Everywhere employees are demanding more of their work. With the breakdown of other sources of community, employees are looking more and more to their workplace to provide them with a sense of meaning and identity. They want to be recognized as individuals. They want a chance to express themselves and to gain meaningful prestige for that expression. Only you, the manager, can create the kind of environment where each person comes to know his or her strengths and expresses them productively.

At the same time, companies are searching for undiscovered reserves of value. Human nature is one of those last, vast reserves of value. If they are to increase their value, companies know they must tap these reserves. In the past they have tried to access the power of human nature by containing it and perfecting it, just as mankind has done with the other forces of nature. We now know why this cannot work: the power of human nature is that, unlike other forces of nature, it is not uniform. Instead its power lies in its idiosyncrasy, in the fact that *each human's nature is different*. If companies want to use this power, they must find a mechanism to unleash each human's nature, not contain it. You, the manager, are the best mechanism they have.

The intersection of these two forces—each company's search for value and each individual's search for identity—will change the corporate landscape forever. You will see new organizational models, new titles, new compensation schemes, new careers, and new measurement systems—all designed around the mantra "Don't try to put in what was left out. Try to draw out what was left in." Some managers may try to resist these forces of change, but they will fail. A company's search for value is as unending and as irresistible as an individual's search for identity. You can slow these gathering forces down. You cannot stop them.

But you can speed them up. You can be the catalyst. The world's best managers have shown you how.

APPENDICES

- Appendix A: The Gallup Path to Business Performance

- Appendix B: What the Great Managers Said

- Appendix C: A Selection of Talents

- Appendix D: Finding the Twelve Questions

- Appendix E: The Meta-analysis

Appendix A: The Gallup Path to Business Performance

"What is the path to sustained increase in shareholder value?"

Through research examining the linkages between key elements of a healthy business, the Gallup Organization has developed a model that describes the path between the individual contribution of every employee and the ultimate business outcome of any company—an increase in overall company value. For publicly traded companies, this is, of course, best measured by increase in stock price and market valuation. Below is a schematic of the path. A brief overview of each step along the path follows.

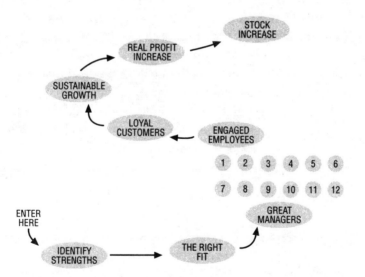

REAL PROFIT INCREASE DRIVES STOCK INCREASE

Many variables influence the market value of a company, including external variables beyond a company's control. But of the variables a company *can* control, real profit increase is the most important driver of stock increase. We emphasize "real," because there are many maneu-vers a company can take to drive short-term profitability. Some are solid operational initiatives, such as improving process efficiency or cutting costs. Others are generously described as creative accounting, such as write-downs, aggressive one-time charges, or forcing orders for prod-ucts at the end-of-period to overstate revenue. However, only sustained profit increase from *normal operations* can drive a sustained increase in stock value.

SUSTAINABLE GROWTH DRIVES REAL PROFIT INCREASE

Real profit increase can only be driven by sustainable growth. Sustainable growth is quite different from "bought growth." A company can buy growth through a variety of techniques: acquiring another company's revenue stream, slashing prices, or, a perennial favorite among fast-growing restaurant or retail chains, opening as many new lo-cations as possible as quickly as possible. All of these techniques create a welcome spike in your revenue, but none of them addresses the issue of sustaining that revenue—in fact, some of them actively undermine it. Sustainable growth is not measured by a short-lived revenue spike. Rather, sustainable growth is measured by metrics such as revenue per store, or revenue per product, or number of services used per customer. These metrics reveal whether or not your revenue stream is robust, whether it will last.

LOYAL CUSTOMERS DRIVE SUSTAINABLE GROWTH

The most critical driver of sustainable growth is an expanding base of loyal customers. In some industries it is also critical to have a growing base of loyal customers who are willing to pay a premium price. It is even better if these loyal customers become advocates, thereby creating a large, vocal, and unpaid sales force.

Customers can be persuaded to try a product or service through ef-fective sales and marketing communications, but true customer loyalty can be created only by treating customers to a superior product and superior service. At Gallup we refer to the sales and marketing communications as the "brand promise," and the quality of the products and services as the "brand experience." A company will be able to create a growing number of loyal customers only if its brand experience matches or exceeds its brand promise.

ENGAGED EMPLOYEES DRIVE CUSTOMER LOYALTY

Jack Welch, the CEO of General Electric, once said, "Any company trying to compete . . . must figure out a way to engage the mind of every employee." This is especially true in service industries, where nearly all of the company's value is delivered to customers by individual employees. But even in pure manufacturing environments, quality products are unlikely to be produced without engaged and committed employees.

The twelve circles in the schematic on page 245 refer to the twelve questions described in chapter 1. A "fully engaged" employee, by our definition, is one who can answer with a strong affirmative to all twelve of those questions. Remember, the four outcome measures we used in our meta-analysis at the business unit level were employee retention, productivity, customer satisfaction, and profitability. While the schematic above only illustrates the link between engaged employees and customer loyalty, there are often very direct links between an increase in the number of engaged employees and profit, either indirectly through an increase in productivity, or directly through major decreases in employee turnover.

THE RIGHT PEOPLE IN THE RIGHT ROLES
WITH THE RIGHT MANAGERS
DRIVE EMPLOYEE ENGAGEMENT

At the entry point of the path, the first steps must be performed almost perfectly or the remaining linkages to customer satisfaction, revenue growth, and profit will not occur. First, you must identify the employee's individual strengths. In step two, you must position that individual to perform a role that capitalizes on these strengths. Failure to meet these two requirements cannot be corrected by either the employee's motivation or by expert coaching. As this book describes in some detail, when we refer to "strengths" we are referring primarily to a person's recurring patterns of thought, feeling, or behavior—his talents—and less to learned skills and acquired knowledge. We believe that when selecting employees, companies have spent far too much time and money focusing on the skills and knowledge of employees and not nearly enough on their talents. Truth be told, most companies trip themselves up right at the start of this path because they have no accurate way of knowing how much talent they are bringing in, nor how well that talent is positioned.

Having successfully taken these first two steps, you arrive at the path's most critical juncture. You must find a way to engage these talented employees. Again, there are many ways to do this—pay them more, provide more generous benefits—but these are low-character solutions. The only way to engage talented employees successfully is to select great managers and then provide these managers with a climate friendly to the Four Keys. In this climate great managers can select the best people, set accurate expectations for them, motivate them, and develop them. Every single employee's talent will be released into customer-focused performance. The company will become strong.

The company that is unable to take this step will be forced off the path. They will lose more talented people than they keep. They will miscast, overpromote, undervalue, and otherwise misuse those talented employees who do stay. Lacking talented people in the right roles, this company will have to revert to less robust routes to performance—an overreliance on marketing, an unquestioned fondness for acquisition, a frantic push for "bought" growth. Pressed by high character competition, these routes will serve this company poorly. And, in the end, lacking great managers to keep it on the right path, this company will lose.

Appendix B: What the Great Managers Said

*"What did great managers say to the three questions
quoted in chapter 2?"*

"As a manager, which would you rather have: an independent, aggressive person who produced $1.2 million in sales or a congenial team player who produced about half as much? Please explain your choice."

Great managers replied that they would prefer an independent, aggressive person rather than the half-as-productive team player. They reasoned that the independent, aggressive person was probably more talented but harder to manage. The team player was probably less talented for the role but much easier to manage. Great managers are not looking for people who are easy to manage. They are looking for people who have the talent needed to be world class. Therefore they prefer the challenge of taking a talented person and focusing him or her toward productivity to the challenge of trying to make a less productive person talented.

"You have an extremely productive employee who consistently fouls up the paperwork. How would you work with this person to help him/her be more productive?"

Great managers would find out why this employee is fouling up the paperwork. Perhaps she is new to the role, perhaps she could benefit from some training. But if they find out that the problem is lack of talent for paperwork, they will work to find a solution that enables the employee to manage around her weakness for administration and focus on her productivity instead.

"You have two managers. One has the best talent for management you have ever seen. The other is mediocre. There are two openings available: the first is a high-performing territory, the second is a territory that is struggling. Neither territory has yet reached its po-

tential. Where would you recommend the excellent manager be placed? Why?"

Great managers would always place the most talented manager in the higher-performing territory. The key phrase in the question is "neither territory has yet reached its potential." Great managers use excellence as their measure. They know that only the talented manager working in the higher-performing territory has a chance to help that territory reach its true potential. Taking that territory to excellence is just as much of a challenge for the talented manager as is moving the struggling territory up above average. Furthermore, the former is much more fun and much more productive. With the talented manager positioned in the higher-performing territory, great managers say they would then remove the poor manager and select a talented turnaround expert to fix the lower-performing territory.

To those who would do the opposite, great managers offer this cautionary word: Your less talented manager will never make the most of the higher-performing territory, and the lower-performing territory may well defeat your talented manager. In this case, with the best of intentions, you have set up two people to fail and halved your productivity.

Appendix C: A Selection of Talents

"Which talents are found most frequently across all roles?"

During our research Gallup has had the opportunity to study excellence in hundreds of distinct roles. The talents needed to excel in these roles vary greatly. But in response to requests from managers, we list here the most commonly found talents with a short definition of each. You can use these definitions to guide your thinking as you decide which talents you should be selecting for.

Striving Talents

Achiever: A drive that is internal, constant, and self-imposed

Kinesthetic: A need to expend physical energy

Stamina: Capacity for physical endurance

Competition: A need to gauge your success comparatively

Desire: A need to claim significance through independence, excellence, risk, and recognition

Competence: A need for expertise or mastery

Belief: A need to orient your life around certain prevailing values

Mission: A drive to put your beliefs into action

Service: A drive to be of service to others

Ethics: A clear understanding of right and wrong which guides your actions

Vision: A drive to paint value-based word pictures about the future

Thinking Talents

Focus: An ability to set goals and to use them every day to guide actions

Discipline: A need to impose structure onto life and work

Arranger: An ability to orchestrate

Work Orientation: A need to mentally rehearse and review

Gestalt: A need to see order and accuracy

Responsibility: A need to assume personal accountability for your work

Concept: An ability to develop a framework by which to make sense of things

Performance Orientation: A need to be objective and to measure performance

Strategic Thinking: An ability to play out alternative scenarios in the future

Business Thinking: The financial application of the strategic thinking talent

Problem Solving: An ability to think things through with incomplete data

Formulation: An ability to find coherent patterns within incoherent data sets

Numerical: An affinity for numbers

Creativity: An ability to break existing configurations in favor of more effective/appealing ones

Relating Talents

Woo: A need to gain the approval of others

Empathy: An ability to identify the feelings and perspectives of others

Relator: A need to build bonds that last

Multirelator: An ability to build an extensive network of acquaintances

Interpersonal: An ability to purposely capitalize upon relationships

Individualized Perception: An awareness of and attentiveness to individual differences

Developer: A need to invest in others and to derive satisfaction in so doing

Stimulator: An ability to create enthusiasm and drama

Team: A need to build feelings of mutual support

Positivity: A need to look on the bright side

Persuasion: An ability to persuade others logically

Command: An ability to take charge

Activator: An impatience to move others to action

Courage: An ability to use emotion to overcome resistance

Appendix D: Finding the Twelve Questions

"How did Gallup find the twelve questions?"

We began with focus groups. Each focus group included employees from each company's most productive departments. An occupational psychologist from Gallup conducted the groups, asking open-ended questions about the workplace. Each focus group was tape-recorded. Over the last twenty-five years Gallup has conducted thousands of such focus groups.

From these focus groups we developed lengthy surveys, including questions on all aspects of the employees' work experiences. These surveys were administered to over one million employees. After each study we performed analyses to identify the factors within the data.

Five factors consistently emerged:

1. **Work Environment/Procedures.** This factor addressed issues relating to the physical work environment—issues such as safety, cleanliness, pay, benefits, and policies.
2. **Immediate Supervisor.** This factor addressed issues relating to the behavior of the employees' immediate supervisor—issues such as selection, recognition, development, trust, understanding, and discipline.
3. **Team/Co-workers.** This factor addressed issues relating to the employees' perceptions of team members—issues such as cooperation, shared goals, communication, and trust.
4. **Overall Company/Senior Management.** This factor addressed issues relating to company initiatives and leaders—issues such as the employees' faith in the company's mission and strategy or in the competence of the leaders themselves.
5. **Individual Commitment/Service Intention.** This factor addressed issues relating to the employees' sense of their own commitment to the company and to the customers—issues such as the employees' pride in the company, likelihood to recommend the company to friends as a place to work, likelihood to stay with the company for their whole career, and desire to provide excellent service to customers.

Although other subfactors were found—subfactors like "communication" or "development"—these five major factors explain virtually all of the variance in the data. And of the five major factors, by far the most powerful is the immediate supervisor factor. It explains a disproportionately large percentage of the variance in the data.

Following this factor analysis, we performed various regression analyses on the data to identify some of the most powerful questions within the data set. During these analyses three dependent variables were used: rating of overall satisfaction; the five best questions from the individual commitment factor; and the performance outcomes of the business units.

Before selecting the final list of twelve questions, we added a final criterion: The questions had to be simple and easy to affect. They had to be "actionable" questions, not emotional outcome questions like "Overall how satisfied are you with your work environment?" or "Are you proud to be working for your company?"

Having identified the twelve most powerful questions, we then subjected them to rigorous confirmatory analyses. The meta-analysis presented in the book was one such study. In the next section we will describe it in detail.

Appendix E: The Meta-analysis

"What are the details of the meta-analysis?"

An excerpt from "A Meta-analysis and Utility Analysis of the Relationship between Core Employee Opinions and Business Outcomes"

Prepared by:
James K. Harter, Ph.D.
Ame Creglow, M.S.

Background to the Core Items

Over the course of the last 25 years, Gallup researchers have qualitatively and quantitatively assessed the most salient employee perceptions of management practices. In addition to designing customized surveys for nearly every organization with which Gallup works, Gallup researchers have sought to define a core set of statements that measure important perceptions across a wide spectrum of organizations. They have also tried to do so in a way that is not overly complicated or cumbersome for business professionals who are already deluged with other business-related responsibilities.

Researchers with the Gallup Organization have conducted thousands of qualitative focus groups across a wide variety of industries. The methodology underlying this research has been centered on the study of success. The Gallup Organization has studied productive work groups and productive individuals for more than 25 years. In developing measures of employee perceptions, researchers have focused on the consistently important human resource issues on which managers can develop specific action plans. The 13 Core statements evolved from a number of qualitative and quantitative studies. The quantitative data have been combined in the current meta-analysis. The 13 Core statements are as follows:

1. Overall Satisfaction—On a five-point scale, where "5" is *extremely satisfied* and "1" is *extremely dissatisfied,* how satisfied are you with (Name of Company) as a place to work?

2. I know what is expected of me at work.
3. I have the materials and equipment I need to do my work right.
4. At work, I have the opportunity to do what I do best every day.
5. In the last seven days, I have received recognition or praise for doing good work.
6. My supervisor, or someone at work, seems to care about me as a person.
7. There is someone at work who encourages my development.
8. At work, my opinions seem to count.
9. The mission/purpose of my company makes me feel my job is important.
10. My associates (fellow employees) are committed to doing quality work.
11. I have a best friend at work.
12. In the last six months, someone at work has talked to me about my progress.
13. This last year, I have had opportunities at work to learn and grow.

Meta-analysis

A meta-analysis is a statistical integration of data accumulated across many different studies. As such, it provides uniquely powerful information, because it controls for measurement and sampling errors and other idiosyncrasies that distort the results of individual studies. A meta-analysis eliminates biases and provides an estimate of true validity or true relationship between two or more variables. Statistics typically calculated during meta-analyses also allow the researcher to explore the presence, or lack thereof, of moderators of relationships. More than 1,000 meta-analyses have been conducted in the psychological, educational, behavioral, medical, and personnel selection fields. The research literature in the behavioral and social sciences includes a multitude of individual studies with apparently conflicting conclusions. Meta-analysis, however, allows the researcher to estimate the mean relationship between variables and make corrections for artifactual sources of variation in findings across studies. It provides a method by which researchers can ascertain whether validities and relationships generalize across various situations (e.g., across firms or geographical locations).

This paper will not provide a full review of meta-analysis. Rather, the authors encourage readers to consult the following sources for both background information and detailed descriptions of the more recent meta-analytic methods: Schmidt (1992); Hunter and Schmidt (1990); Lipsey and Wilson (1993); Bangert-Drowns (1986); and Schmidt, Hunter, Pearlman and Rothstein-Hirsh (1985).

Hypothesis and Study Characteristics

The hypotheses examined for this meta-analysis were as follows:

1. Employee perceptions of quality of management practices measured by the 13 Core items are related to business unit outcomes (i.e., units with higher scores on these items have, in general, more favorable business outcomes).
2. The validity of employee perceptions of quality of management practices measured by the 13 Core items generalizes across the organizations studied.

A total of twenty-eight (28) studies are included in Gallup's database—studies conducted as proprietary research for various organizations. In each study, one or more of the Core items were used, and data were aggregated at the business unit level and correlated with aggregate performance measures:

- customer satisfaction/loyalty
- profitability
- productivity
- turnover

That is, in these analyses the unit of analysis was the business unit, not the individual employee.

Pearson correlations were calculated, estimating the relationship of business unit average measures of employee perceptions to each of these four general business outcomes. Correlations were calculated across business units within each company, and these correlation coefficients were entered into a database for each of the 13 items. The researchers then calculated mean validities, standard deviations of validities, and validity generalization statistics for each item for each of the four business unit outcome measures.

Here is a summary of the studies composing this meta-analytic study.

- There were eighteen (18) studies that examined the relationship between business unit employee perceptions and customer perceptions. Customer perceptions included customer satisfaction scores, patient satisfaction scores, student ratings of teachers, and quality ratings by those posing as customers (mystery shoppers). Customer instruments varied from study to study. The general index of customer satisfaction/loyalty was an average score of the items included in each measure.

- Profitability measures were available for fourteen (14) studies. Definition of profitability typically was a percentage profit of revenue (sales). In several companies, the researchers used, as the best measure of profit, a difference score from the prior year or a difference from a budgeted amount, because it represented a more accurate measure of each unit's relative performance. As such, a control for opportunity was used when profitability figures were deemed less comparable from one unit to the next. For example, a difference variable involved dividing profit by revenue for a business unit and then subtracting a budgeted percentage from this percentage. In every case, profitability variables were measures of margin, and productivity variables were measures of amount produced.

- Fifteen (15) studies included measures of productivity. Measures of business unit productivity consisted of either revenue figures, revenue-per-person figures, revenue per patient, or a managerial evaluation which was based on all available productivity measures and management judgment as to which business units were most productive. In many cases, this was a dichotomous variable (top performing business units = 2, less successful units = 1).

- Turnover data were available for fifteen (15) studies. These studies consisted of the annualized percentage of employee turnover for each business unit.

The overall study involved 105,680 individual employee responses to surveys and 2,528 business units, an average of 42 employees per business unit and 90 business units per company.

Here is a summary of studies (per company) sorted by industry and type of business unit.

- Twenty-eight percent of all business units in this meta-analysis were from financial organizations, 21 percent were from health care business units, and 18 percent were from restaurants. The remaining industries included in the meta-analysis were entertainment, grocery, research, telecommunications/publishing, medical sales, electronics, hospitality, government, and education.
- Thirty-one percent of all business units were retail operations and 28 percent were financial organizations; 21 percent were health care units, 9 percent were education units, and 11 percent were other businesses.

There is considerable variation among companies in the extent to which employee perception data and business performance data can be aggregated at enough levels to provide comparable analyses. Retail businesses and financial organizations provide numerous opportunities for this type of analysis, as they typically include a large number of business units that use similar measures.

Meta-analytic Methods Used

Analyses included weighted average estimates of true validity, estimates of standard deviation of validities, and corrections made for sampling error and measurement error in the dependent variables for these validities. The most basic form of meta-analysis corrects variance estimates only for sampling error. Other corrections recommended by Hunter and Schmidt (1990) include correction for measurement artifacts, such as range restriction and measurement error in the performance variables gathered. The definitions of the above procedures are provided in the sections that follow.

For this study, the researchers gathered performance variable data for multiple time periods to calculate the reliabilities of the business performance measures. Since these multiple measures were not available for each study, the researchers utilized artifact distributions meta-analysis methods (Hunter & Schmidt, 1990, pp. 158–197) to correct for measurement error in the performance variables. The artifact distributions developed were based on annual test-retest reliabilities, where they were available, from various studies.

At the time of the study there were no population estimates of standard deviations of items for each of the scale types used. Therefore, no corrections for range restriction were made. Similarly, no corrections were made for measurement error in independent measures (the 13 Core items). To adequately correct for item-level independent variable measurement error, test-retest reliabilities (with a short time interval) would be necessary. Such estimates were unavailable at the time of this study. For composite dimensions (provided later in the report), true score correlation estimates were calculated by using Cronbach's alpha estimates for independent variable reliability values.

As noted, no corrections were made in the item validities or variances due to measurement error in the independent variables and for range restriction. The following item analyses should therefore be considered conservative estimates, and estimates of true variance should be considered as slightly larger than actual true variance.

In any given meta-analysis there may be several artifacts for which artifact information is only sporadically available. For example, suppose measurement error and range restriction are the only relevant artifacts beyond sampling error. In such a case, the typical artifact distribution-based meta-analysis is conducted in three stages:

- First, information is compiled on four distributions: the distribution of the observed correlations, the distribution of the reliability of the independent variable, the distribution of the reliability of the dependent variable, and the distribution of the range departure. There are then four means and four variances compiled from the set of studies, with each study providing whatever information it contains.
- Second, the distribution of correlations is corrected for sampling error.
- Third, the distribution corrected for sampling error is then corrected for error of measurement and range variation (Hunter & Schmidt, 1990, pp. 158–159).

In this study, corrections for measurement error in the dependent variable were made in all analyses. The meta-analysis for each item and each performance variable includes an estimate of the mean sample size weighted validity and the variance across the correlations—again weighting each validity by its sample size. The amount of variance predicted for weighted correlations on the basis of sampling error was also computed. The following is the formula to calculate variance expected from sampling error in "Bare Bones" meta-analyses, utilizing the Hunter/Schmidt technique referred to in the previous paragraph:

$$\acute{O}_e^2 = (1 - \bar{r}^2)^2 / \bar{N} - 1)$$

True score standard deviations were calculated by subtracting the amount of variance due to sampling error and the amount of variance due to measurement error in the dependent variable from the observed variance. Taking the square root of this figure, a correction for the attenuation effect in the dependent variable was then made. The amount of variance due to sampling error and measurement error was divided by the observed variance to calculate the total percent variance accounted for. One rule of thumb adopted from the literature is that, if over 75 percent of variance in validities across studies is due to sampling error and other artifacts, the validity is assumed generalizable. Since two measurement error artifacts could not be corrected for in this study, the researchers chose to use a figure of 70 percent or more in determining whether validities generalized across organizations.

Results

Below is a summary of the meta-analysis for each of the 13 Core items with regard to customer satisfaction/loyalty criteria. Statistics included the number of business units contained in the analysis, the number of correlations, the weighted mean observed correlation, the observed standard deviation, the true validity standard deviation (subtracting out variance due to sampling error and measurement error in the performance variables), the percent variance due to sampling error, the percent variance accounted for, and the 90 percent credibility value (the point above which 90 percent of the true validities fall).

Results indicate that, across all 13 items, true validity estimates are in the positive direction. Validity estimates range from a low of .057 to a high of .191. If an item had a positive 90 percent credibility value, it was considered generalizable in the sense that we are confident the true validity is positive (in the hypothesized direction). Items in which over 70 percent of the variance in validities was accounted for were considered generalizable in the sense that the validity did not vary across studies.

Eleven (11) of the 13 items had positive 90 percent credibility values, and six (6) did not vary across studies.

Interestingly, for item number 12 ("In the last six months, someone at work has talked to me about my progress"), the calculations indicate 148 percent of the variance in validities across studies is due to sampling error. The interpretation of this is: By chance there was less variability across studies in this data set in the observed correlations than predicted from random sampling error, based on the number of business units in each study, and dependent variable measurement error. Two other items also had over 100 percent of variance accounted for due to sampling error alone. The practical significance of the size of correlations depicted here will be discussed following the results section. For item validities that did not appear to generalize across companies, it is possible that there are other variables moderating the strength of the relationship of these employee perceptions to customer satisfaction. For instance, perhaps the moderator for "opinions count" is the extent to which the manager not only listens to the employees' opinions, but also uses them to affect the customer. Items with highest true validities that appear to generalize across companies include:

- I have a best friend at work.
- At work, I have the opportunity to do what I do best every day.
- I know what is expected of me at work.
- My supervisor, or someone at work, seems to care about me as a person.

When multiple generalizability estimates are derived, second order sampling error can slightly influence results. To compute the mean percent variance accounted for, the following formula was used:

$$\text{Variance} = \frac{1}{(\Sigma(1\% \text{ Var.})) / K}$$

On average, 66.96 percent of variance was accounted for across item validities to customer satisfaction criteria. While the mean true validity is clearly positive, the strength of the relationship may be moderated slightly by one or more other variables. It is important to remind the reader that these estimates have not yet been corrected for other artifacts, such as measurement error in the independent variable and range restriction. Once they have been corrected for other artifacts, it is likely that there will be little room left for detecting substantial moderating relationships.

Here is the same summary analysis for items with regard to their relationship to profitability criteria. Ten (10) of the 13 items have positive 90 percent credibility values, and it is possible to account for over 70 percent of the variance in validities for nine items. The mean percent variance accounted for across items is 69.21 percent. Again, there is some room (although little) for possible moderating relationships. Those that may not generalize include "talked about progress," "mission," "materials and equipment," and "best friend." Approximately half of the variance in validities for these items is explained by sampling error and measurement error in the dependent variable. Items that appear to generalize across companies and that tended to have the highest validities to the profitability criteria are:

- Overall Satisfaction
- My associates (fellow employees) are committed to doing quality work.
- At work, I have the opportunity to do what I do best every day.
- My supervisor, or someone at work, seems to care about me as a person.

Here is a summary of the meta-analytic and validity generalization statistics for the 13 Core items relative to productivity criteria. Again, the relationships were positive. All 90 percent credibility values were positive, and we were able to account for over 70 percent of the variance in validities for 11 items. The mean percent variance accounted for across items is 83.72 percent, suggesting very little room for possible moderators. There was variation, however, in the magnitude of true validity estimates across items. Those with highest validity estimates to productivity criteria were:

- I know what is expected of me at work.
- At work, my opinions seem to count.
- The mission/purpose of my company makes me feel my job is important.
- Overall Satisfaction

- My associates (fellow employees) are committed to doing quality work.

Finally, here is a summary of the meta-analytic and validity generalization statistics for items as they relate to turnover. Four items had negative 90 percent credibility values and two were approximately zero. Therefore, for six items, we can be quite certain the direction of the relationship is negative (as hypothesized for turnover). We were able to account for over 70 percent of the variance in validities for ten items. The mean percent variance accounted for across items is 91.96 percent, again suggesting very little room for moderators. Interestingly, one of the highest true validity estimates was Item No. 3 ("I have the materials and equipment I need to do my work right"). Employee perceptions with regard to this item, as they relate to turnover, do not vary substantially across companies. Items with the highest negative correlations that appear to generalize across companies included:

- I have the materials and equipment I need to do my work right.
- Overall Satisfaction
- My supervisor, or someone at work, seems to care about me as a person.

Table 1 now provides a summary of all item statistics calculated for each of the four general performance criterion measures included in the study. This table presents the mean number of studies per variable, the mean number of business units across items, the mean observed correlation per item, and the mean true validity.

In general, items correlated at a similar magnitude with customer, profitability, and productivity criteria, and at a lower level with turnover.

TABLE 1 Summary of Item Statistics

Criterion Measure	No. of Studies	Mean No. of Bus. Units	Mean Observ. r's	Mean True Validity r's
Customer	18	2,170	.107	.122
Profitability	14	1,490	.084	.133
Productivity	15	1,148	.126	.128
Turnover	15	1,552	-.023	-.045

Of the correlations included in these analyses, the average meta-analytic correlation was .107. The practical utility of the magnitude of these correlations is discussed later in Harter and Creglow, 1998.

Table 2 provides a summary of the items that had positive 90 percent credibility values (zero or negative for the turnover measure) and in which over 70 percent of the variance in validities was accounted for. Six items fit this criterion with regard to customer satisfaction. Nine items fit this criterion for profitability outcomes, and eleven items fit this criterion for productivity outcomes. Five of the 13 items met this criterion with regard to turnover.

TABLE 2 Items with Meta-analytic r's
That Are Generalizable across Organizations

Core Item	Customer	Profitability	Productivity	Turnover
1) Overall Satisfaction		x	x	x
2) Know what is expected	x	x	x	x
3) Materials/equipment			x	x
4) Opportunity to do what I do best	x	x		x
5) Recognition/praise	x	x	x	
6) Cares about me	x	x	x	x
7) Encourages development		x	x	
8) Opinions count		x	x	
9) Mission/purpose			x	
10) Committed—quality		x	x	
11) Best friend	x		x	
12) Talked about progress	x		x	
13) Opportunities to learn and grow		x		

Computation of Dimension Correlations

Items were combined into four frequently used theoretical constructs taught by the Gallup School of Management:

Base Camp: "What do I get?"
   Item 2   Know what is expected
   Item 3   Materials/equipment

Camp 1: "What do I give?"
Item 4   Opportunity to do what I do best
Item 5   Recognition/praise
Item 6   Cares about me
Item 7   Encourages development

Camp 2: "Do I belong?"
Item 8   Opinions count
Item 9   Mission/purpose
Item 10 Committed—quality
Item 11 Best friend

Camp 3: "How can we grow?"
Item 12 Talked about progress
Item 13 Opportunities to learn and grow

The reliabilities of the above composite dimensions are reviewed in Harter (1998).

Reliability estimates of the above dimensions and the sum of the 12 items (all except overall satisfaction) were used to correct for independent variable measurement error. In estimating composite dimension correlations with criteria, a distribution of interitem correlations was compiled at the aggregate business unit level and combined across 12 studies. While a majority of the 12 items were included in most of the studies, the number of items included varied from study to study. For this reason, item statistics were calculated and the meta-analytic estimates of items were used to compute composite dimension correlations with various criteria. Since both Yes/No/Don't Know scales and one-to-five-point Likert scales were used interchangeably across studies, the researchers calculated weighted average interitem correlations based on the proportion of Yes/No/Don't Know and one-to-five-point scales used.

For the overall sample of studies, 19 studies used a one-to-five-point scale and 9 used a Yes/No/Don't Know scale. The weighted average interitem correlations, based on the above overall study proportions, are provided in Appendix B. Interitem correlations were needed for the composite score estimation (Hunter & Schmidt, 1990, p. 455). Composite scores were calculated as follows:

$$\overline{C}_{xx} = \frac{1 + (n-1)\overline{r}_{xx}}{n}$$

$$r_{x_y} = \frac{r_{xy}}{\sqrt{\overline{c}_{xx}}}$$

$\overline{c}_{xx}$ = the average item covariance

$\overline{r}_{xy}$ = the average item correlation to criterion.

$\overline{r}_{xx}$ = the average item intercorrelation

r_{x_y} = the composite score correlation

For the sum of the 12 items, the true score correlation is .19 to customer satisfaction/loyalty, profitability, and productivity criteria. (For true score correlations, the denominator becomes the square root of the dependent variable reliability multiplied by the square root of the independent variable reliability.) The true score correlation is negative to turnover, but at a lesser magnitude. The dimension correlated highest with turnover is *Base Camp*. As such, business units with employees who indicate they know what is expected of them and have the materials and equipment to do their work right tended to have lower turnover in comparison to other business units. The dimension most highly correlated with profitability was *Camp 1*. Dimensions most highly related to customer satisfaction/loyalty outcomes were *Base Camp* and *Camp 2*. *Camp 3* was least highly correlated with business outcomes, although it was positively related to customer satisfaction, profitability, and productivity.

For more detail on these and other discoveries, please see the report "A Meta-analysis and Utility Analysis of the Relationship between Core Employee Perceptions and Business Outcomes," prepared by Dr. Jim Harter and Ame Creglow, available from our world headquarters at 47 Hulfish St., Princeton, N.J. The excerpt above was written in 1998. The report is updated every year with the latest discoveries from Gallup's research.

Acknowledgments

Dr. George H. Gallup founded the Gallup Organization on the belief that each individual had a right to be heard, that, in his words, "there are four billion ways to live a life and we should study them all." Dr. Donald O. Clifton pioneered the systematic study of individual strengths and developed the concept of talent. This book is the product of the spirit and the inquisitiveness of these two scientists.

A book like this needs focus. It needs clarity and energy and impatience and passion. It needs love. Jim Clifton embodied all of these and so drove the book from start to finish.

Our book took a while to find its form. The first drafts staggered along and collapsed in a heap under the slightest pressure. To help us through these early fumblings we turned to a few, carefully chosen people. Richard Hutton guided us with his sense of pacing, of drama, of humor, and with his disconcerting ability to understand what we were trying to say before we did. Alec Gallup examined the text with his classicist's eye and (we hope) prevented us from letting the style slide into jargon. Jane Buckingham suffered through draft after draft—and so much more—but somehow always managed to keep the point and the spirit clearly in mind. Whatever you think of the book as it is, be thankful that you didn't see it before these three got their hands on it.

The Gallup Organization is world renowned for its political polls. But this book is not about polls. It is about strong workplaces and the managers who build them. Larry Emond is responsible for helping the world extend its understanding of Gallup to include all of our discoveries in the area of employee opinion and employee talent. This book owes much to his astonishing ability to articulate.

The Gallup Organization has been asking questions for seventy years. Sarah Van Allen's experience and sensibility kept this book rooted in the Gallup tradition of measuring and reporting with integrity.

In this book we have organized a body of knowledge that already existed within Gallup. Our colleagues Dr. Jim Harter, Jan Miller, Dr. Mick Zangari, Dr. Kathie Sorensen, Dr. Glen Phelps, and Graeme Bucking-ham discovered much of this knowledge and, over the years, shared it with us. We owe them a great debt.

Until someone thinks to organize all facts and make them available the TheTruth@Facts.com, authors will need pearl divers. The most effective pearl divers are persistent, charming, resourceful, and blithely optimistic—"The exact depth of the sunken Mercury space capsule? I'm sure I can find that." We had the best in Antoinette Southwick.

Over the last seventy years the Gallup Organization has worked with some of the world's finest organizations. We have learned a great deal from these partnerships, but perhaps our greatest boon was the opportunity to forge relationships with some outstanding executives. For their vision, their concepts, and their passion for building people-centered workplaces, Ronni Fridman, Kevin Cuthbert, and Mel Warriner stand out in our minds. Thank you for all of those wonderful conversations. We look forward to many more.

This is not a book of theory. The voices of one million employees and eighty thousand managers can be heard in this book. Their time and their opinions have been invaluable to us. But a few managers gave us even more. They gave us stories and vignettes and details, which we have used to help bring the messages of the book to life. To protect them from unwanted attention we have changed their names and with-held the specifics of their organizations. They know who they are. Thank you.

And a special thank-you to Linda and Mitch Hart—part family, part manager, but always complete supporters.

When we began this project we were familiar with our material but ill at ease in the unfamiliar terrain of the book world. Joni Evans, our agent at William Morris, was our guide, helping us differentiate between the friends and the foes, the truths and the mirages. Candid when we would have tiptoed, assertive when we would have shied away, clear-eyed when we would have stumbled, and, above all, so confident, Joni, and her inspirational associate Tiffany Erickson, led us toward the right book and the right partners. Without her, nothing good would have happened.

Fred Hills was our editor at Simon & Schuster. When we learned, early on, that he had been Vladimir Nabokov's editor, our insecurities reached an all-time low. But he pulled us up then, as he did on many other occasions, and refocused us on the book we needed to write. His wisdom and his relentless expertise, combined with the insight of his associate Priscilla Holmes, have fashioned our best efforts into the book you are now holding. Its strengths are his, its weaknesses our own.

You don't write a book without some people very close to you believing that you can. When things slowed to a slumped halt, our families' belief inched us forward and upward and over the hump, until we were happily careening down the other side. Thank you, Jane and Michael, Graeme, Jo, Neil, Pippa, Nader and Ingrid, Tim, Miles and Steve, Tammy, Katie, Claire, and Clayton: we owe you so much.

About the Authors

MARCUS BUCKINGHAM is the leader of The Gallup Organization's twenty-year effort to identify the core characteristics of great managers and great workplaces. He is also a senior lecturer in Gallup's Leadership Institute.

CURT COFFMAN is the global practice leader for The Gallup Organization's Workplace Management Practice. He consults regularly on the development of productive, customer-oriented workplaces.

For more than sixty years, The Gallup Organization has been a world leader in the measurement and analysis of human attitudes, opinions, and behavior. Although the company is best known for the Gallup Poll, most of Gallup's work is in providing measurement, consulting, and education to many of the world's largest companies. Gallup's clients include Audi, BankAmerica, Best Buy, Blockbuster, Carlson, Citigroup, Delta Air Lines, Fidelity, Marriott, Searle, Sears, Swissôtel, and Toyota.

70083196